Remembering Los Angeles

Dana Lombardy

TURNER
PUBLISHING COMPANY

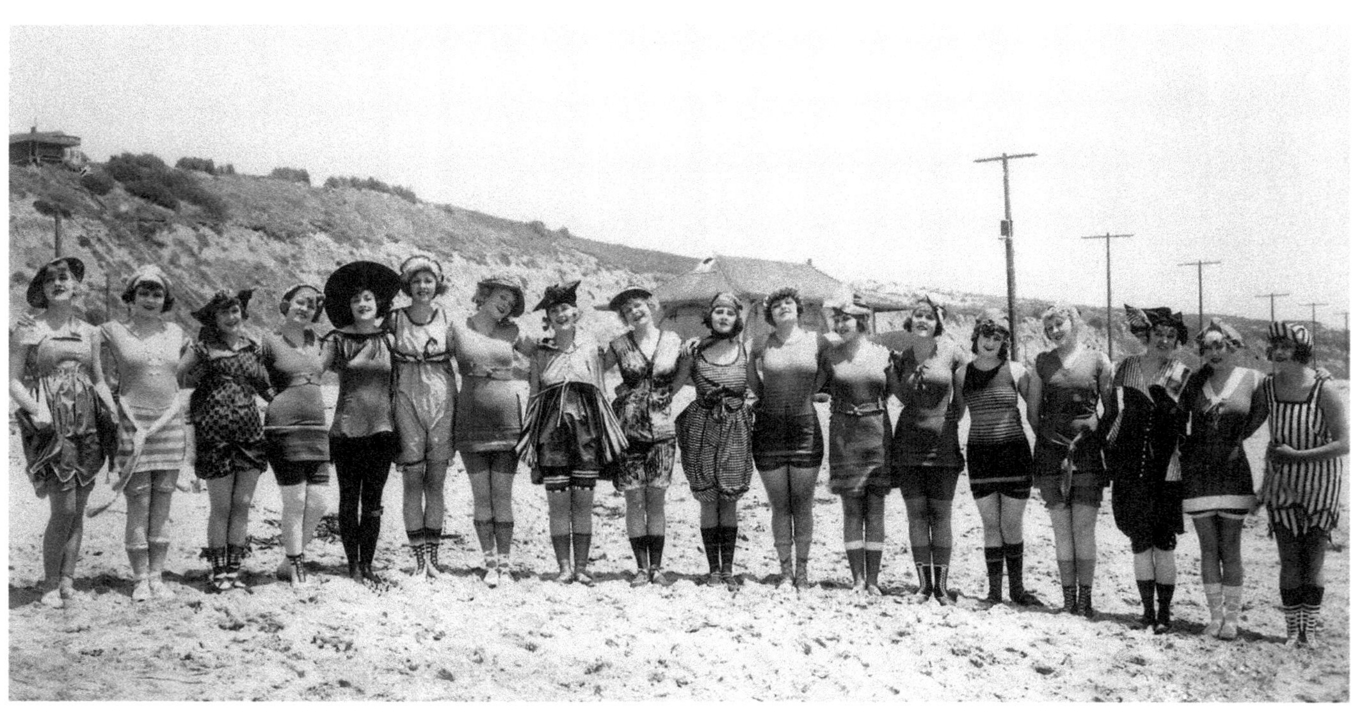

One of the early movie pioneers of Hollywood was Mack Sennett (1880–1960). He founded Keystone Studios in 1912 with history's first totally enclosed film stage and studio, which still exists. Mack Sennett Productions became famous for slapstick comedies with wild car chases and pie fights, and for the Sennett Bathing Beauties such as these young women photographed on an L.A. beach about 1917.

Remembering
Los Angeles

Turner Publishing Company
4507 Charlotte Avenue • Suite 100
Nashville, Tennessee 37209
(615) 255-2665

Remembering Los Angeles

www.turnerpublishing.com

Library of Congress Control Number: 2007929596

ISBN: 978-1-59652-682-2

Printed in the United States of America

ISBN-13: 978-1-68336-851-9 (pbk)

Contents

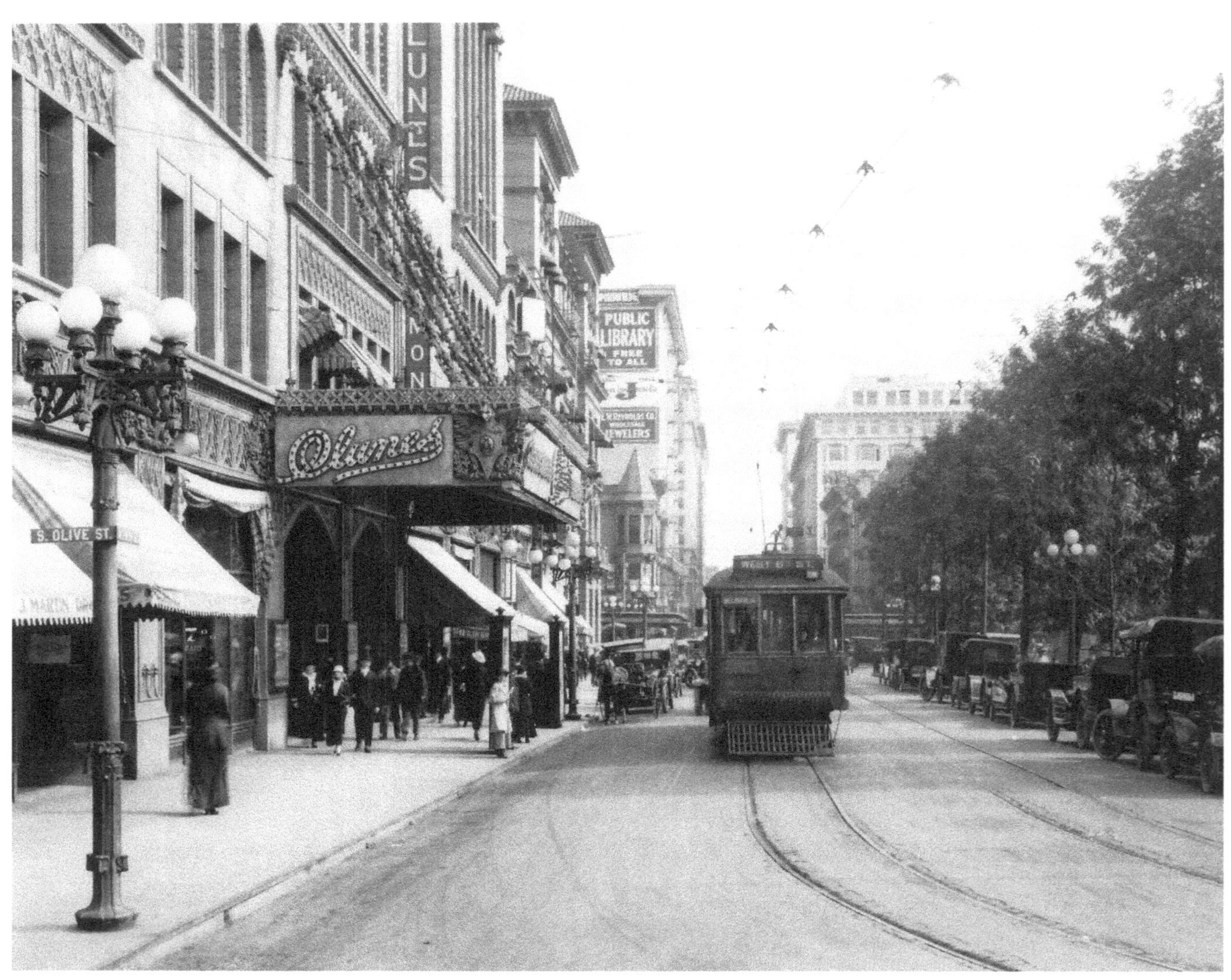

Fifth Street in Los Angeles. Harris Newmark (1834–1916), one of L.A.'s entrepreneurs and philanthropists, wrote about advertising excesses during one of the early real estate booms in his *Sixty Years in Southern California, 1853-1913,* published in 1916: "If every conceivable trick in advertising was not resorted to, it was probably due to oversight."

Acknowledgments

With the exception of cropping images where needed and touching up imperfections that have accrued over time, no other changes have been made to the photographs in this volume. The caliber and clarity of many photographs are limited by the technology of the day and the ability of the photographer at the time they were made.

This volume, *Historic Photos of Los Angeles,* is the result of the cooperation and efforts of many individuals, organizations, and corporations. It is with great thanks that we acknowledge the valuable contribution of the following for their generous support:

The Bancroft Library, University of California, Berkeley
Korean Heritage Library, University of Southern California
Library of Congress
Los Angeles Public Library
National Archives
Southern California Library for Social Studies and Research
University of Southern California, USC Special Collections

We would also like to thank the following individuals for valuable contributions and assistance in making this work possible:

Michael Hanlon
Bill Jaffe
Howie Muir

This book is a tribute to my family and memories of Los Angeles. Most important, it is for Anne and Iggy, who help me chase my dreams. —*Dana Lombardy*

Preface

I grew up in Southern California. My immediate and extended family lived in various Los Angeles and San Diego suburbs, and many family members still live in both cities. Every time I return I look forward to sampling the tremendous variety of great restaurants. Although I can still navigate the familiar freeways and main streets of L.A., each subsequent visit seems to require more and more time to travel from one part of town to another, due to the continuing increase in traffic on those highways.

When the opportunity was presented to write this book, I wondered what might be possible for the text beyond a collection of captions for a broad selection of old photos. Was it possible to write a story about L.A. through the presentation of these sometimes unrelated pictures? I considered it a challenge.

In this book you will read about how the phenomenal growth of Los Angeles occurred, transforming a desert into a dynamic metropolitan super-city. From the 1910s on, there are regular reminders of the city's movie industry and entertainment celebrities, plus examples of L.A.'s tradition of architectural experimentation. These are all things for which Los Angeles is world famous.

The notorious side of L.A., the corruption and crime that accompanied this rapid growth, is also presented in words and photos. The disasters—both natural such as earthquakes, and man-made such as the race riots—can also be found in this volume.

What you won't see in this book is a nostalgic tribute to a beloved city. People will readily recognize songs like "California Girls" and "California Dreamin'," but after "Hooray for Hollywood" appeared in 1937, no song specifically about Los Angeles attained the status of a popular standard, as occurred for San Francisco, Chicago, and New York. This seems a bit odd, considering that Los Angeles (Hollywood, actually) claims to be "the entertainment capital of the world." Most of the nice things about L.A., such as the beaches, gorgeous sunsets, and beautiful weather, are often qualified or counterbalanced with a disparaging remark by critics about some negative aspect of the city—traffic congestion, poor or nonexistent urban planning, air pollution, and so on.

The "City of the Angels" may be the most maligned large city in America—at least in the descriptions of many literary and sociological sources. Other big American cities also suffer from corruption, crime, and areas of urban decay. However, in L.A. these problems seem exacerbated by the perceived hypocritical and phony social façade and relentless promotion, or "hype," of Hollywood specifically and Los Angeles in general.

I did not intend to write a controversial book about Los Angeles. However, the recurring negativity about L.A. in the twentieth century is readily apparent from the magnitude of critical opinions and disdain in the writing of the famous, the talented, and the influential. To ignore this would present an incomplete picture of Los Angeles.

Perhaps this negativity stems from the disappointment that follows high expectations. Los Angeles attracts dreamers as well as schemers. Angelenos love their sunshine, beaches, movies, celebrities, cars, and freeways. These icons of L.A. and the sometimes less than successful interaction between nature, civilization, and various groups of people in the city's sprawling vastness inspired a diverse collection of writers. These writers' words, and the photos in this book, combine to create a fascinating, if not always favorable, portrait of America's second largest city.

—Dana Lombardy, Author

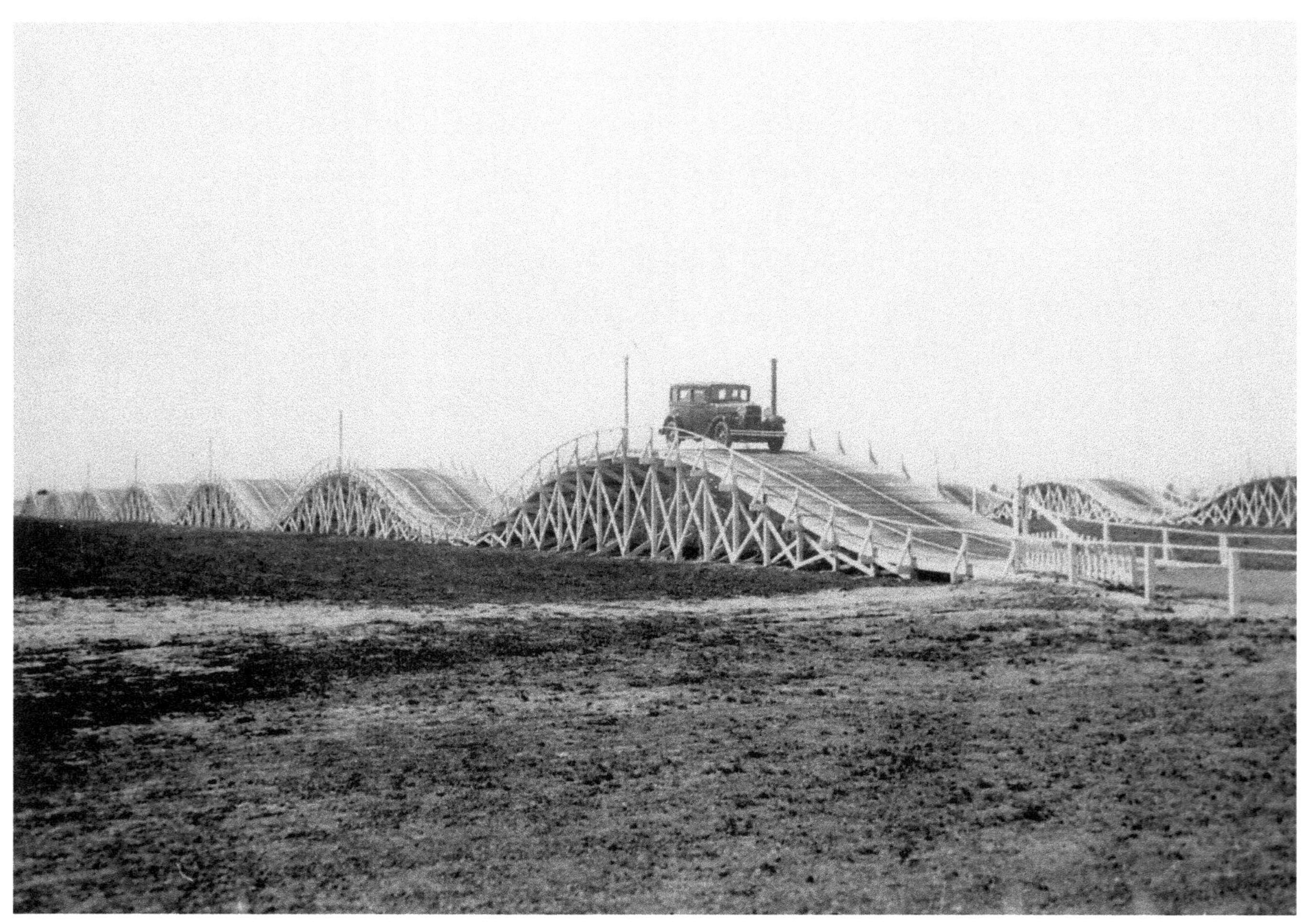

Americans went crazy for their cars in the 1920s. This is an unusual automobile course at Los Angeles photographed by a visiting French team for World Wide Photos. Architect Frank Lloyd Wright (1867–1959), for one, embraced the automobile as a revolutionary, liberating force. Wright built several houses in the Los Angeles area, including the Hollyhock House in Hollywood and the shops at Anderton Court in Beverly Hills.

A Sleepy Pueblo Becomes an American Town

(1870–1899)

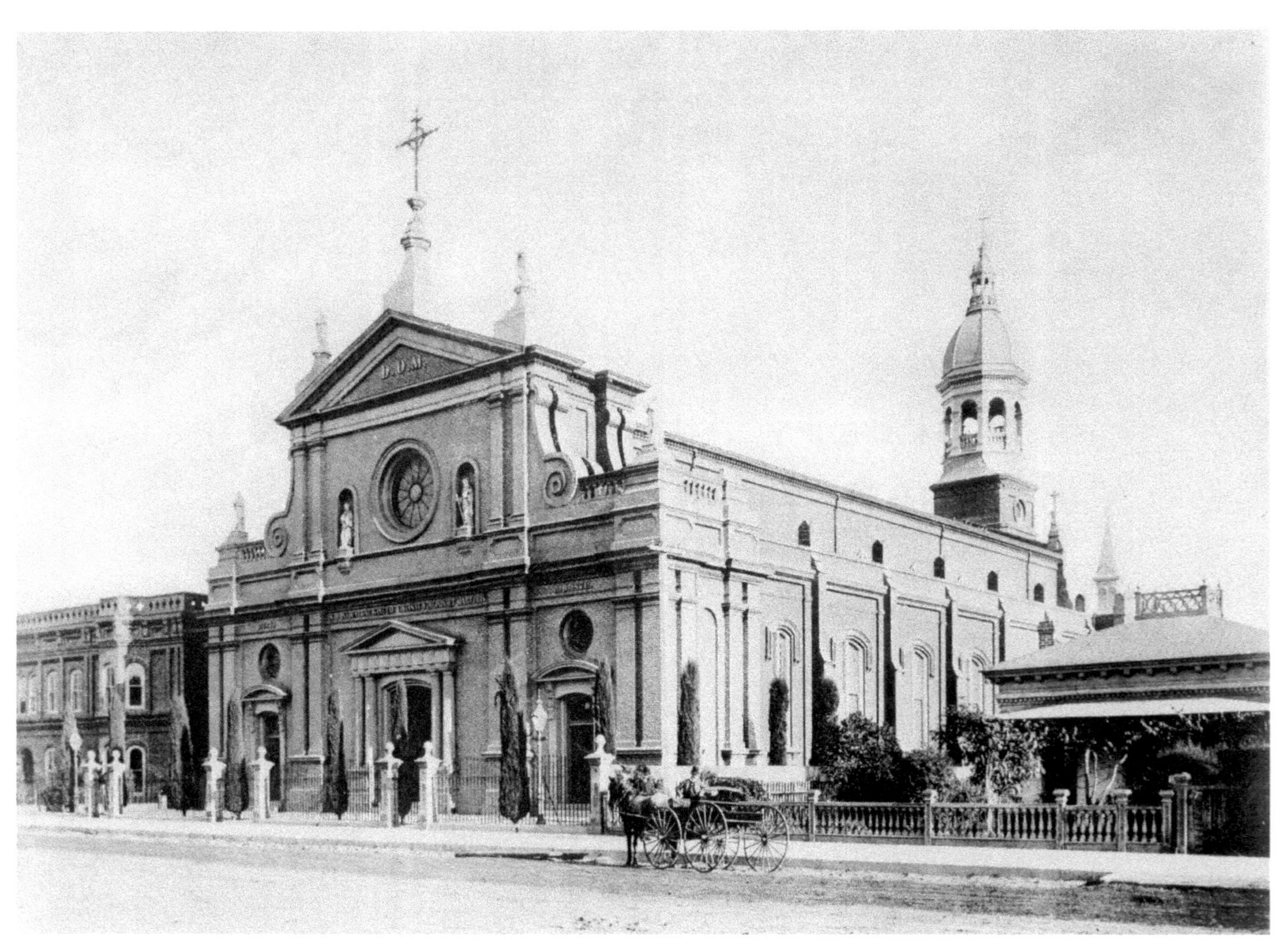

St. Vibiana's Catholic Cathedral, located at Second and Main streets in Los Angeles, was dedicated in 1876. As of 2008 it is the seat of the Los Angeles Archdiocese.

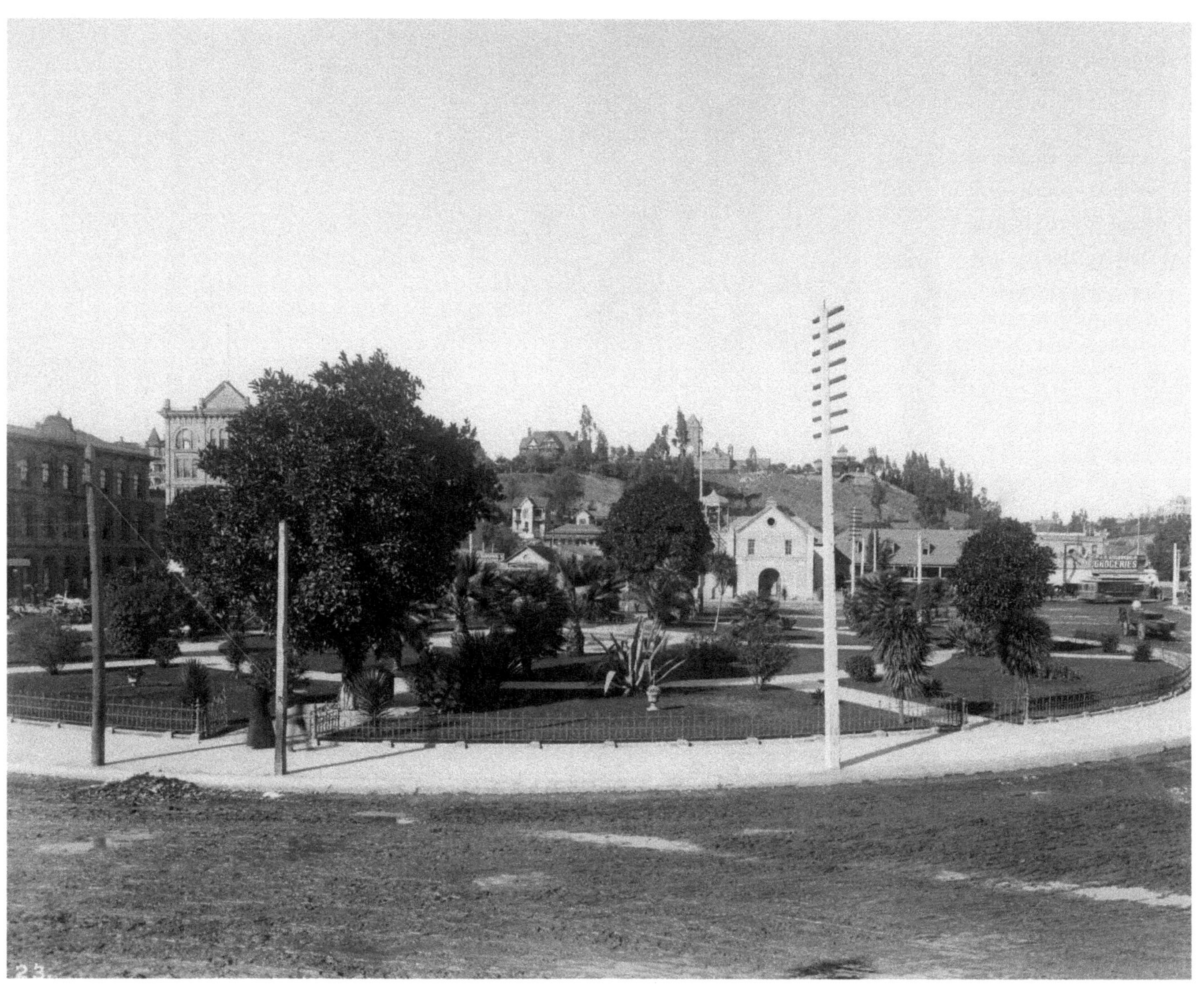

L.A.'s first park, seen here in 1890, was located in the center of Pueblo de los Angeles, founded by Spanish Governor Felipe de Neve in 1781. The park was later named Los Angeles Plaza.

Spring Street in Los Angeles as it was shown on a stereo card intended to be viewed with a stereoscope to provide the illusion of a three-dimensional image. This technique of viewing photographs was very popular in the mid-1800s.

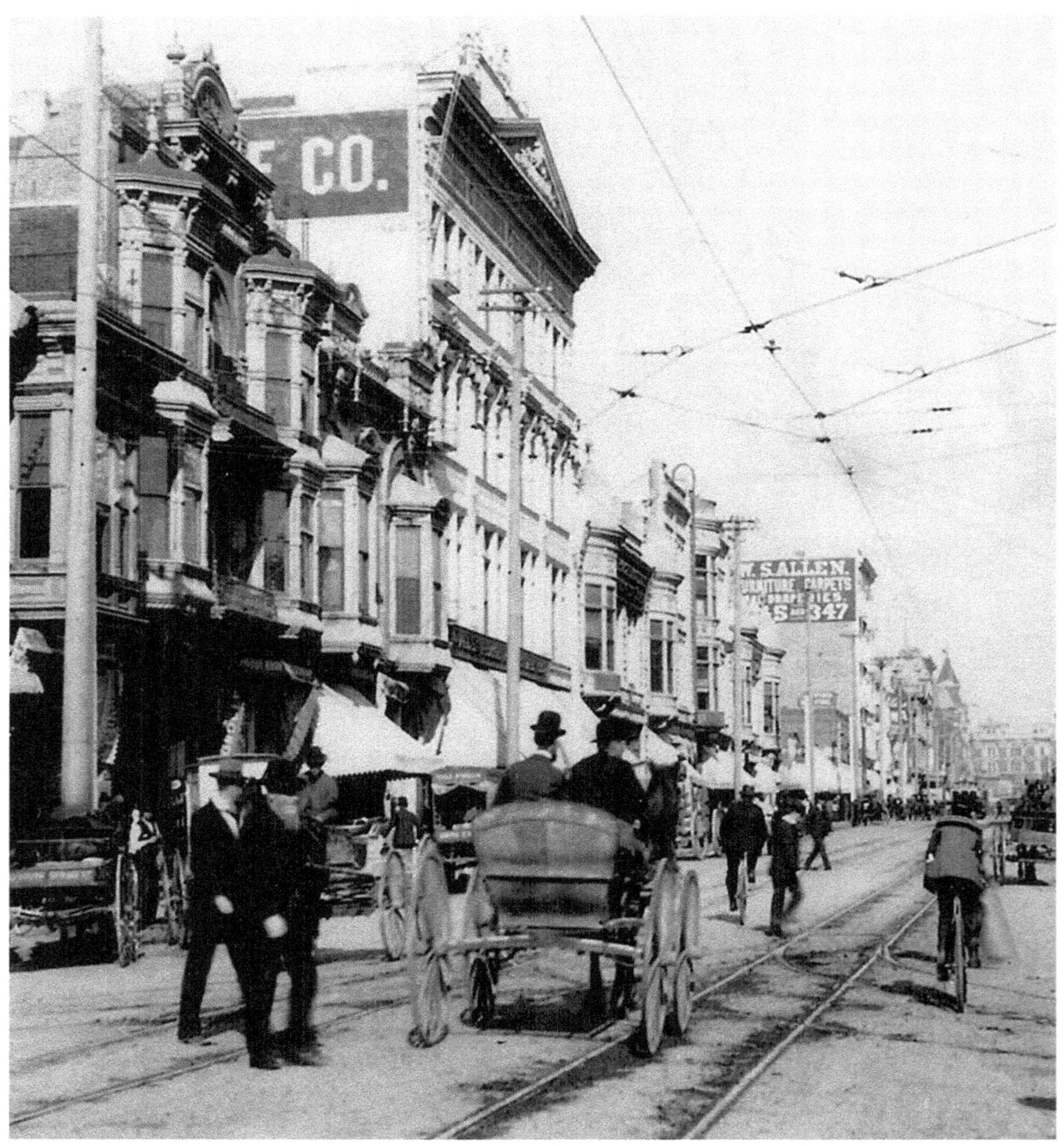

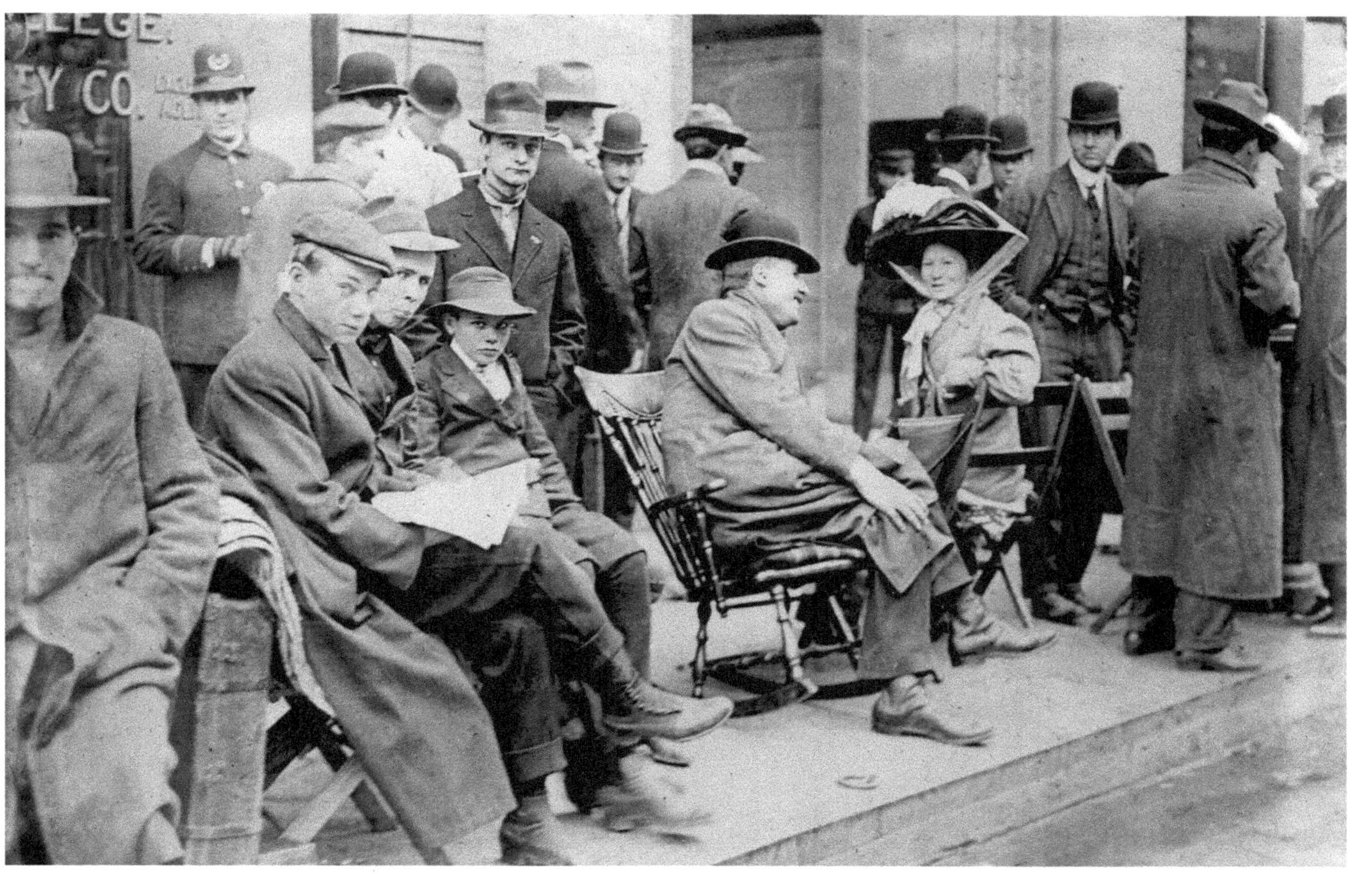

Some standing, some seated, people wait to file Yuma Land claims in Los Angeles, around 1900. Land runs or land rushes were events where previously restricted land of the United States was opened for homesteading on a first-come basis, or by lottery, or was sold by bid. The most famous of these was the Oklahoma Land Run of 1889, but others took place, including for areas seized from the Yuma Indian tribe in California and other states.

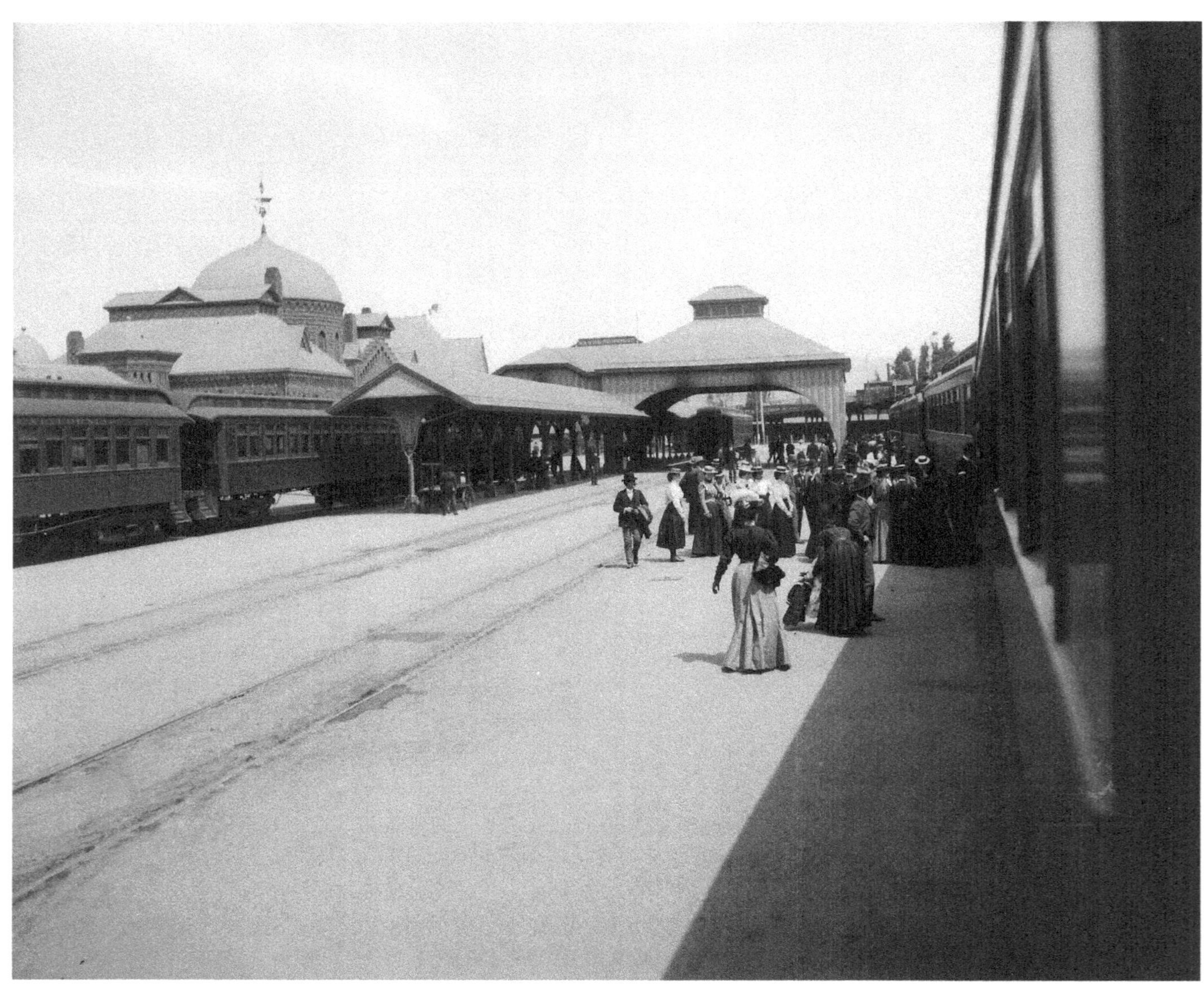

Travelers board the overland for departure from Los Angeles, around 1890. During this period, the arrival of the railroad lines dramatically transformed the city. In particular, the 1890s to 1920s were described by one sociologist as a "golden era" for African Americans in Los Angeles. Migrants from the South and Southwest found better opportunities for home-ownership and employment in parts of Los Angeles.

Defeating Rival San Diego for West Coast Dominance

(1900–1909)

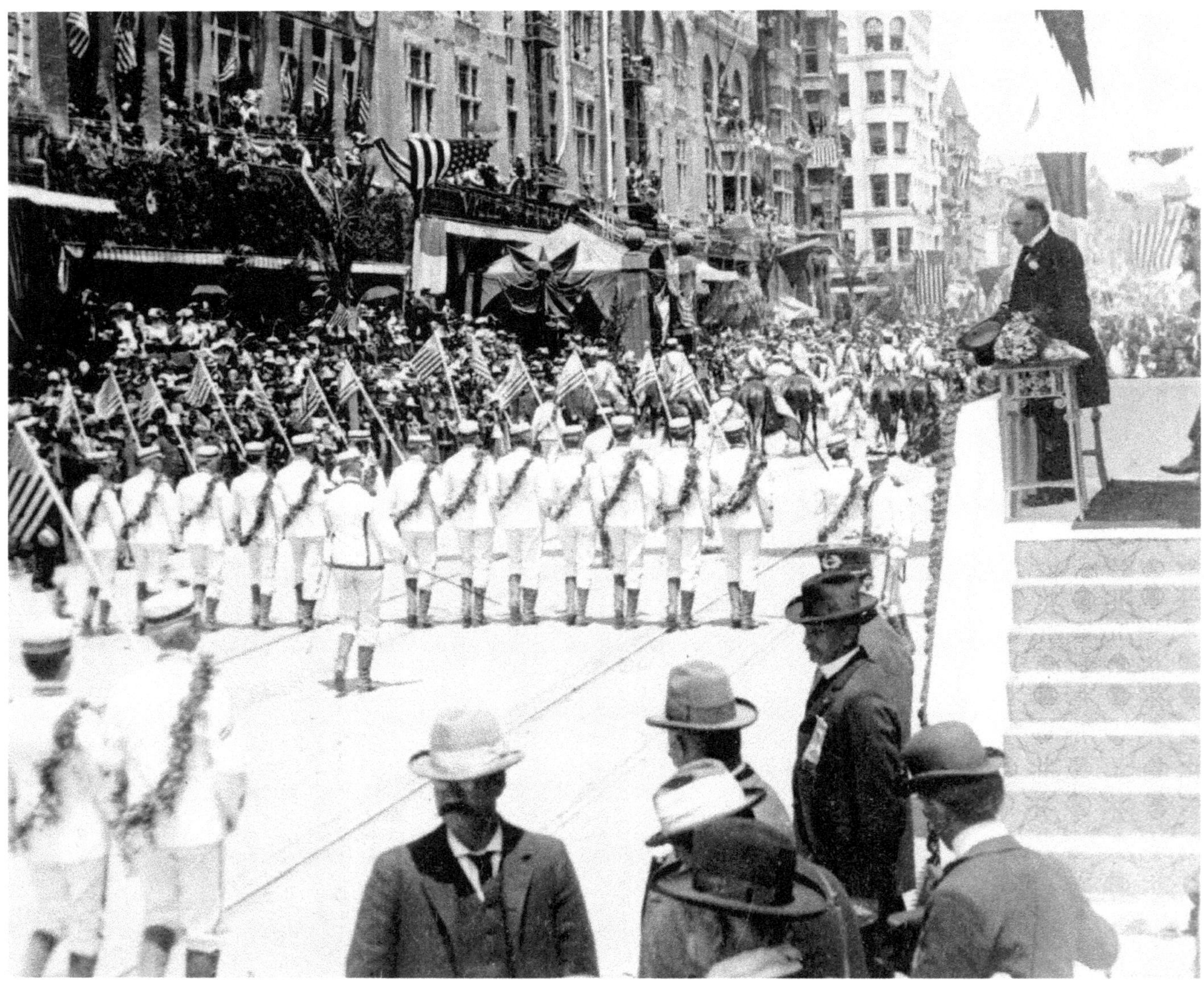

A crew prepares to "crop" tobacco on a Nash County farm in the early 1900s. They will remove the yellowing lower leaves from the plant and place them into the mule-powered "drag." At the barn, waiting hands will tie the leaves to tobacco sticks for curing, then grading, then delivery to market. Whether cropping tobacco or picking cotton, only hard work and low wages awaited field hands, black and white alike, in North Carolina.

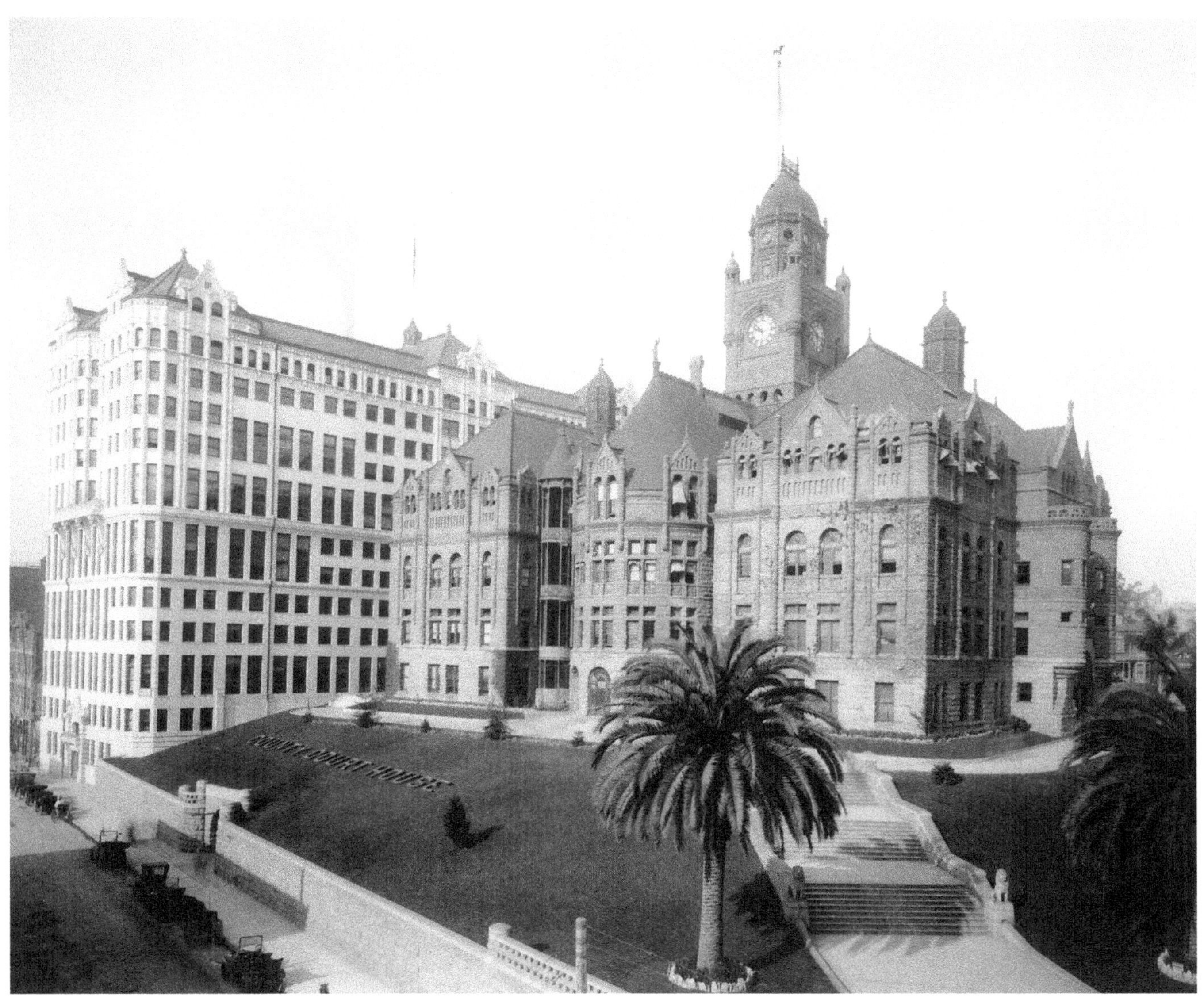

Los Angeles Court House and Hall of Records in the early twentieth century. L.A.'s drive to obtain more water for future growth was not always seen as positive. Mary Austin (1868–1934), writer and poet, described the conflict between developing a desert terrain and conserving diminishing water resources in her story "The Land" (1909). Austin lived in the Owens Valley where the "notorious" plan to divert water from the Owens River destroyed many farming communities.

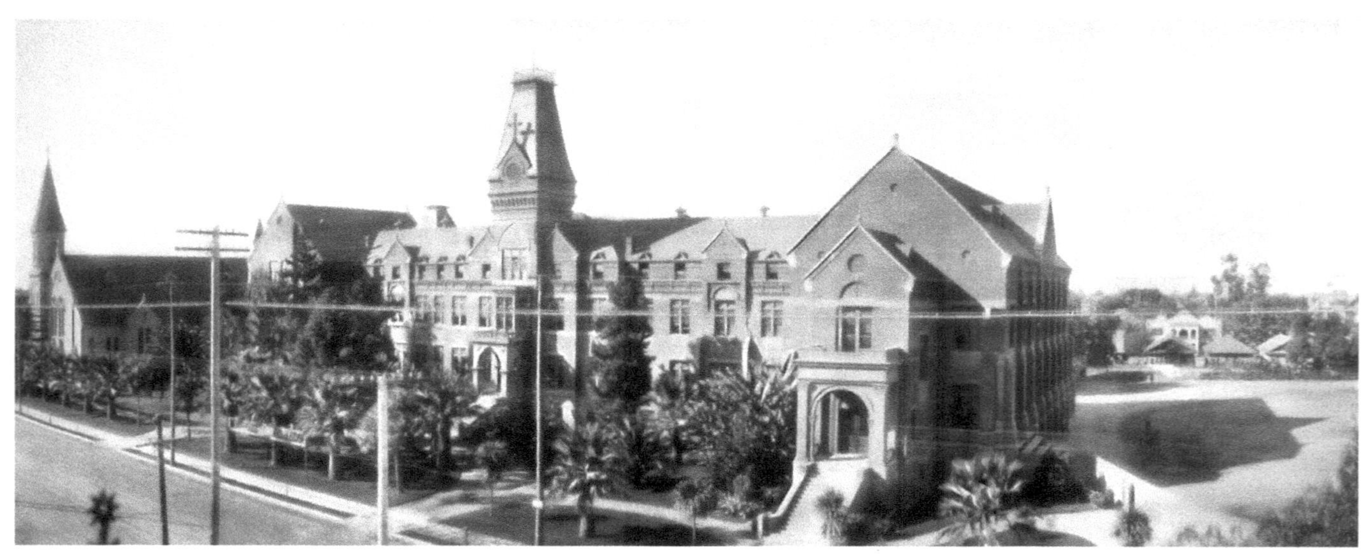

A panorama view of St. Vincent's College around 1908. The school was founded in Los Angeles in 1865 at the behest of the Roman Catholic Archdiocese Bishop Thaddeus Amat, a member of the Vincentian order. In 1917 the school moved and in 2008 was known as Loyola High School of Los Angeles, a Jesuit preparatory school for young men.

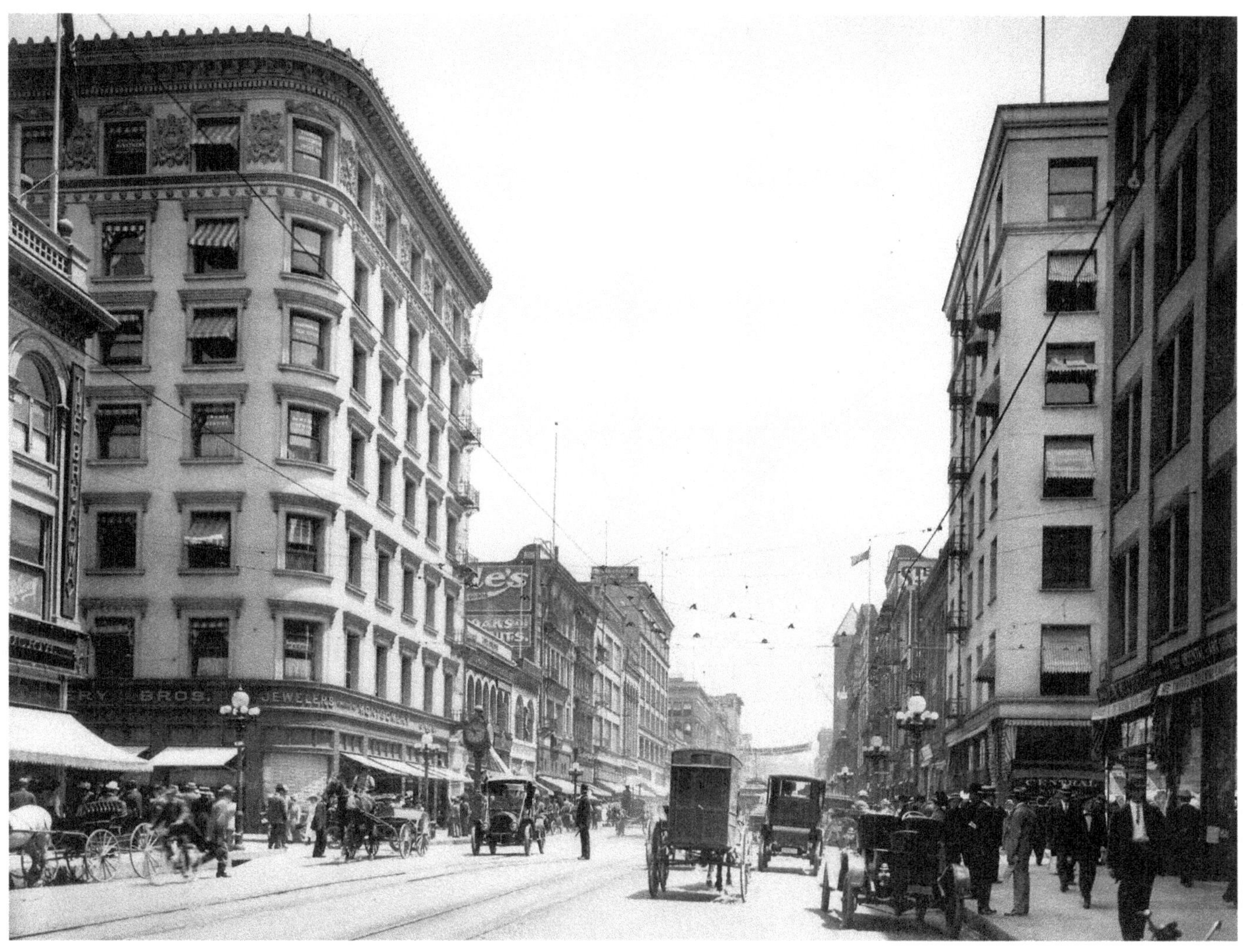

Some of the first automobiles in America appear in this Los Angeles photograph of Broadway looking north from 4th Street. Due in large part to Henry Ford's (1863–1947) innovative, assembly-line production techniques, ownership of motor cars expanded dramatically over the next several decades.

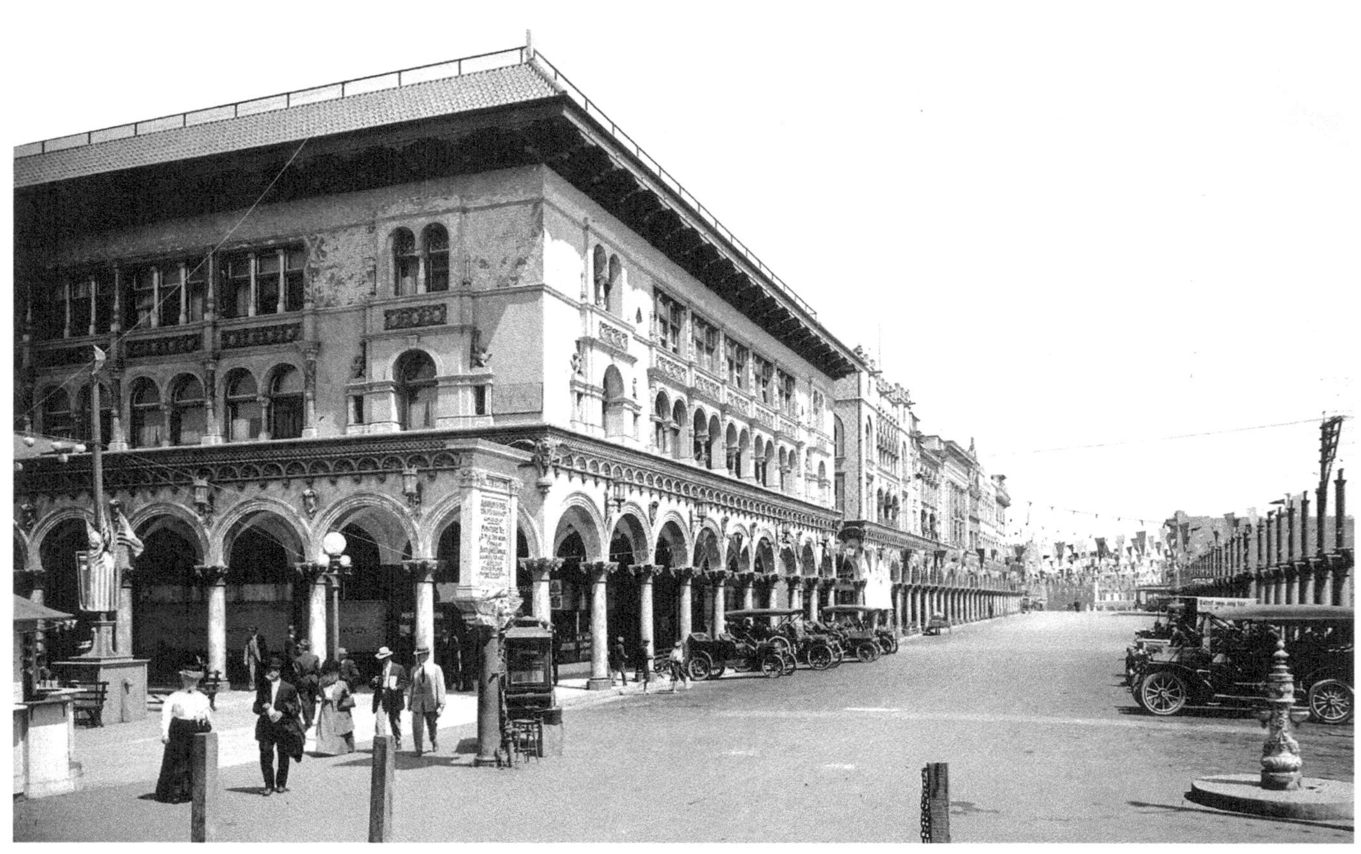

Southern California, with its beautiful weather, was often compared to Italy, "A Mediterranean land without the marshes and malaria." Venice, California, was built by Abbot Kinney (1850–1920), a wealthy tobacco mogul, to resemble its Italian namesake. By 1906 the resort and amusement park was completed, and it became known as the "Coney Island of the Pacific." With the Hotel St. Mark at left, this Venice street scene could easily pass for the famous European city of the same name.

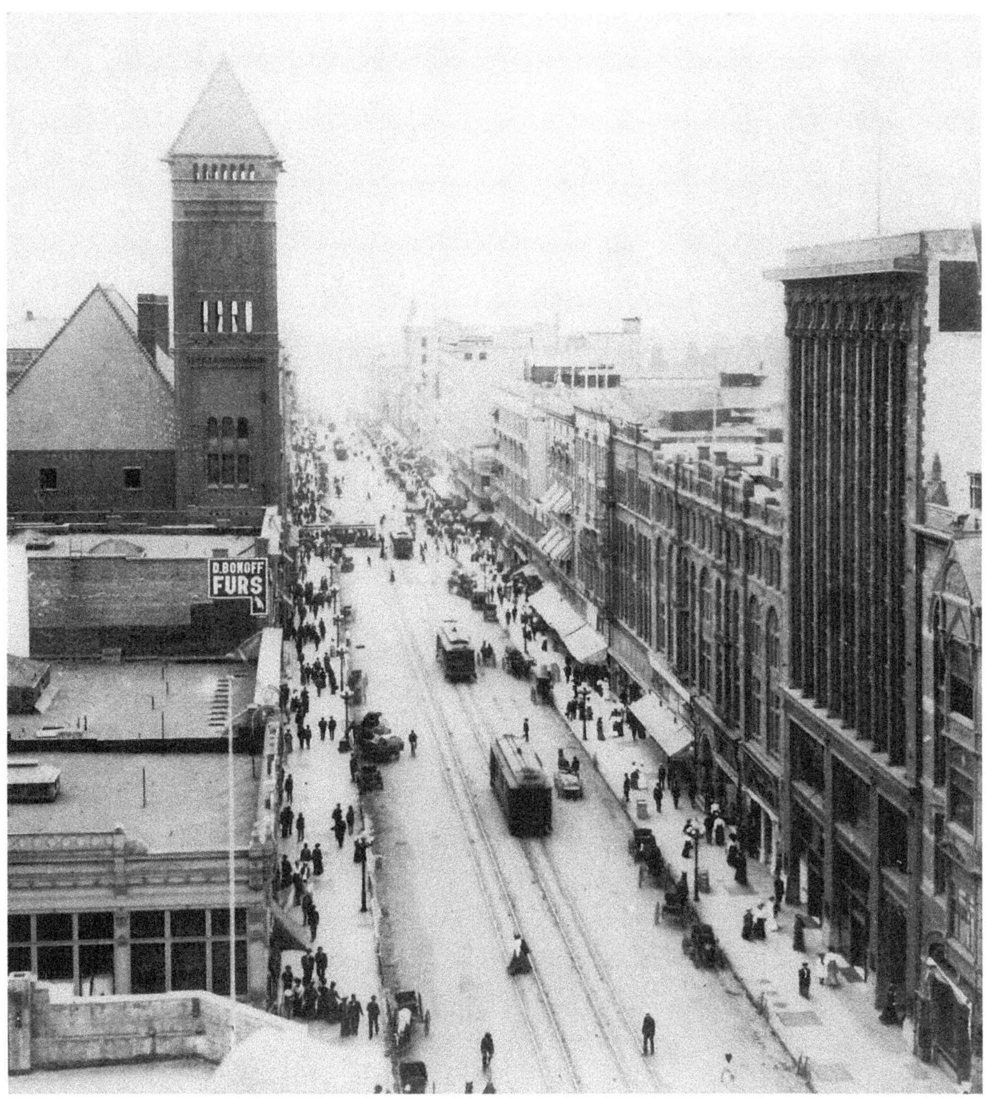

A stereo-card view of Broadway in Los Angeles as seen from the Chamber of Commerce Building. The Chamber of Commerce displayed the Coronel Collection, donated in 1901 by Doña Mariana, the widow of Don Antonio Coronel, which contained relics of the Spanish and Mexican regimes in California.

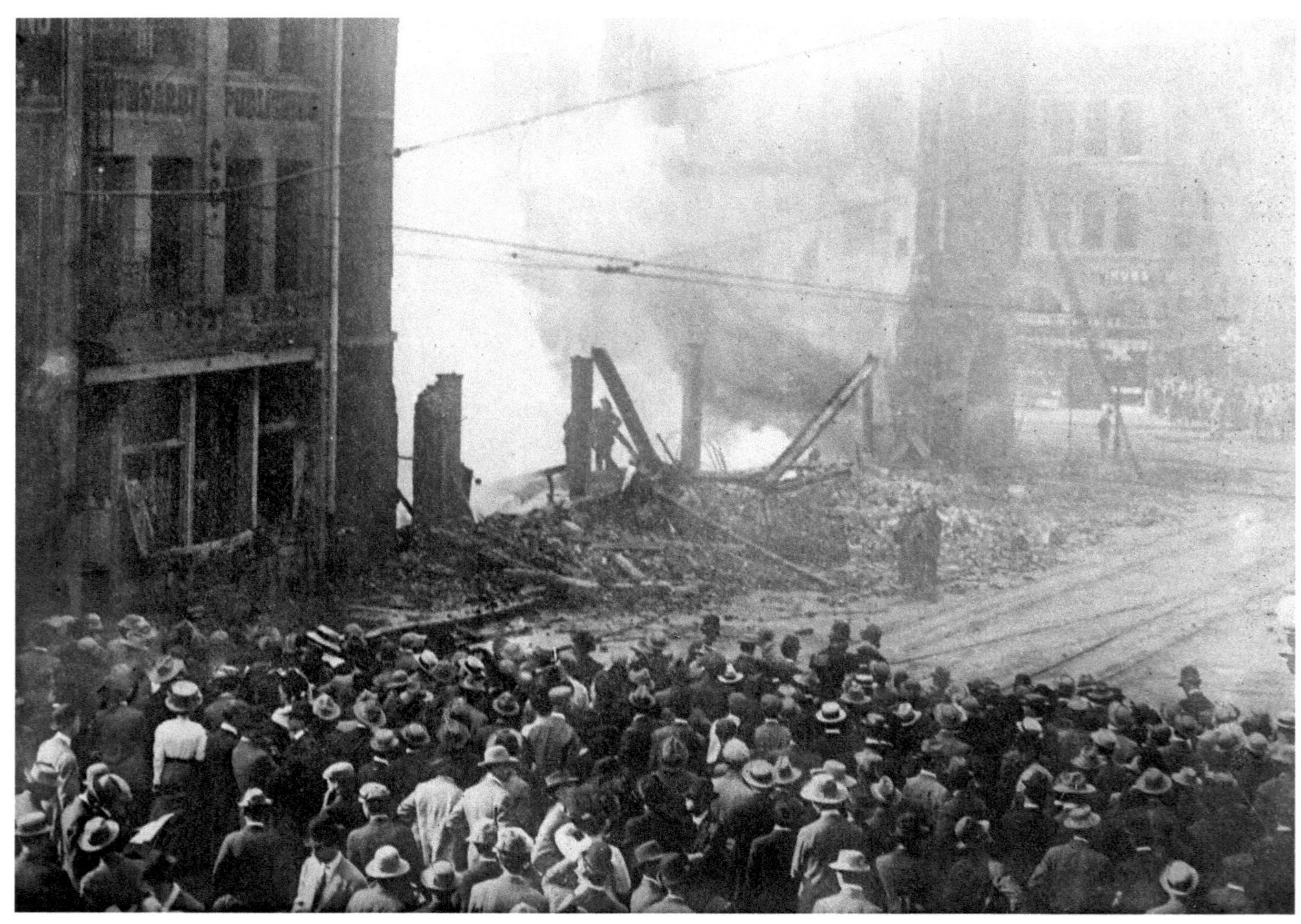

This wreckage is all that remained of the *Los Angeles Times* building after dynamite was detonated at the anti-union newspaper on October 1, 1910. Twenty-one employees were killed and many more injured in the explosion and fire. James and John McNamara, Irish American trade unionists, were arrested and initially pleaded not guilty. The unions hired Clarence Darrow (1857–1938) as their lawyer.

The Rise of Hollywood and the Great War

(1910–1919)

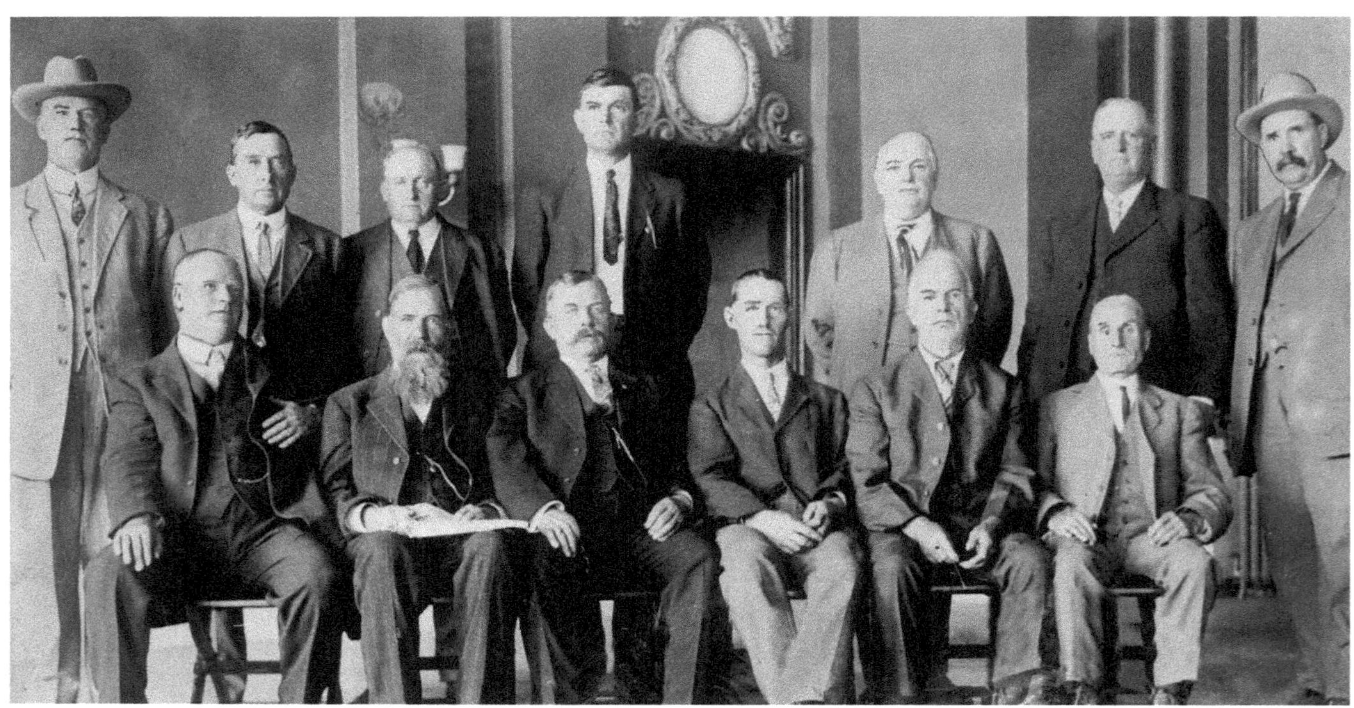

Overwhelming evidence against the McNamara brothers for destroying the *Los Angeles Times* building caused them to change their plea to guilty. The outcome of the McNamara case destroyed Socialist candidate Job Harriman's chances of being the next governor of California. Because no trial occurred, prospective jurors, such as these "talesmen" (a person who is summoned under a "writ of tales"), were not needed.

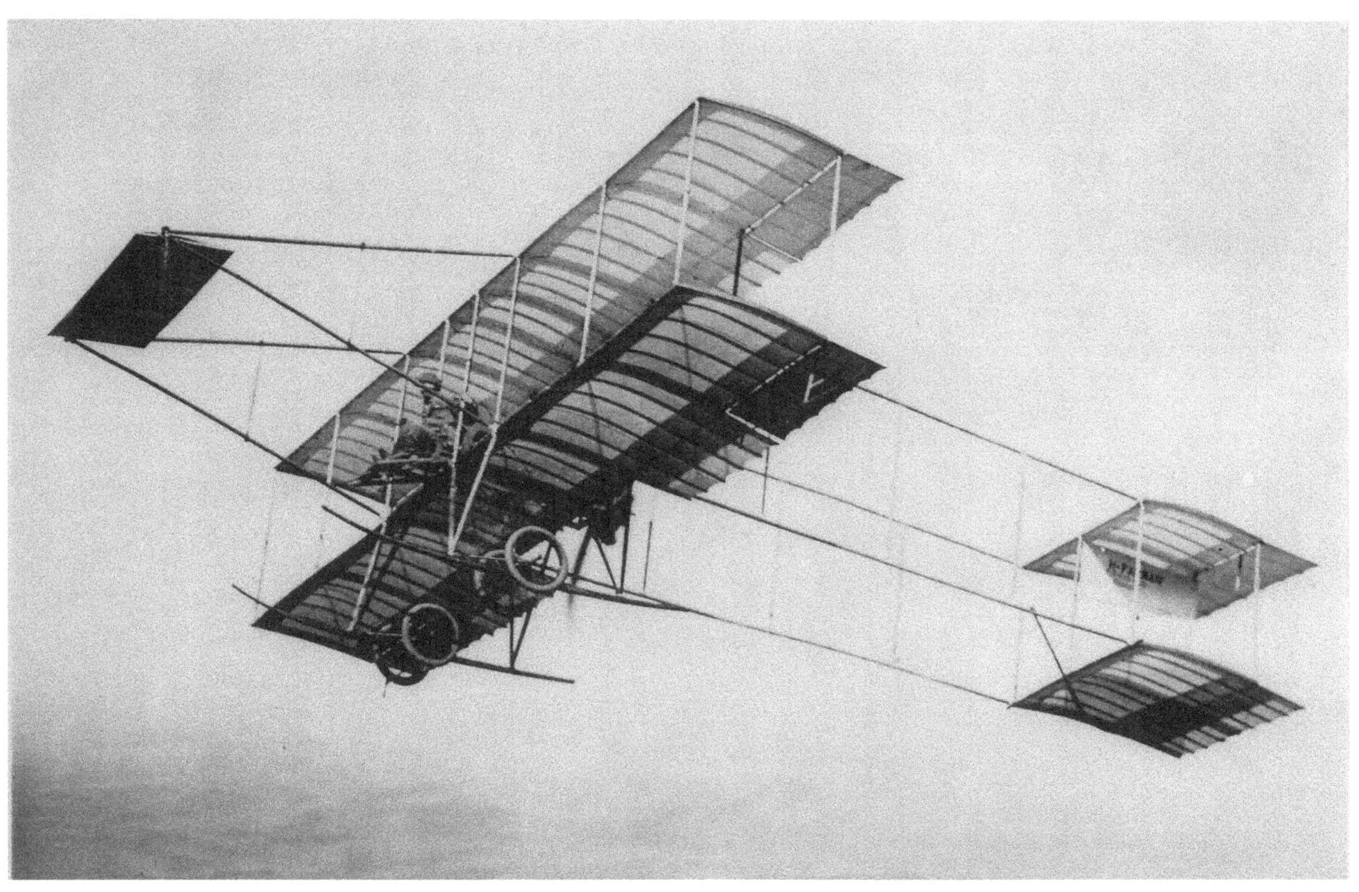

Americans Orville and Wilbur Wright are credited with inventing and building the world's first successful airplane and making the first controlled, powered, and sustained heavier-than-air human flight on December 17, 1903. Daredevil pilots soon followed to capture the public's imagination. One of these was French aviator Louis Paulhan (1883–1963), shown in this photo, who won $10,000 in prize money and the title "King of the Air" for establishing a new altitude record of 4,165 feet at the Los Angeles Air Meet in January 1910.

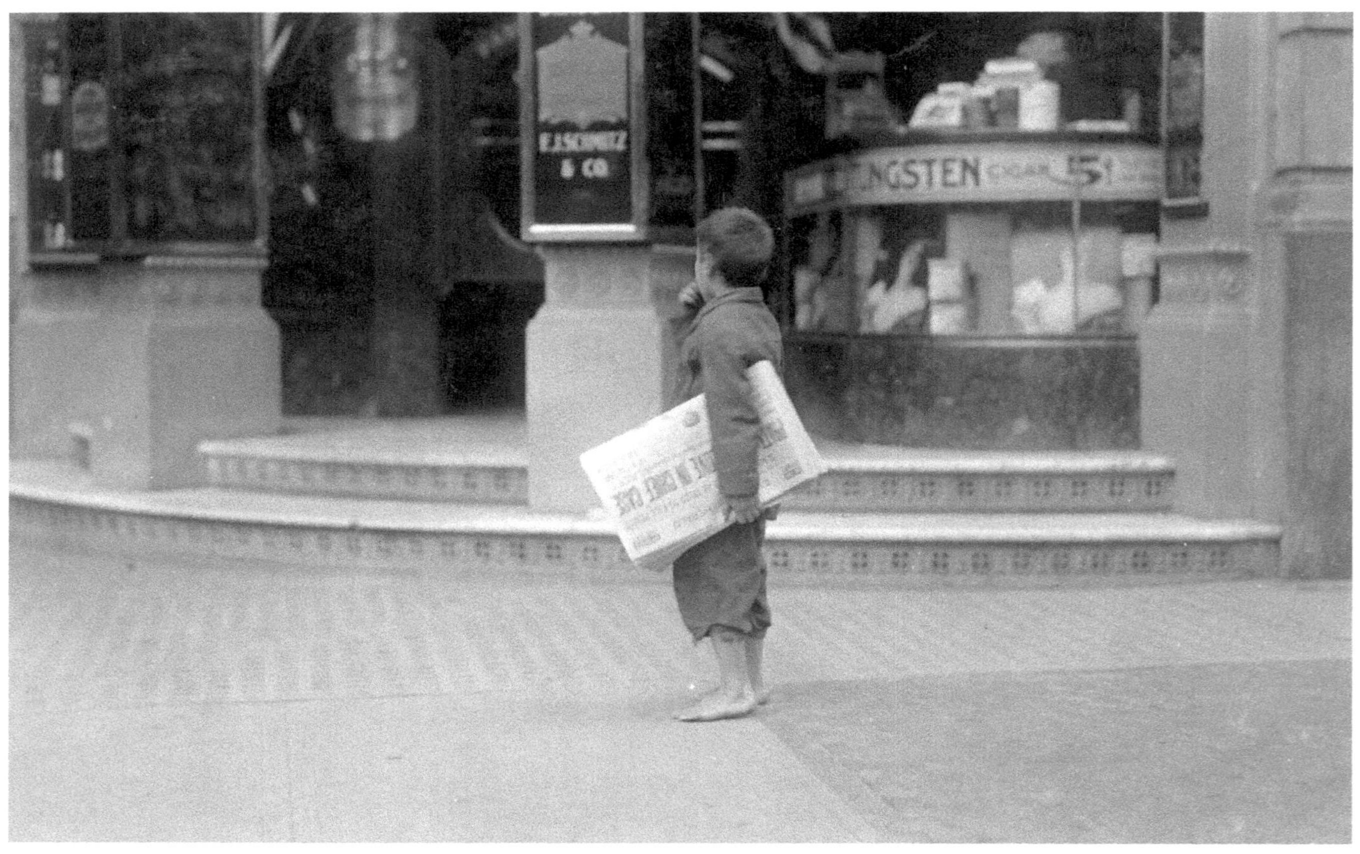

A barefoot newsie sells papers to earn a few pennies. The fierce competition for circulation motivated newspapers to practice "yellow journalism"—a type of reporting that featured scandal-mongering, sensationalism, jingoism, and unethical and unprofessional writing.

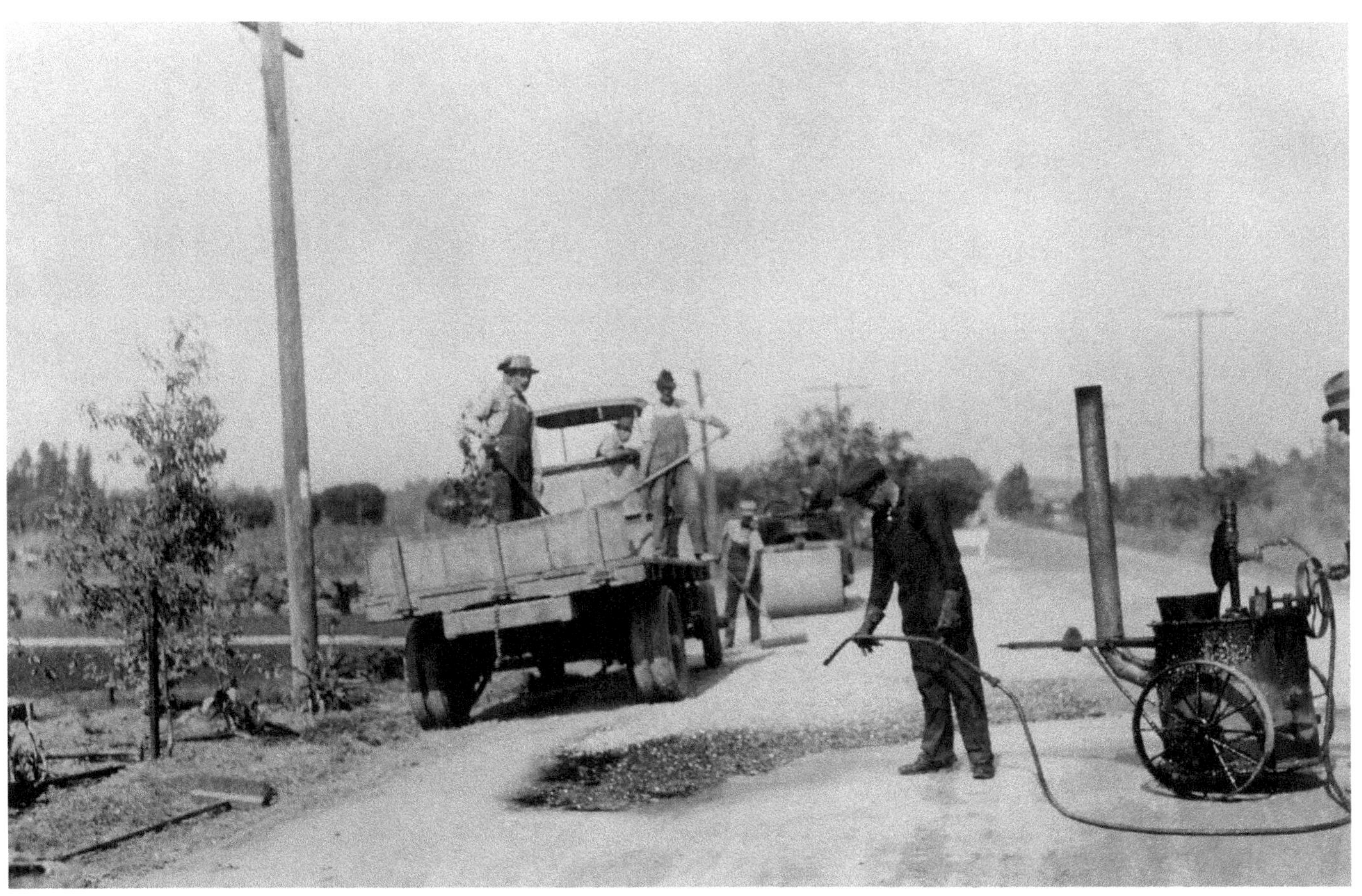

Automobile ownership in America increased tremendously during the second decade of the twentieth century. Private cars and business-owned trucks kept repair crews like this "heavy maintenance" squad constantly busy. The crew here is placing a three-inch-deep patch on oiled macadam around 1915.

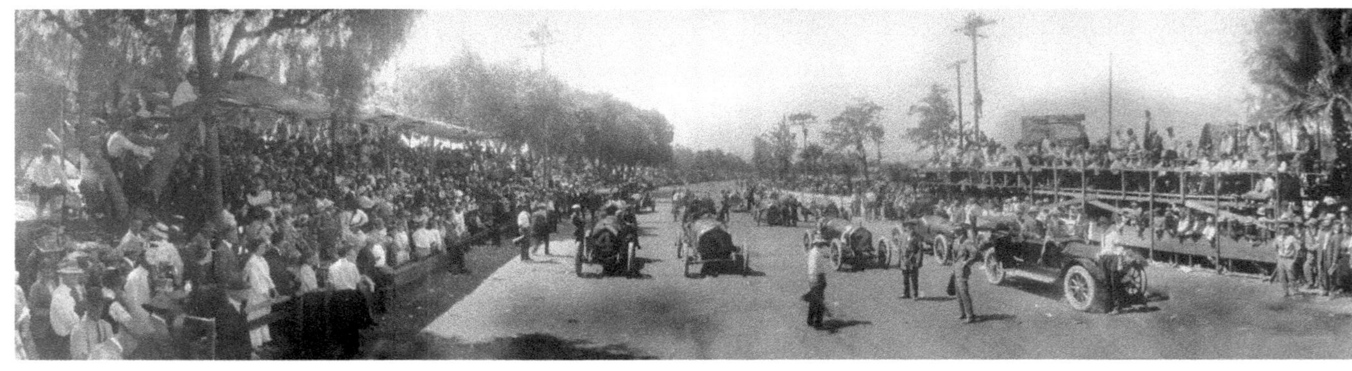

Within a few years after the automobile was invented, car races became popular. This panorama view shows the start of a "medium and heavyweight" auto race at the Corona Speedway around 1913.

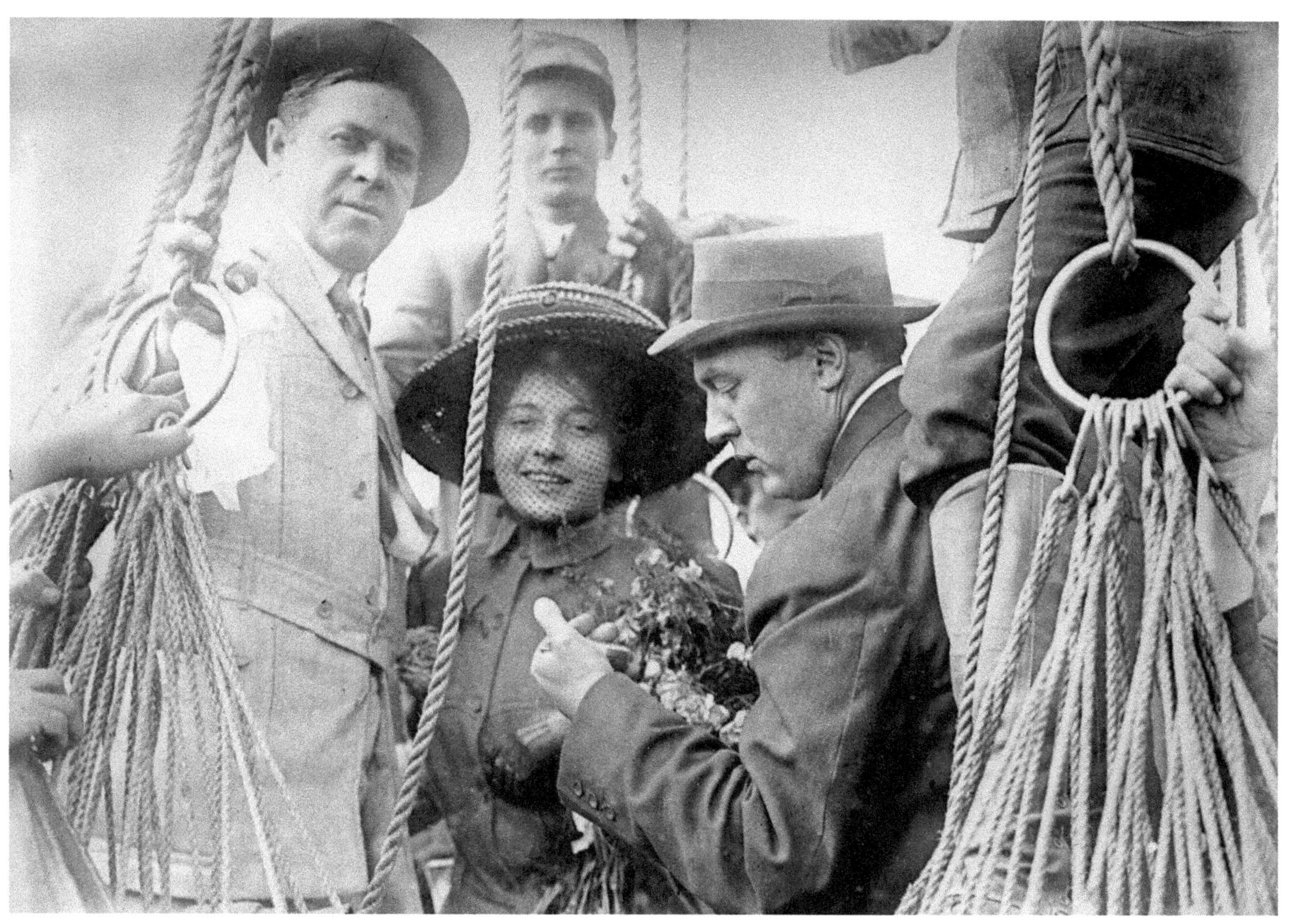

One of America's earliest news picture agencies was the Bain News Service. George Grantham Bain (1865–1914) created a business that documented sports events, celebrities, crime, strikes, disasters, political activities, and so on, from the 1860s through the 1930s. The bulk of the collection covers life in New York City, but other cities were included. This Bain image shows C. A. Coey and his bride in Los Angeles in the 1910s.

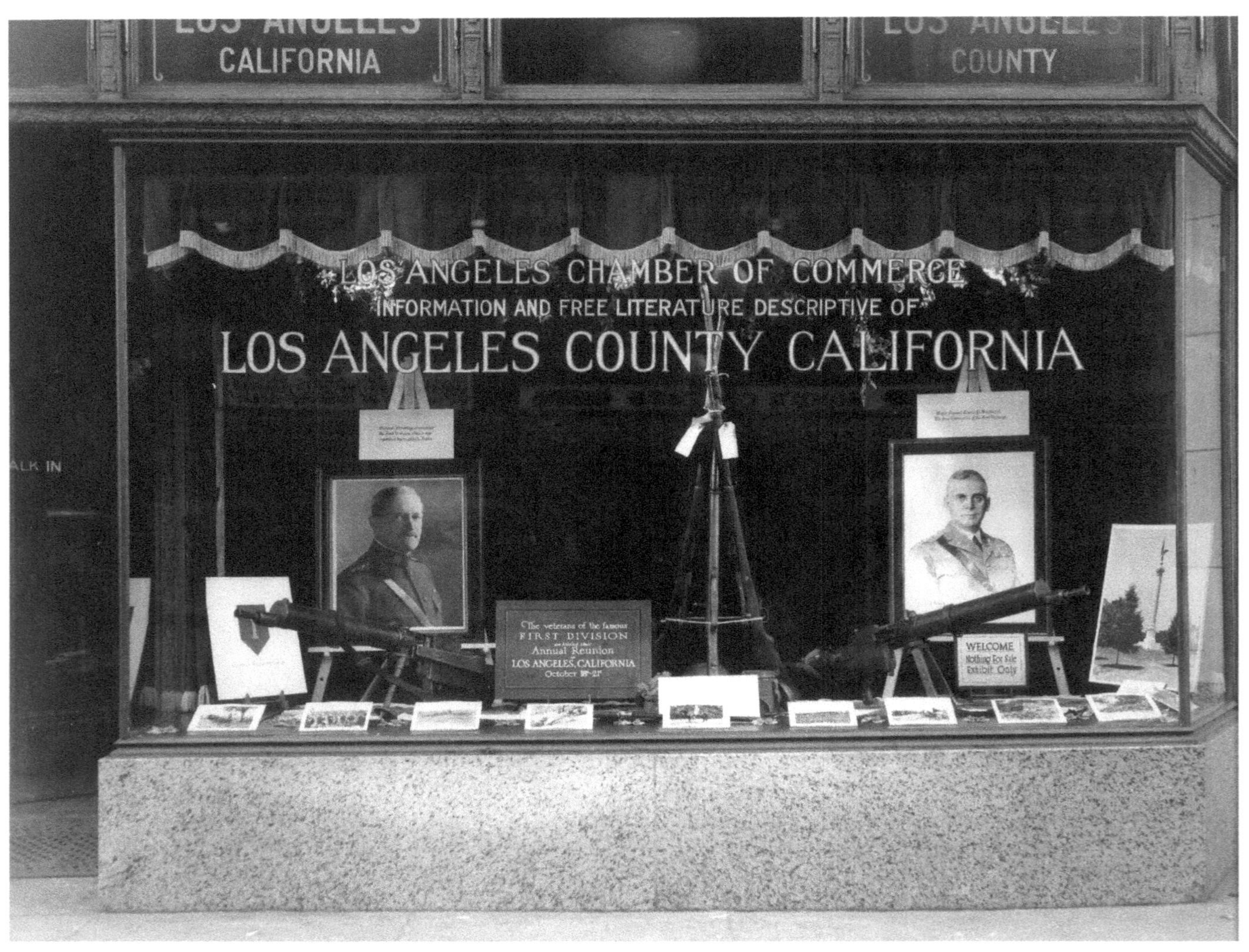

After President Woodrow Wilson delivered his "war message" speech on April 2, 1917, Congress declared war against Germany. By June, the first American military units arrived in France, including the First Division. A window display for a First Division reunion appeared in the office of the Los Angeles Chamber of Commerce.

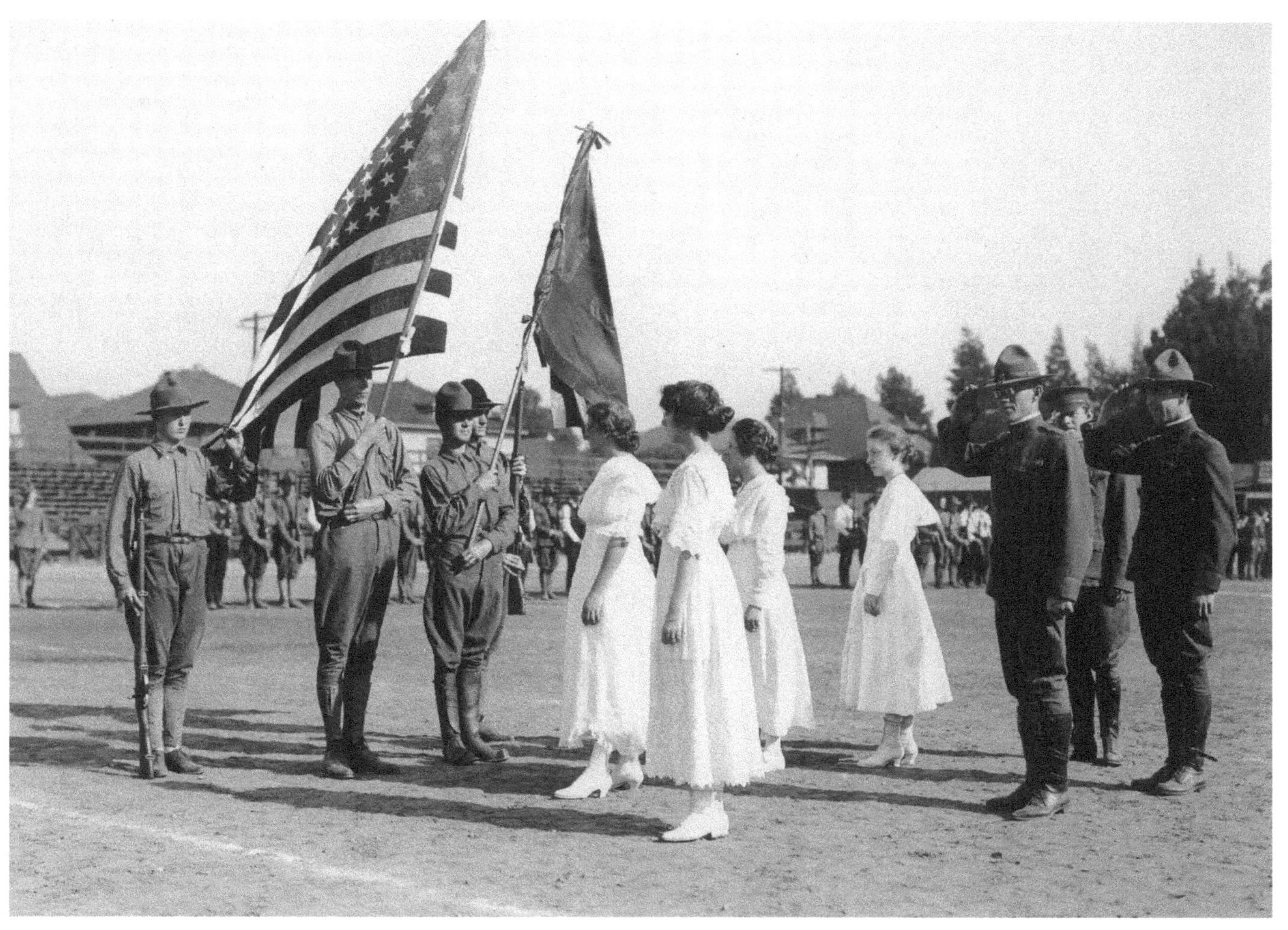

Presentation of the colors and standard of the USC (University of Southern California) Battalion to a committee of women students. The American Expeditionary Force (AEF) sent to fight in Europe lost 116,708 soldiers of the nearly six million dead lost by the Allied powers as a whole. Following the war, more than 650,000 Americans died in the influenza pandemic of 1918–1919.

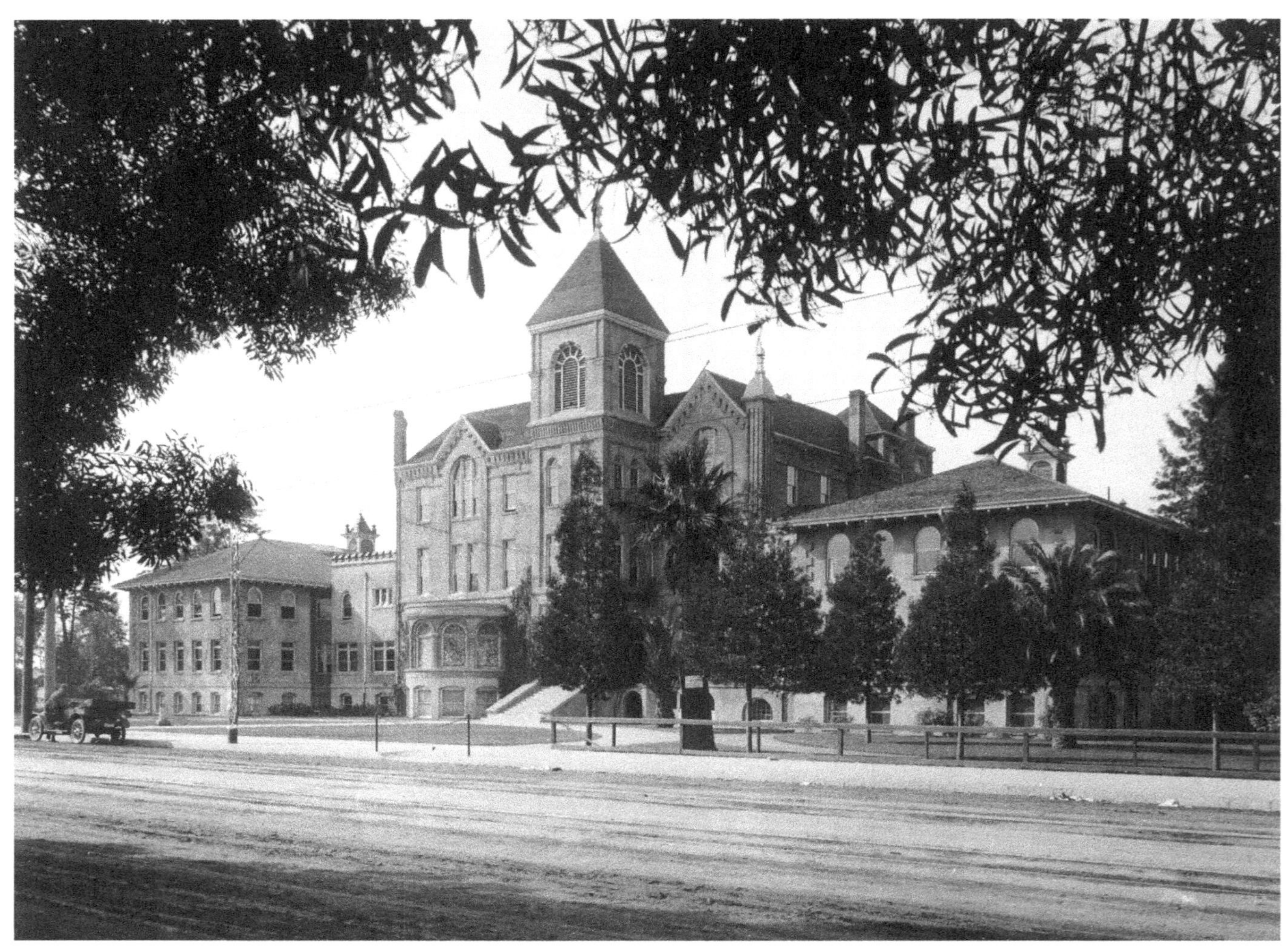

The University of Southern California, commonly referred to as USC, was founded in 1880, making it California's oldest private research university. This photograph from the 1910s shows the Administration Building of the College of Liberal Arts at USC. The school consistently ranks among the top American colleges, with students from all 50 states as well as more than 115 countries.

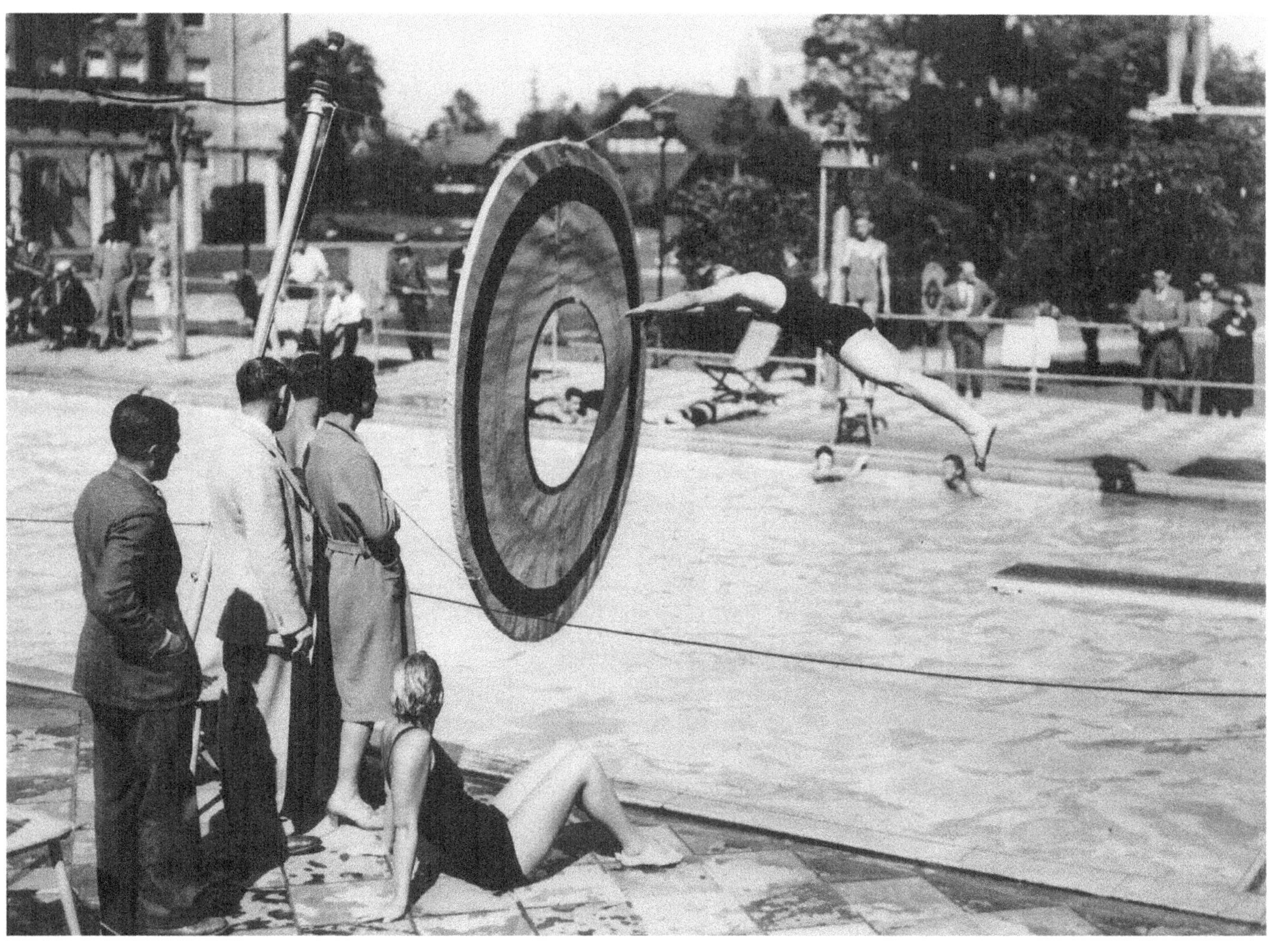

In this acrobatic “target diving” stunt in Los Angeles, Johnny Riley, national 10-foot-diving champ, takes flight as a “human arrow.”

The tower of Los Angeles City Hall can be seen in the background as a Hispanic woman obtains water at a fountain on Olvera Street, an area described as a "Mexican shopping lane." In 1910, Mexican immigration to Los Angeles increased dramatically as many people fled the turmoil and violence of the Mexican Revolution, the first large revolution of the twentieth century. Reaction to the tide of illegal immigrants from Mexico led to the 1913 California Alien Land Law that prevented ownership of land by "aliens ineligible for citizenship."

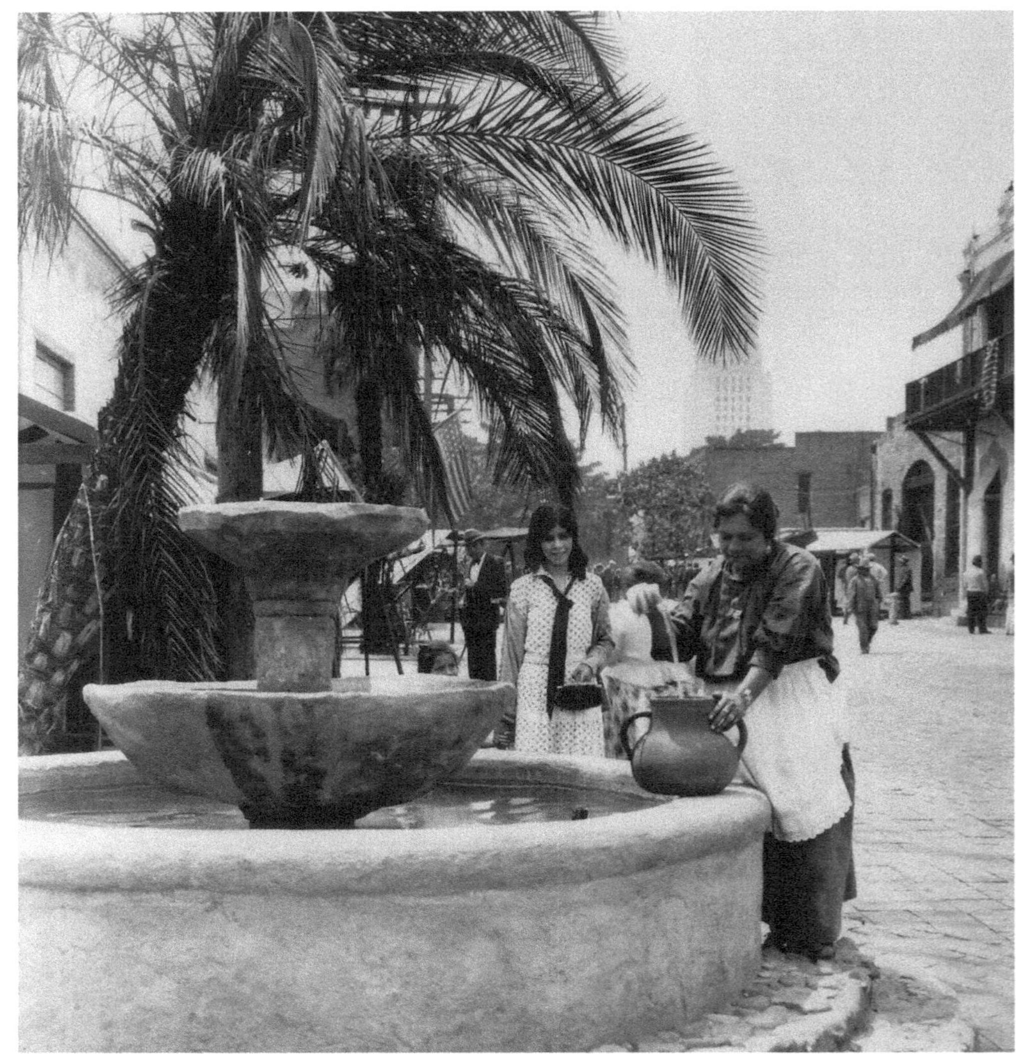

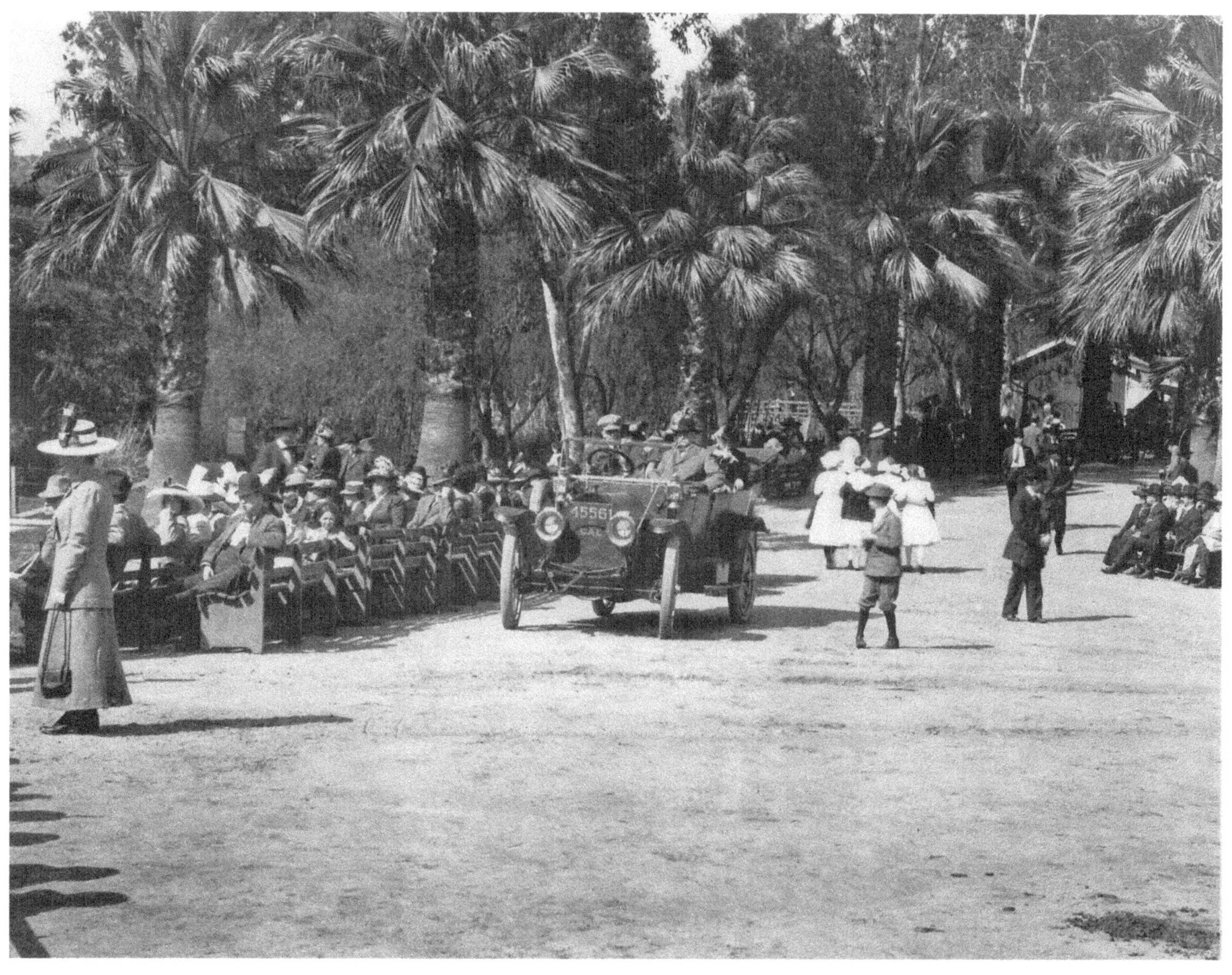

An early photo of Lincoln Park, initially called East Los Angeles Park and then Eastlake Park in 1901. It quickly became a major amusement center, and one of its main attractions was the area's first zoological display. In 1917, the L.A. City Council responded to a petition from residents and renamed it Lincoln Park after a local high school.

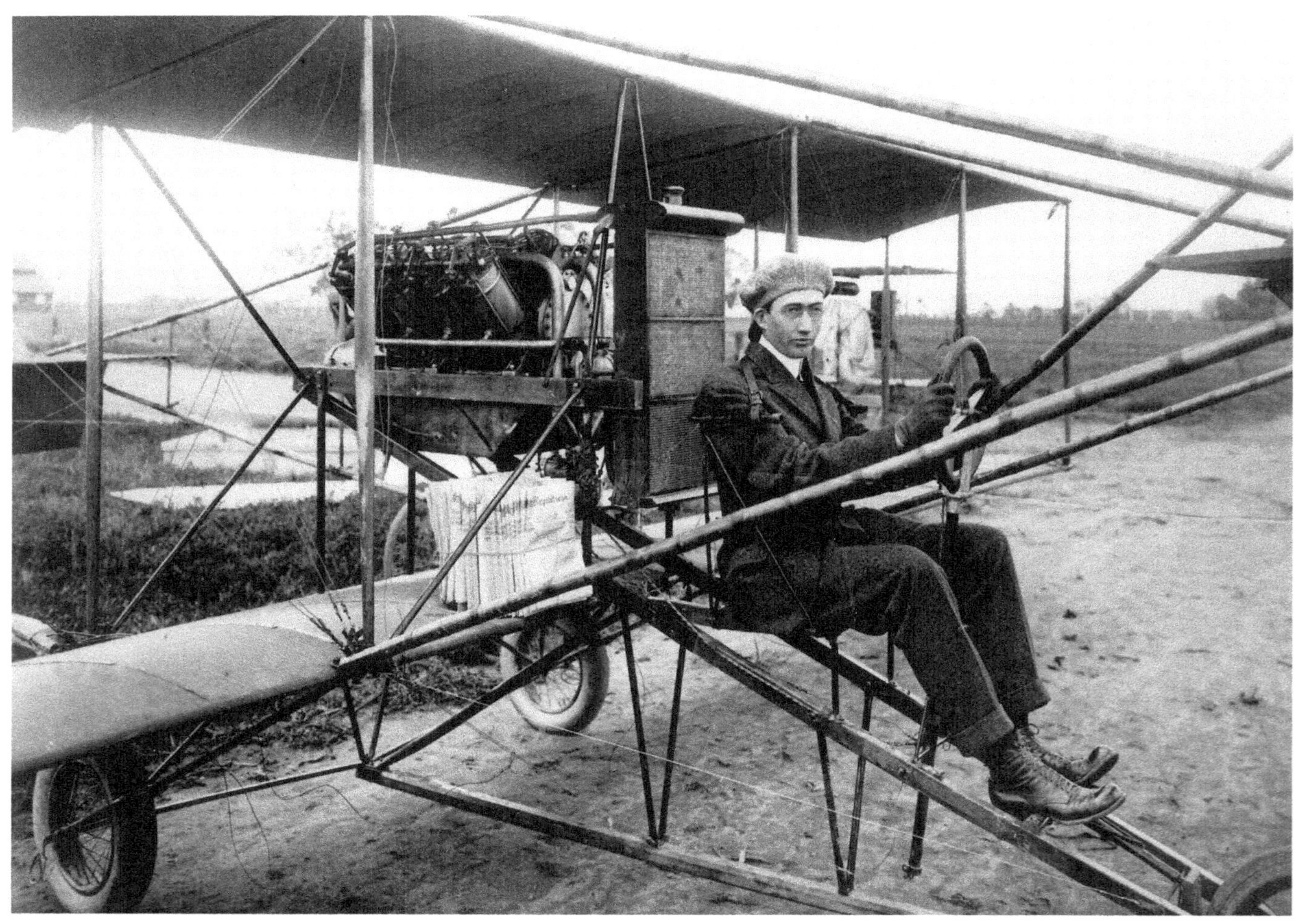

Aviation pioneer Glenn Martin (1886–1955) is shown delivering newspapers to Los Angeles in his airplane in 1911. He founded a company that initially made military trainers in Santa Ana, then eventually relocated to Maryland where he produced military aircraft until after World War II. His company went through several mergers and in 1995 became part of Lockheed Martin, a leading multinational aerospace manufacturer and advanced technology company.

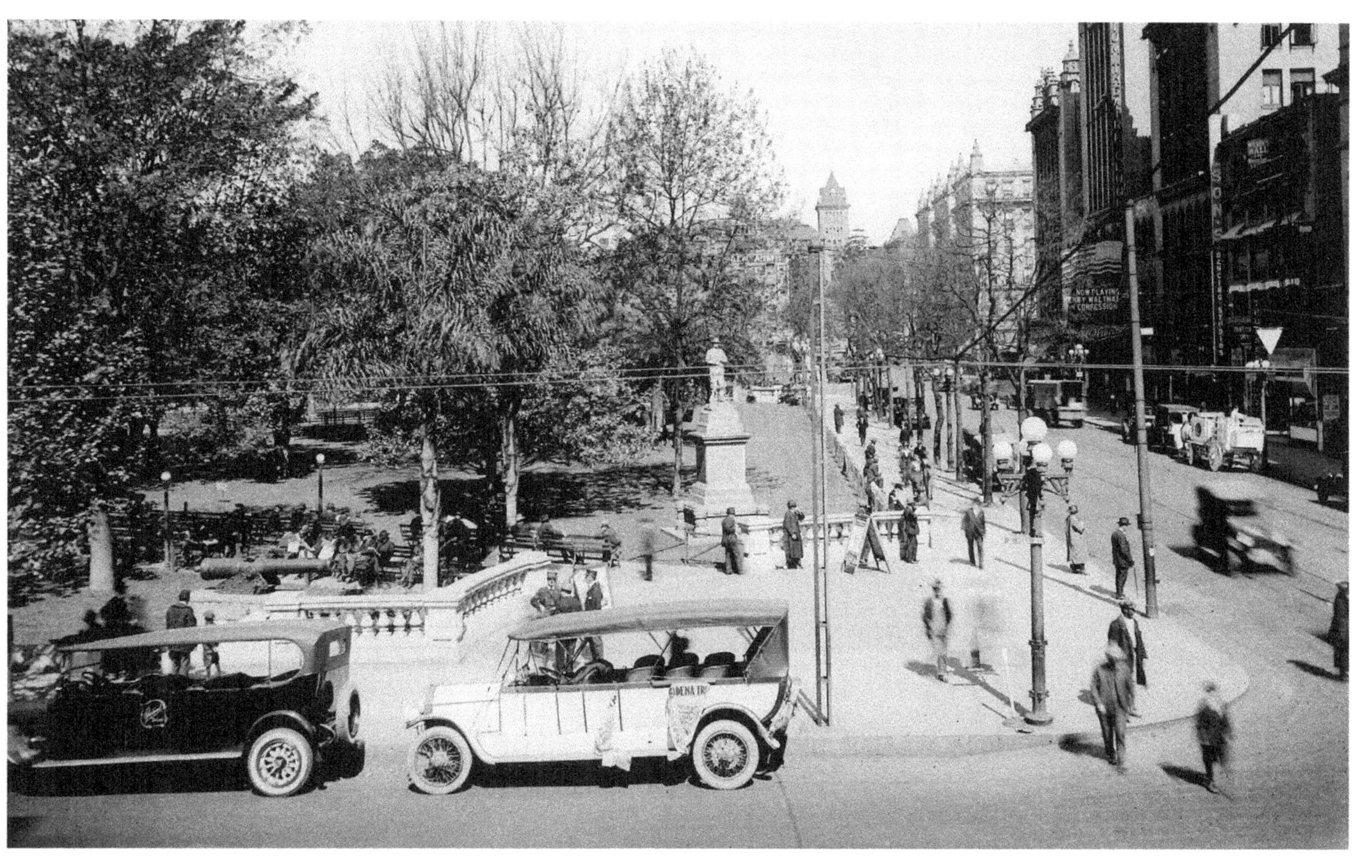

This photo shows Central Park, one of the oldest parks in Los Angeles, with its Spanish-American War Memorial honoring the Seventh California Volunteer Infantry Regiment. The monument, reputedly the first work of public art in L.A., was dedicated in 1900. The park was renamed Pershing Square in 1918 to honor General John Joseph "Black Jack" Pershing, the commander of the American Expeditionary Force that fought in Europe. In 2008 the park was a concrete plaza located on the roof of a parking garage.

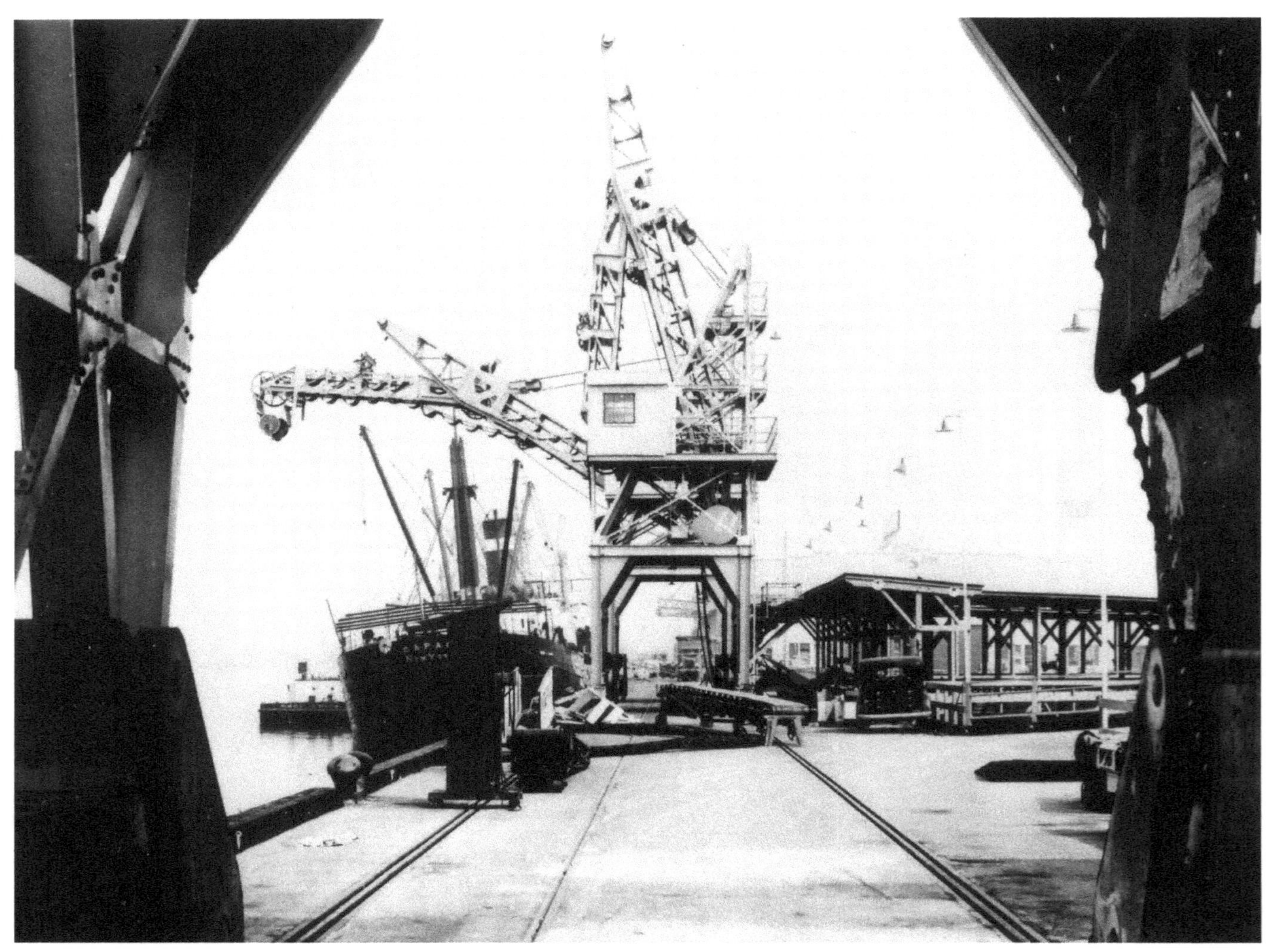

Los Angeles did not originally have a deep harbor like San Diego or San Francisco. In the early 1900s repeated bonds were issued by the L.A. Harbor Commission to create a viable Port of Los Angeles. Over many years the Army Corps of Engineers widened the channel near San Pedro and Wilmington and constructed a deep basin. Here, traveling cranes stand at ready on a Los Angeles pier.

The Roaring Twenties, Prohibition, and Gangsters

(1920–1929)

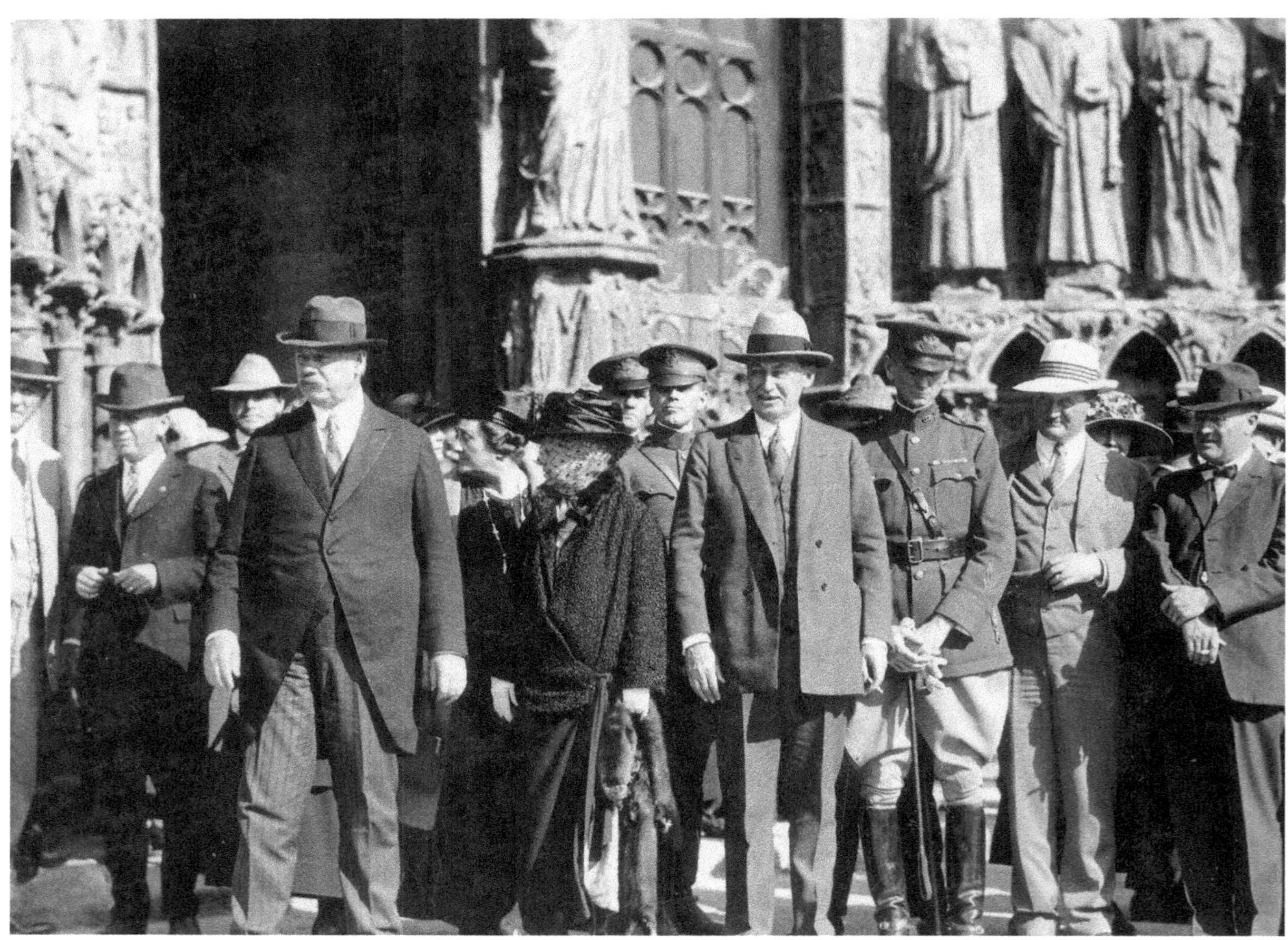

A Congressional party visits the Universal Motion Picture Studio in Los Angeles while on a tour to Panama and Alaska in 1924. Although immorality was presented in burlesque houses and dime novels, many religious groups and other organizations were concerned that moving pictures had much greater influence. Congress was therefore pushed to censor movie content, and a ruling by the Supreme Court confirmed that films were subject to censorship and could not claim protection under the First Amendment.

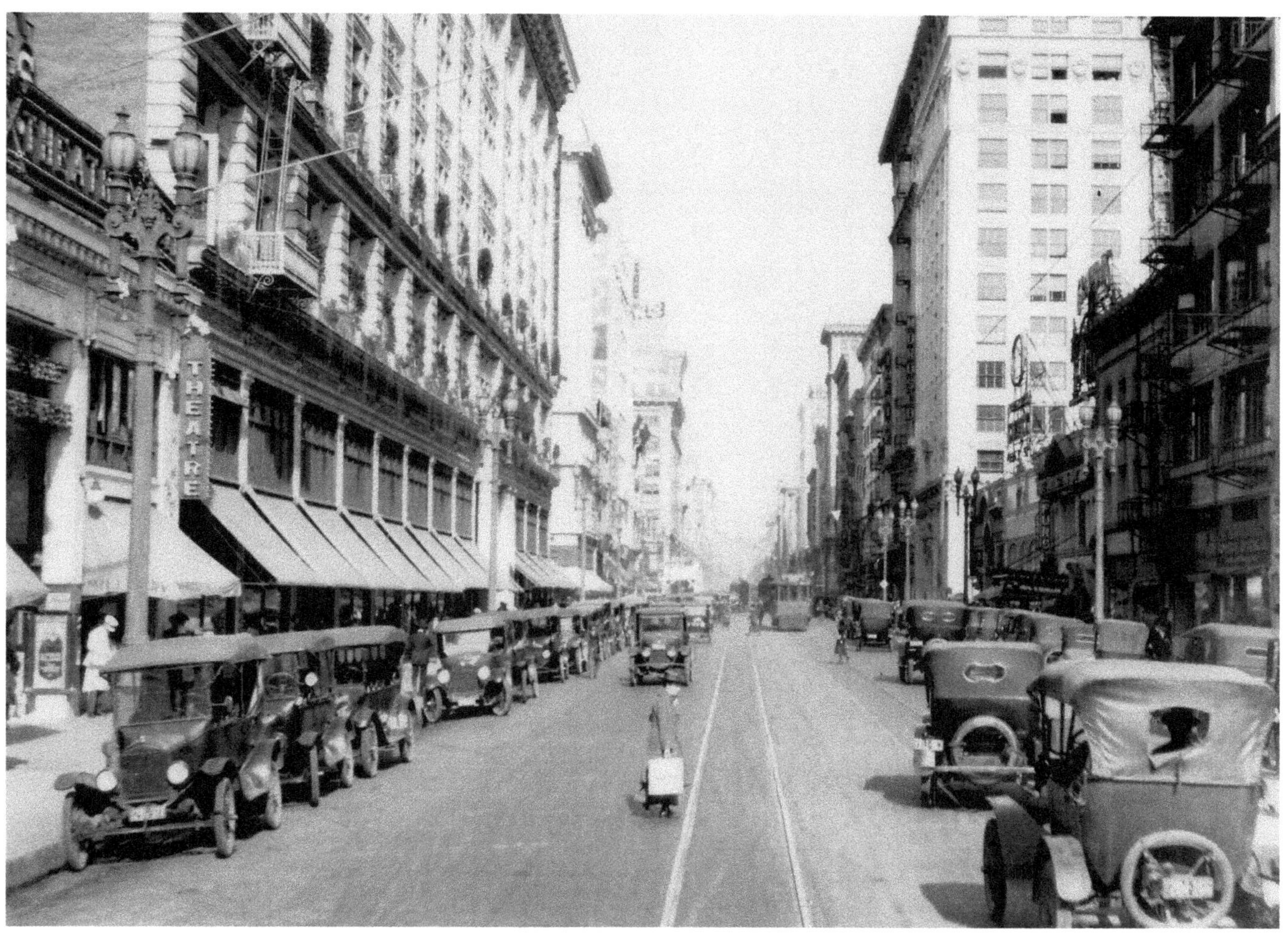

Broadway at 8th Street in downtown Los Angeles around 1920. The dramatic increase in roads and cars created the suburban boom of the 1920s and affected nearly a hundred American cities. This growth was welcomed not only by real estate developers; housing reformers believed that poverty and crime resulted from overcrowding in centralized cities.

An artist at his easel, Avenue of the Palms in Los Angeles. Louis Adamic (1899–1951), an émigré writer and labor activist from Slovenia, eked out a living in Los Angeles in the 1920s. His bitter view of L.A., expressed through such works as *Laughing in the Jungle,* was that of a remorseless city where dishonest promoters grew rich exploiting deluded idealists looking for a nonexistent paradise. Similar sentiments of Los Angeles would echo in the works of many other writers.

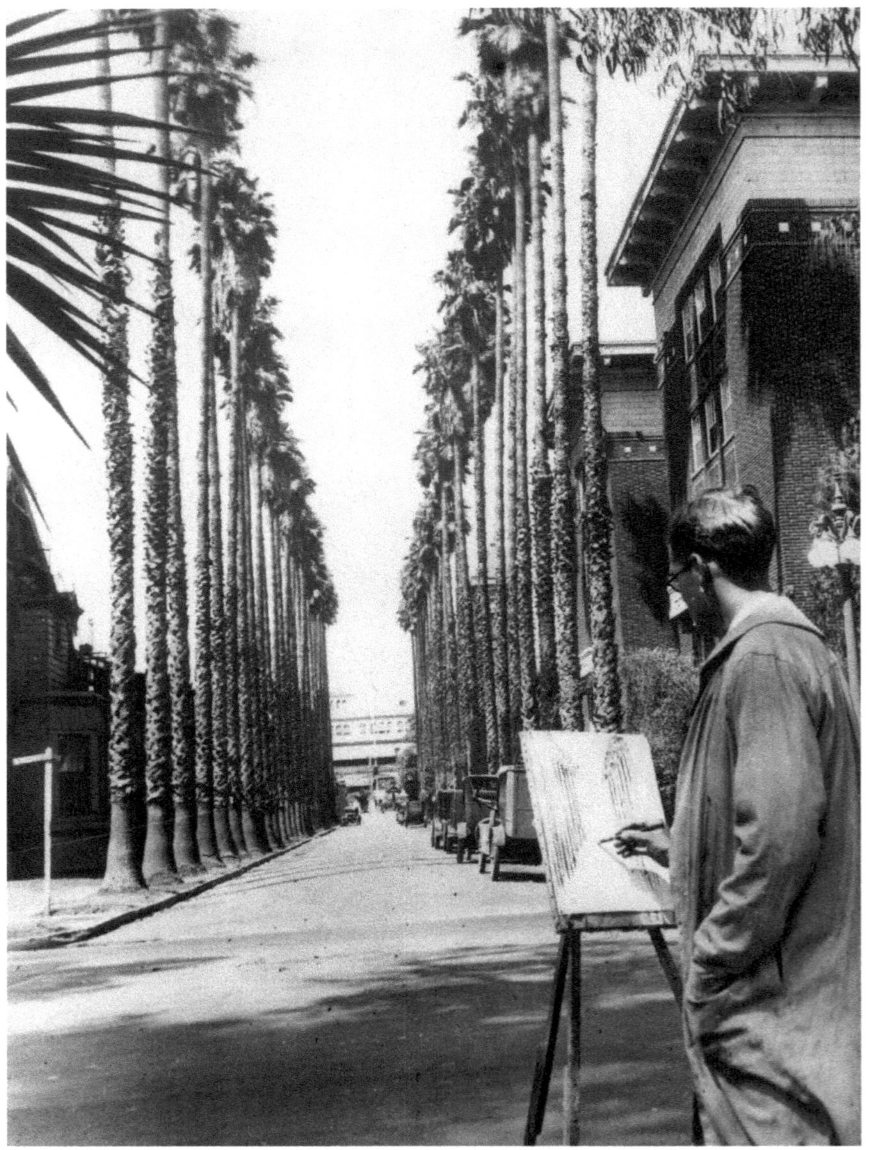

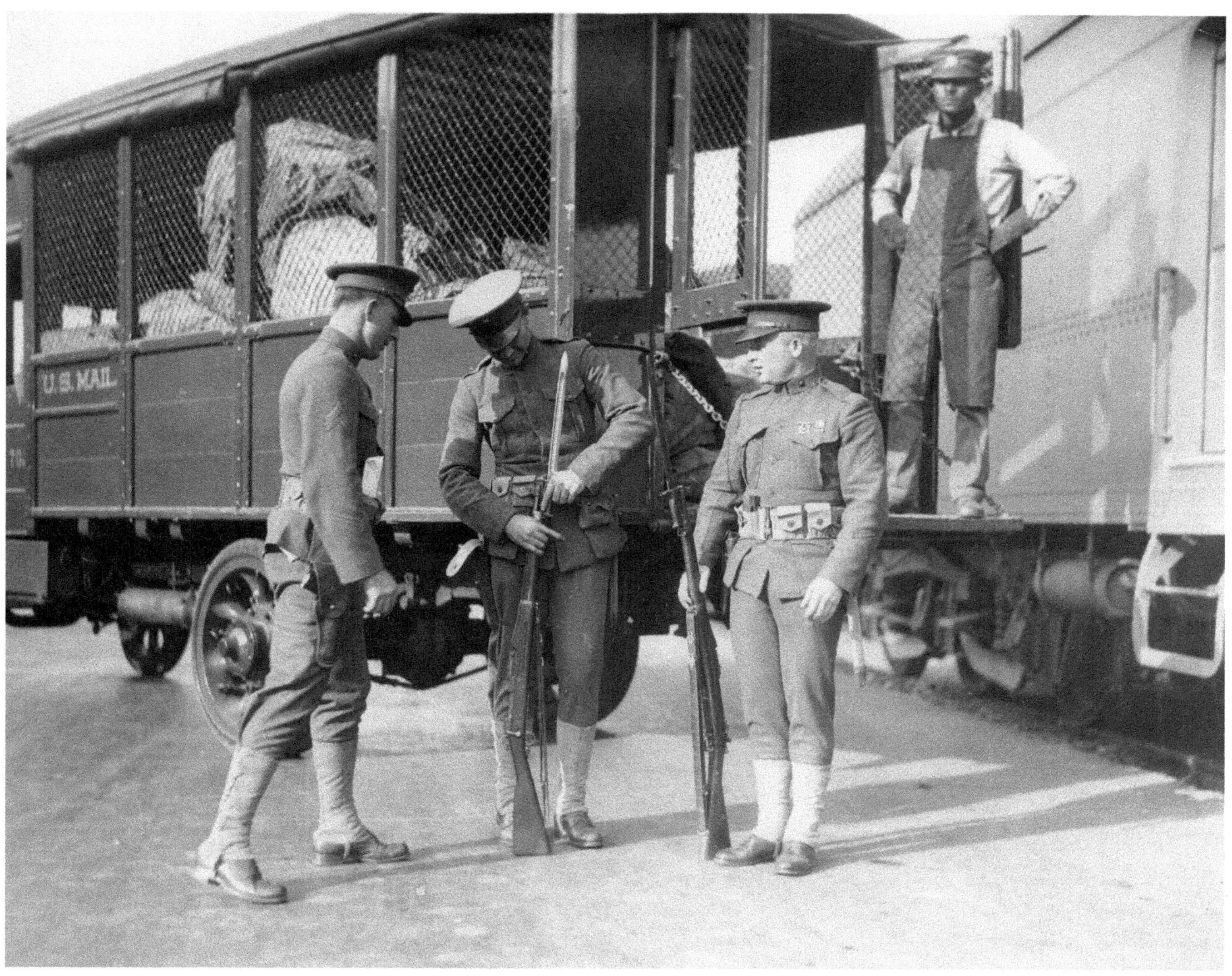

Prohibition unintentionally created criminal networks throughout many American cities. Although Los Angeles was not controlled by gangsters as Chicago was, L.A. still had its share of ruthless thugs, corrupt policemen, and petty crime. In 1926, so many mail robberies occurred that 2,500 Marines were assigned to guard the mail in 23 cities. Marines equipped with semiautomatic pistols, shotguns, rifles, and machine guns guarded the U.S. mail in Los Angeles with instructions to shoot to kill.

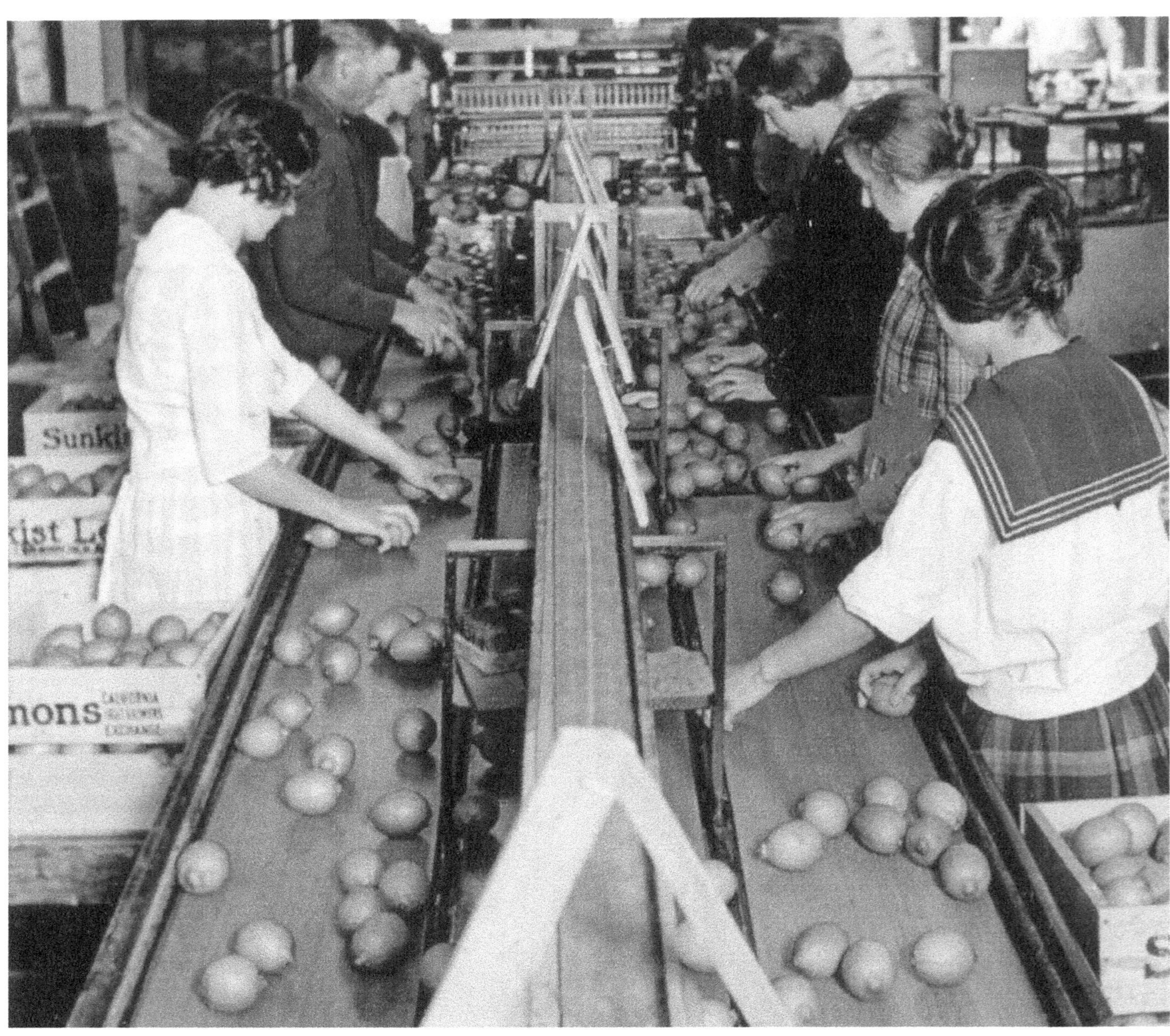

In Lamanda Park, lemons coming from a washer are hand-graded according to their color. Such labor in the 1920s, as today, was often done by migrant workers.

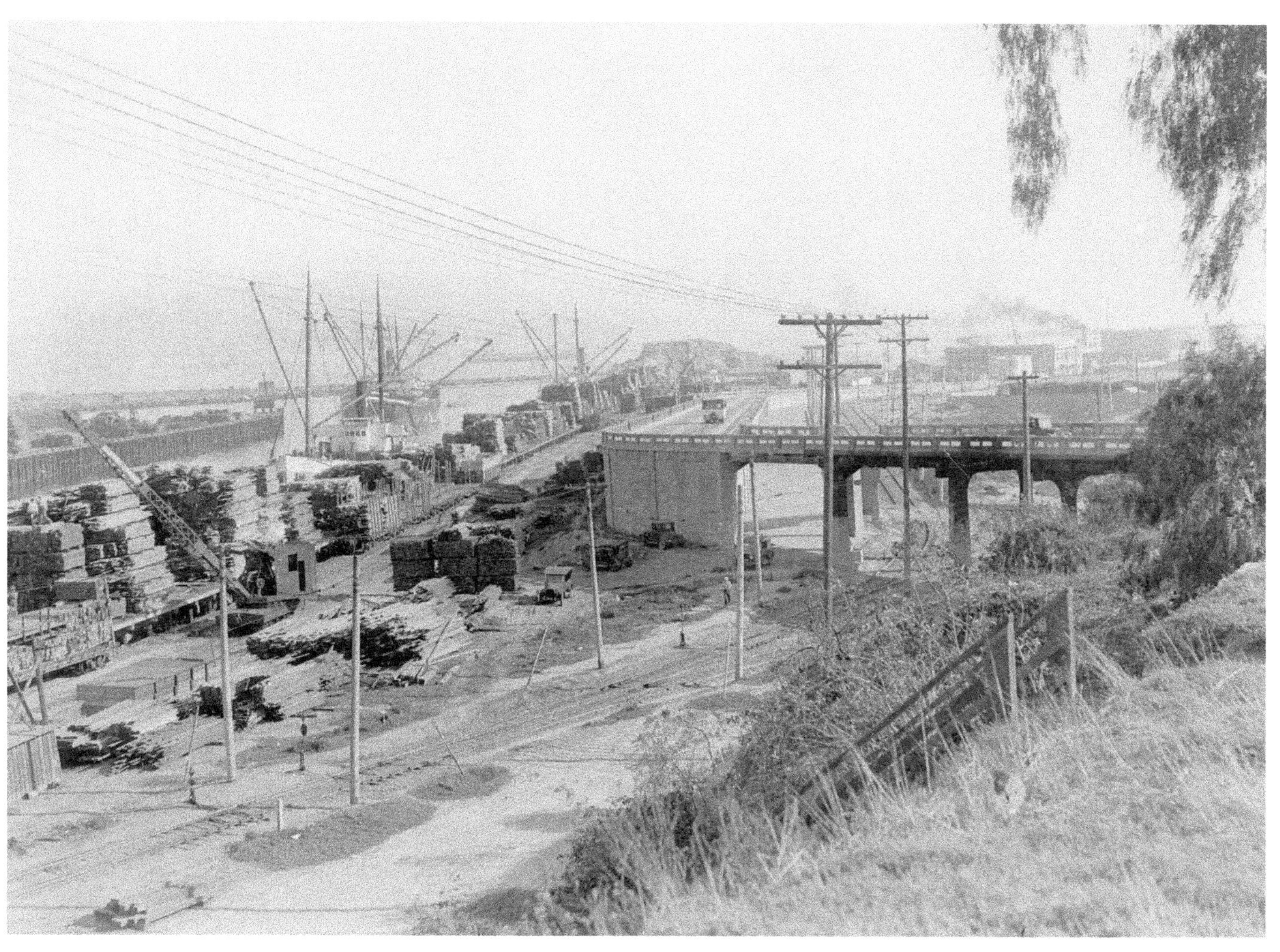

A view of Los Angeles harbor, whose phenomenal growth in this decade made it the second greatest port in America. L.A.'s shipping trade was exceeded only by New York and exports alone during 1926 were more than $100 million, nearly fourteen times greater than exports through L.A. in 1915.

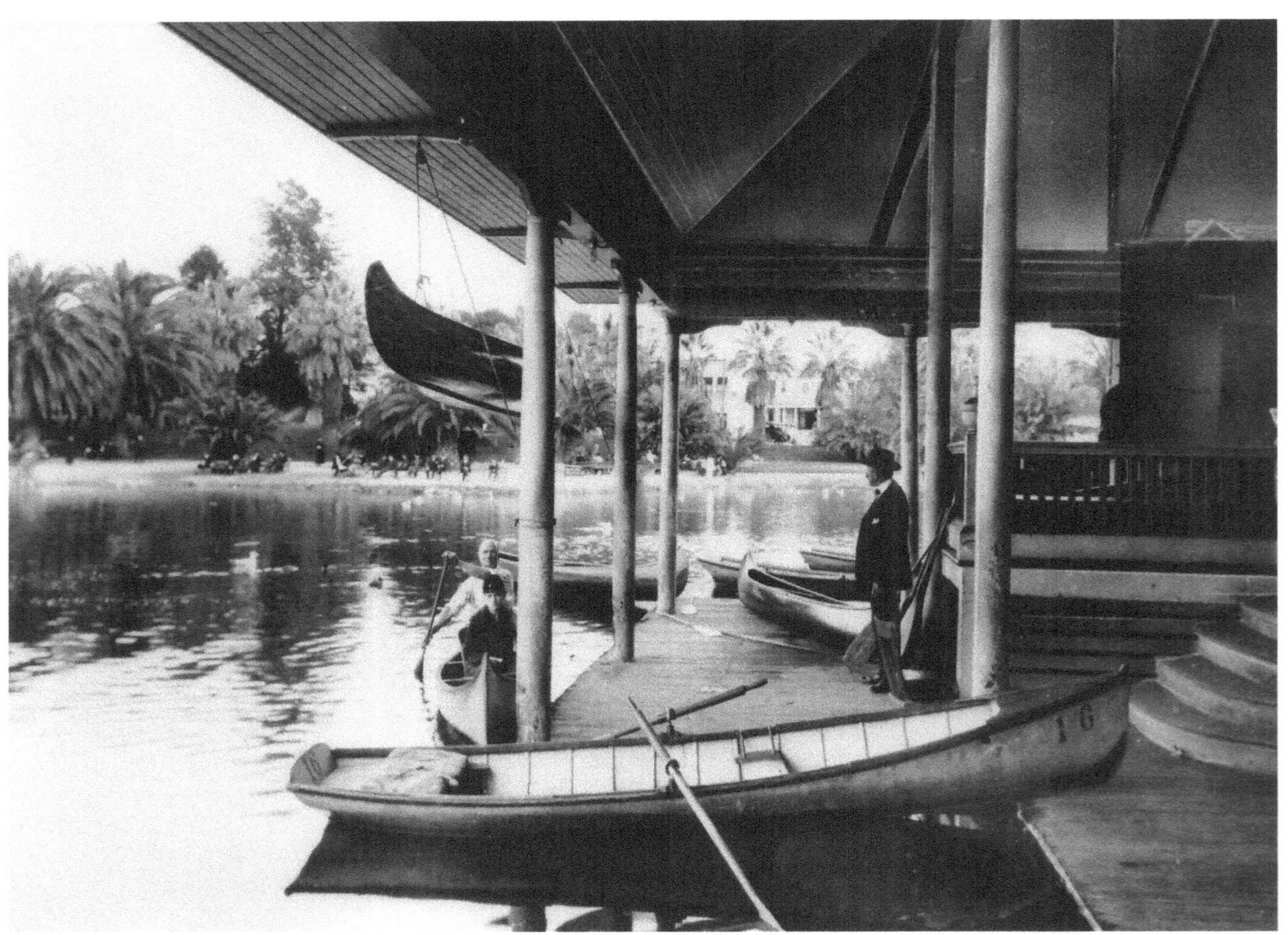

Canoes in the water at Westlake Park. This placid scene belies the stress that the economic boom and rapid expansion of Los Angeles had on the average Angeleno. One woman wondered: “how soon the wheels of progress are going to stop rattling long enough for us to hear ourselves think, catch our breath and develop some sort of cohesive social organism.”

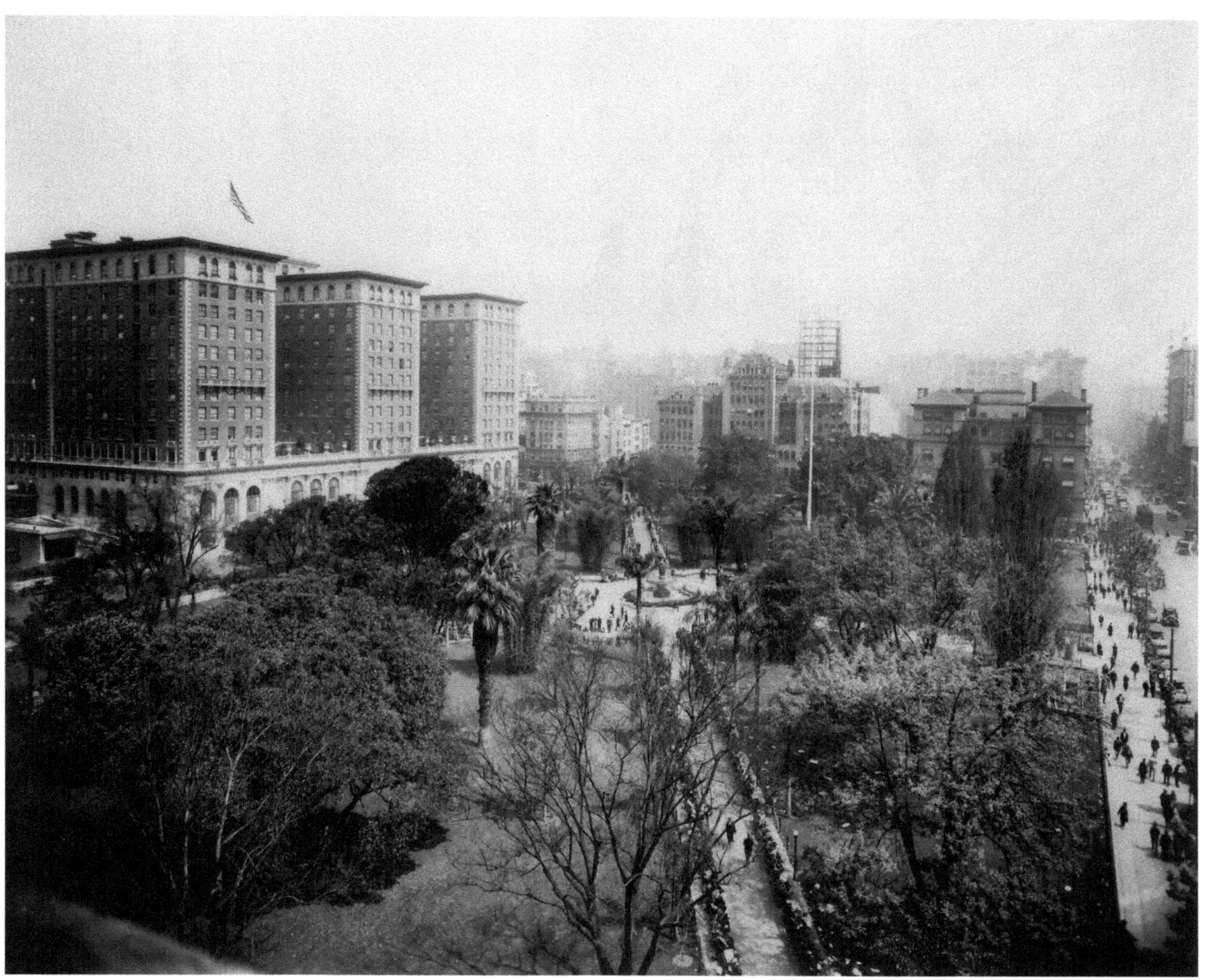

Pershing Square and the Biltmore Hotel in Los Angeles in the 1920s. The nearby Long Beach oil boom was one of the driving forces of L.A.'s dramatic economic growth in this decade. Upton Sinclair (1878–1968) was an author, investigator, and Socialist best known for his 1906 exposé of the meatpacking industry. In 1916 he settled in the L.A. area and wrote a muckraking novel about the corrupting effects of the boom.

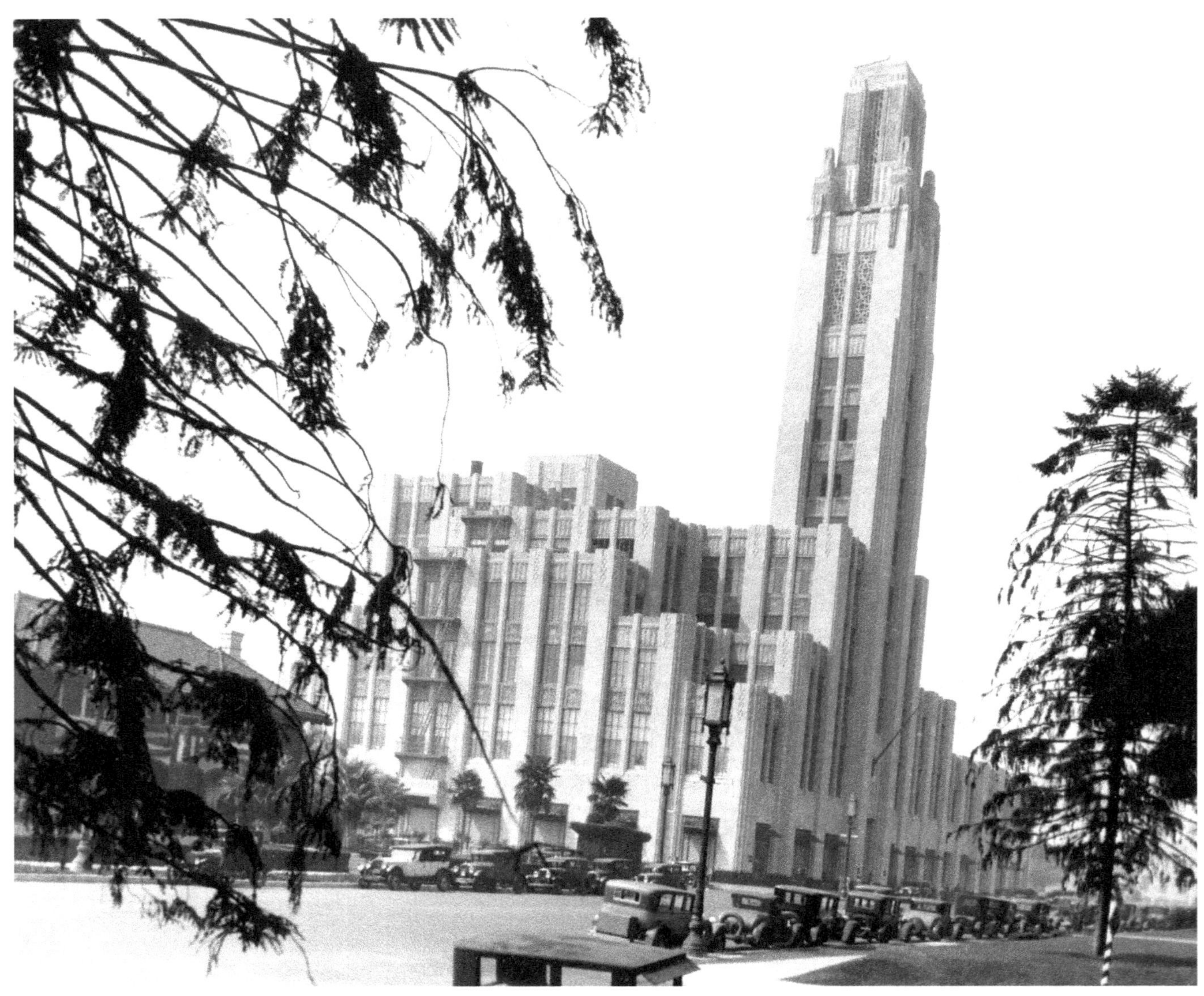

The same month that the stock market collapsed in 1929, Bullock's opened a Wilshire Boulevard retail operation the company claimed was the most beautiful such establishment in the world. The store's brightly illuminated tower could be seen for miles along Wilshire at night.

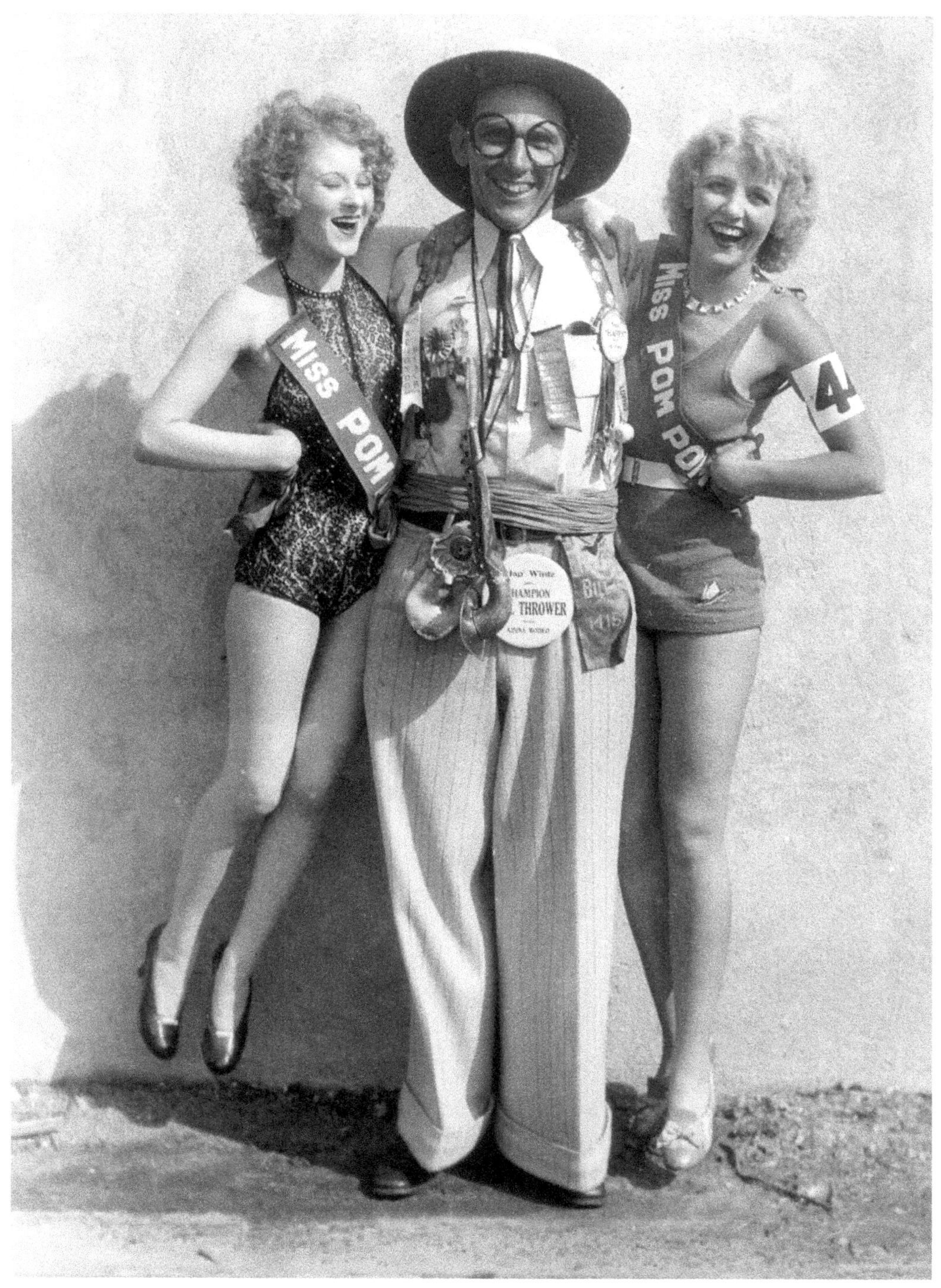

Flanked by two entrants in a "bathing beauty contest," this Elks Lodge member poses during a 1929 Elks convention in Venice.

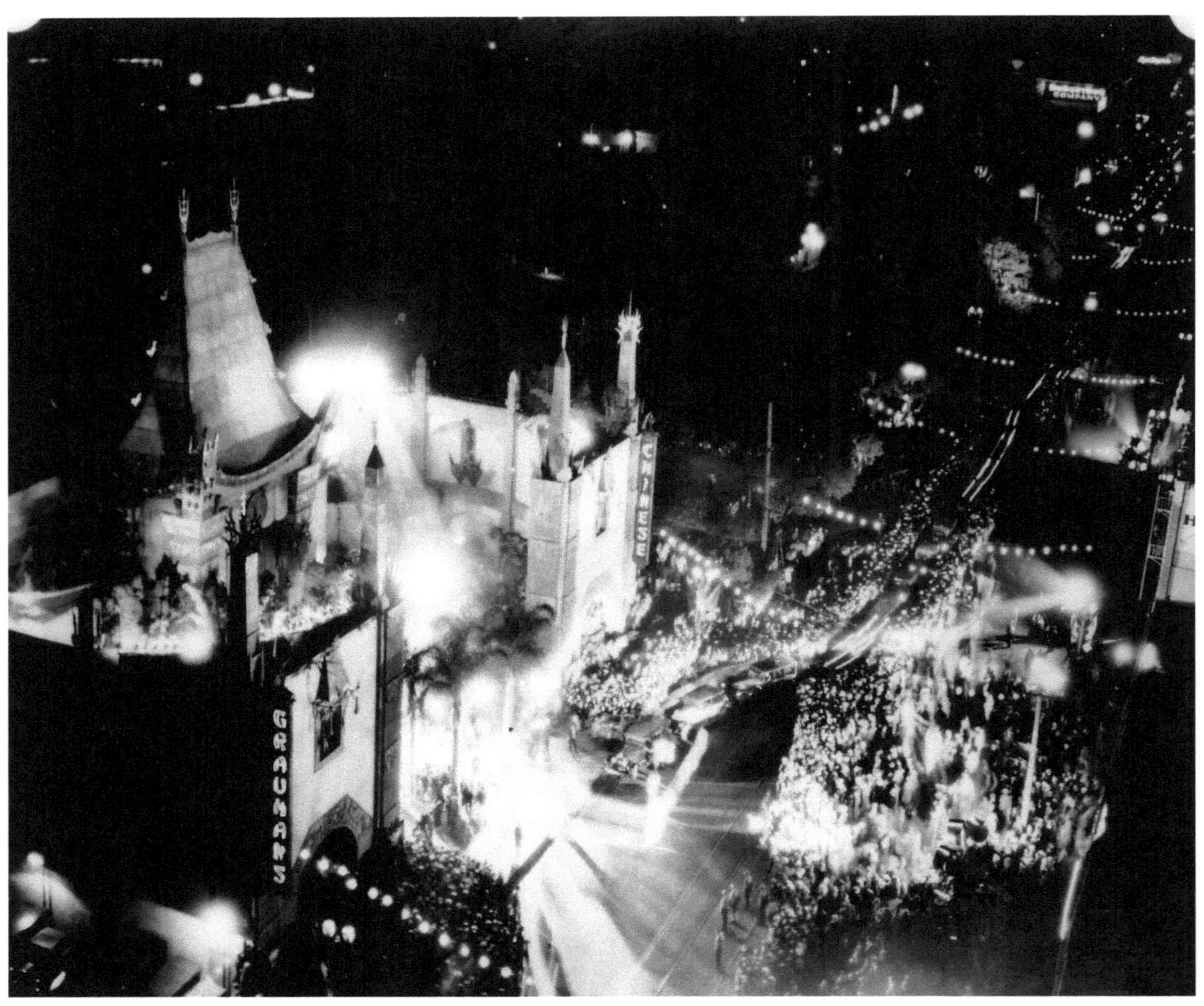

On the night of May 18, 1927, Grauman's Chinese Theatre in Hollywood held its grand opening—touted as the most spectacular theater opening in motion picture history. Thousands of fans lined Hollywood Boulevard to see the movie stars and other celebrities arrive for the opening. *The King of Kings,* directed by Cecil B. DeMille, was the film premiered that night.

The Great Depression and Recovery

(1930–1939)

Hollywood, seen here in the 1930s, had 200,000 residents of the 1.2 million people who lived in greater Los Angeles. The movie industry made millions of dollars for the studios and star celebrities, but not everyone was happy with the types of movies that were produced. In 1933, Reverend Amleto Cicognani asked fellow Catholics to launch "a united and vigorous campaign for the purification of the cinema, which has become a deadly menace to morals." Nine million Catholics joined the Legion of Decency, pledged to boycott films that the Legion's rating board condemned.

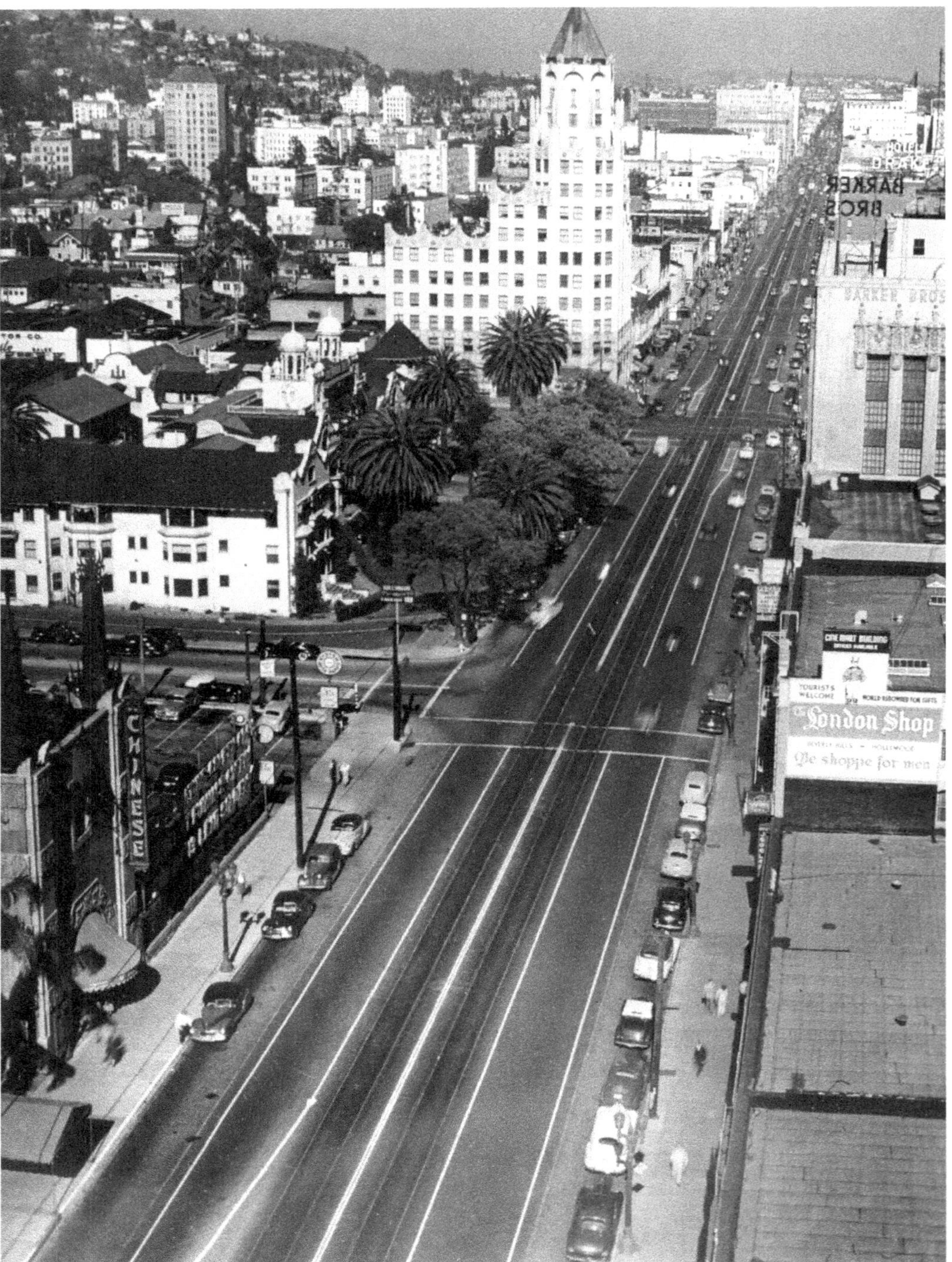

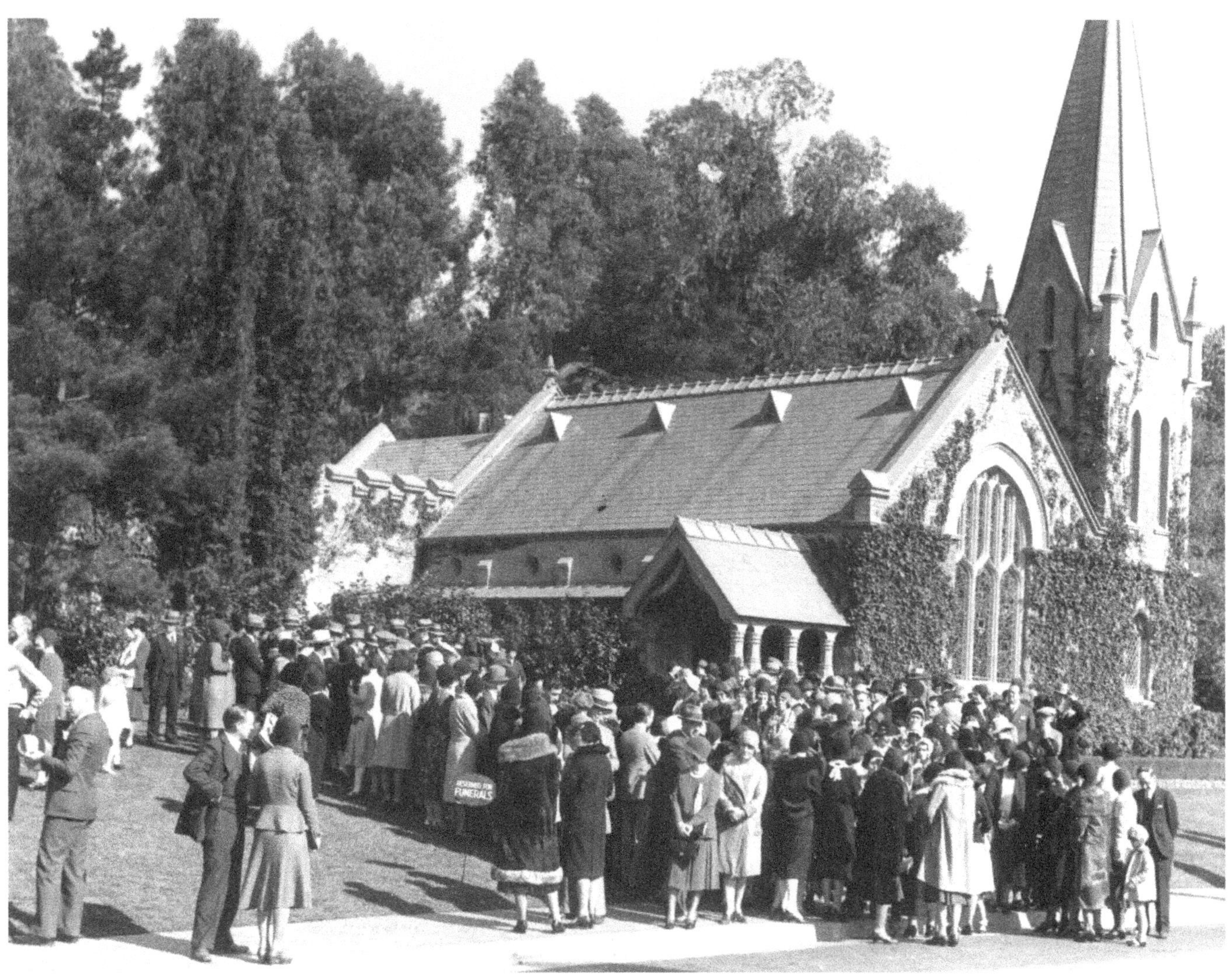

A crowd outside the Church of the Little Flower at the Forest Lawn Memorial Cemetery, where services were conducted for silent film star Alma Rubens (1897–1931). Rubens died January 22, 1931, from pneumonia. Forest Lawn, founded in 1906, was managed from 1917 by Dr. Hubert Eaton. Eaton was an innovator who said that most cemeteries were "unsightly, depressing stoneyards" and designed Forest Lawn to be "a great park devoid of misshapen monuments and other signs of earthly death."

Vice-president Charles Curtis opened the X Olympiad on July 30, 1932, in Los Angeles Olympic Stadium, which was completed in 1923 as a memorial to Great War veterans. Approximately 1,300 athletes participated, representing 37 countries. The 1932 Olympic Games introduced the first photo-finish cameras as well as the victory platform. Los Angeles hosted the Summer Olympics again in 1984.

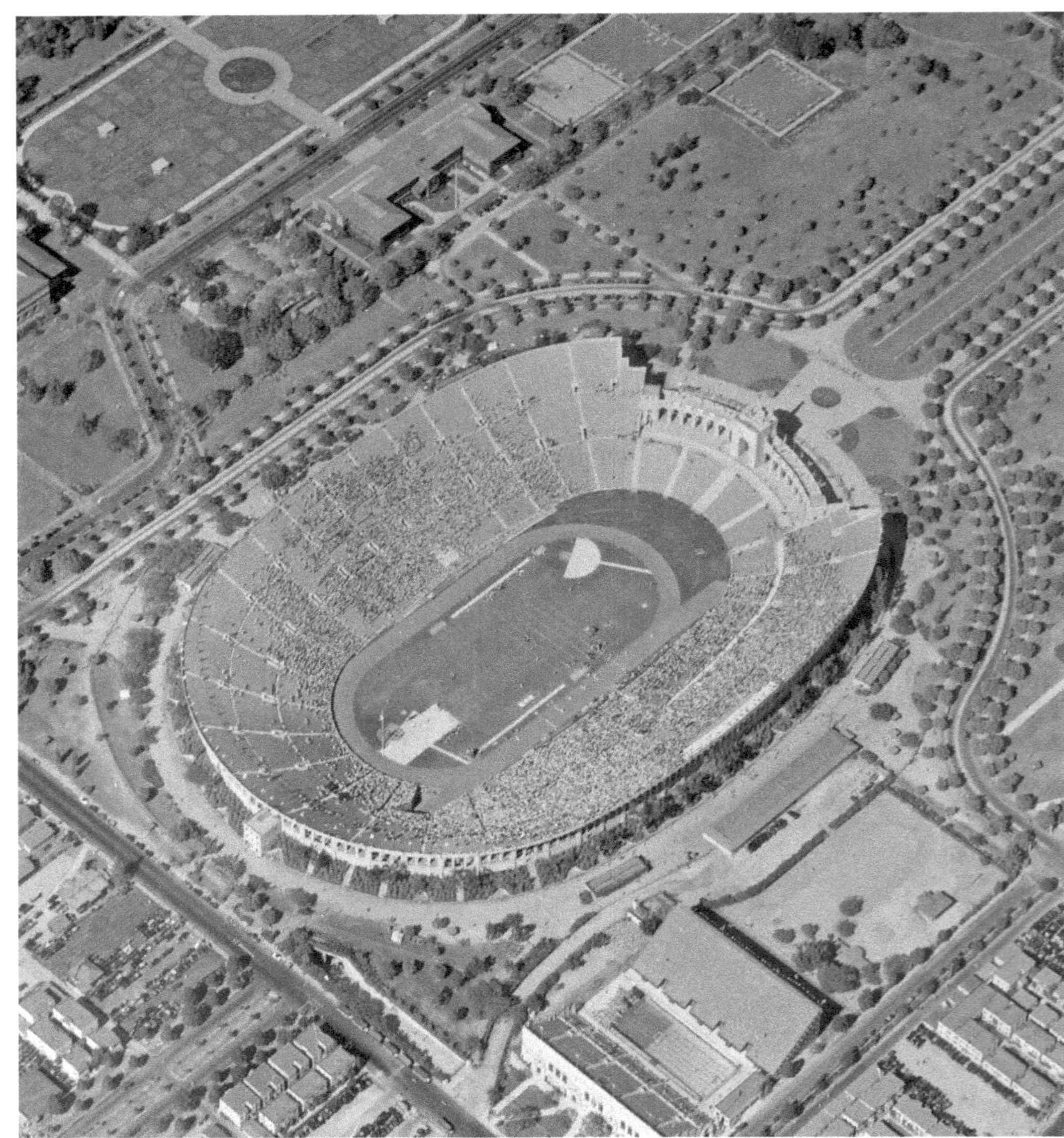

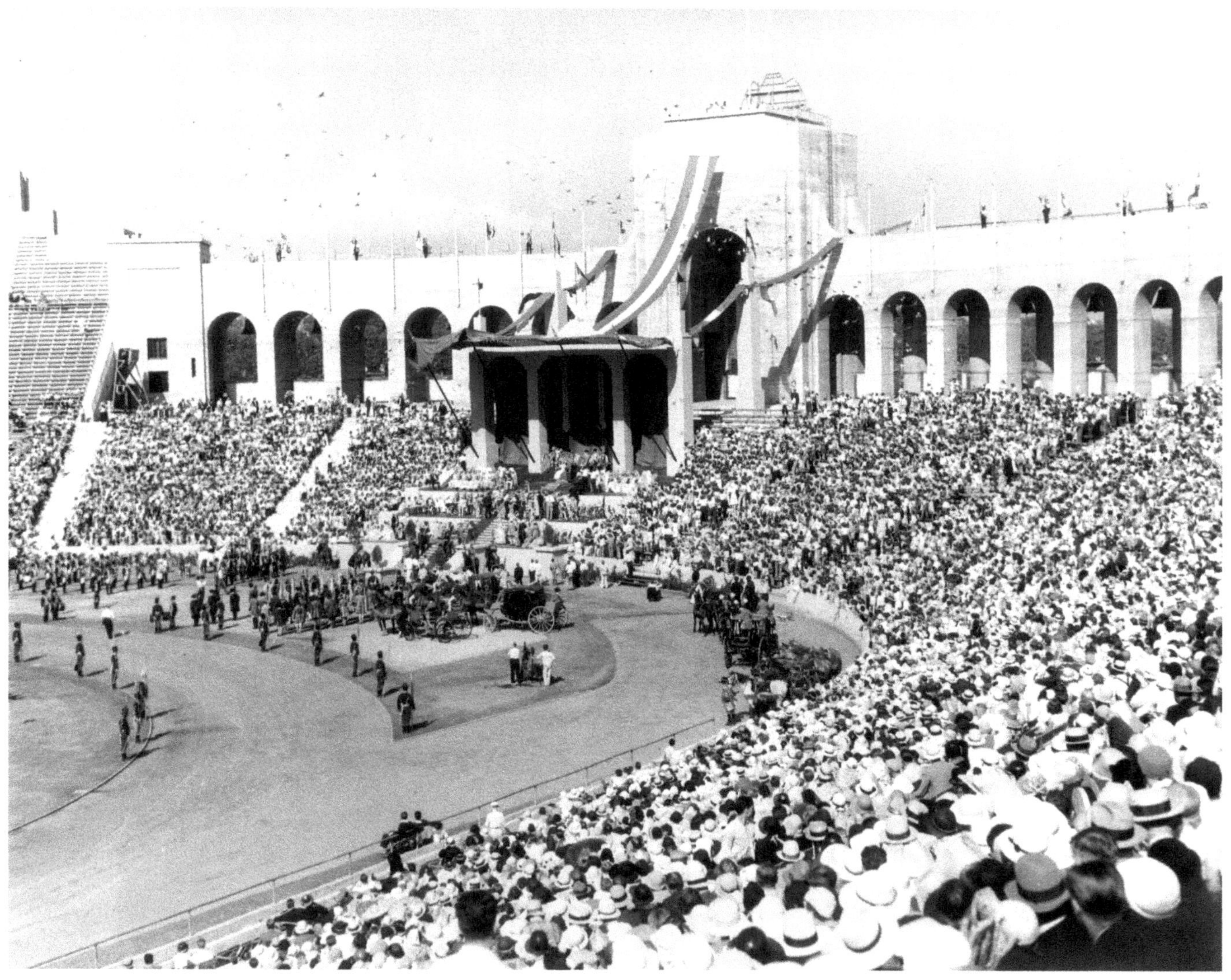

Los Angeles Olympic Stadium hosted many other events, such as the crowning of Mrs. Elizabeth Hicks Green as Queen of La Fiesta de Los Angeles that marked the 150th anniversary of the city. The scene of medieval pomp and ceremony was witnessed by a large crowd that jammed the stadium.

A special telephone exchange was put into service for the Los Angeles Olympic Games. The operators could speak English, German, Spanish, and French.

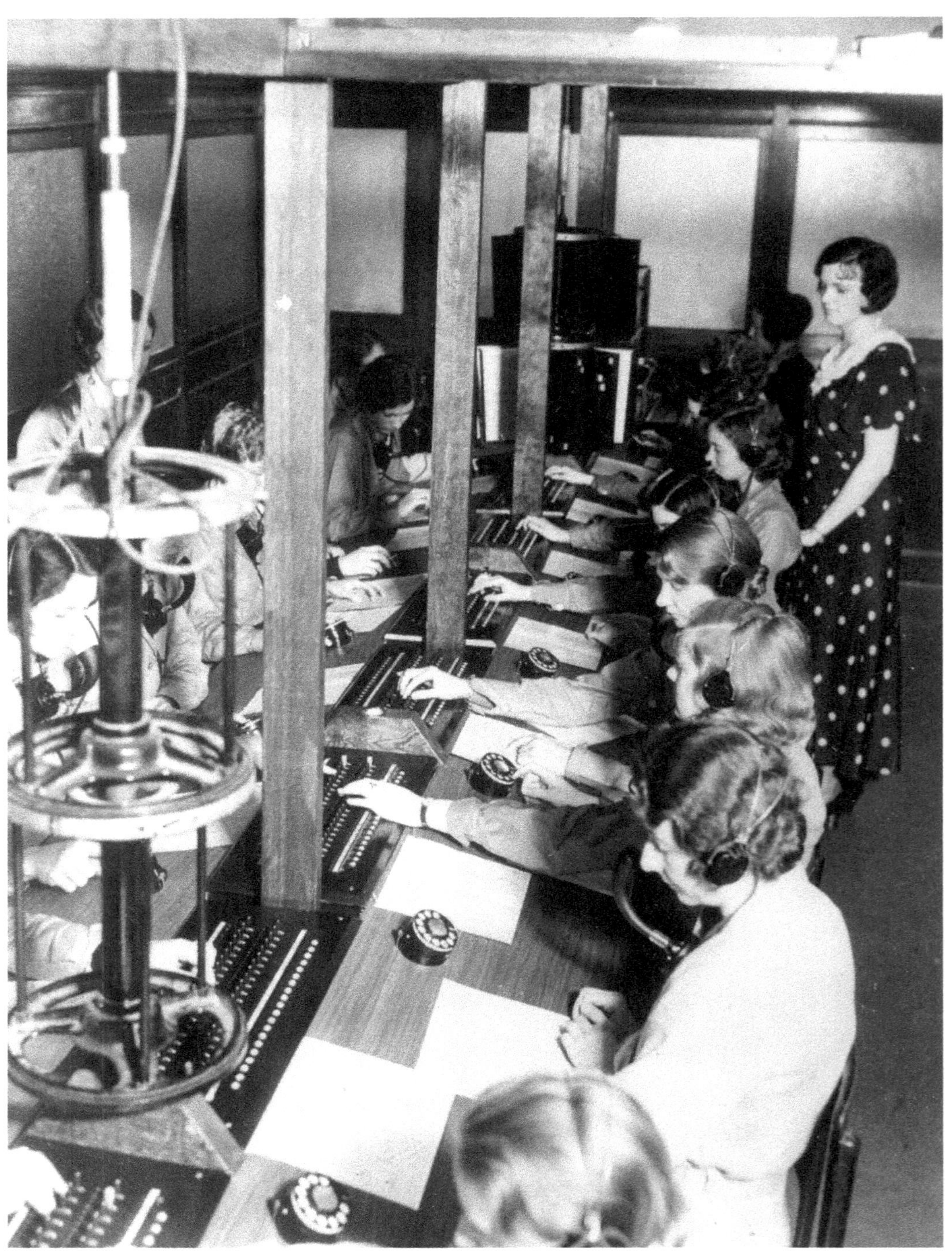

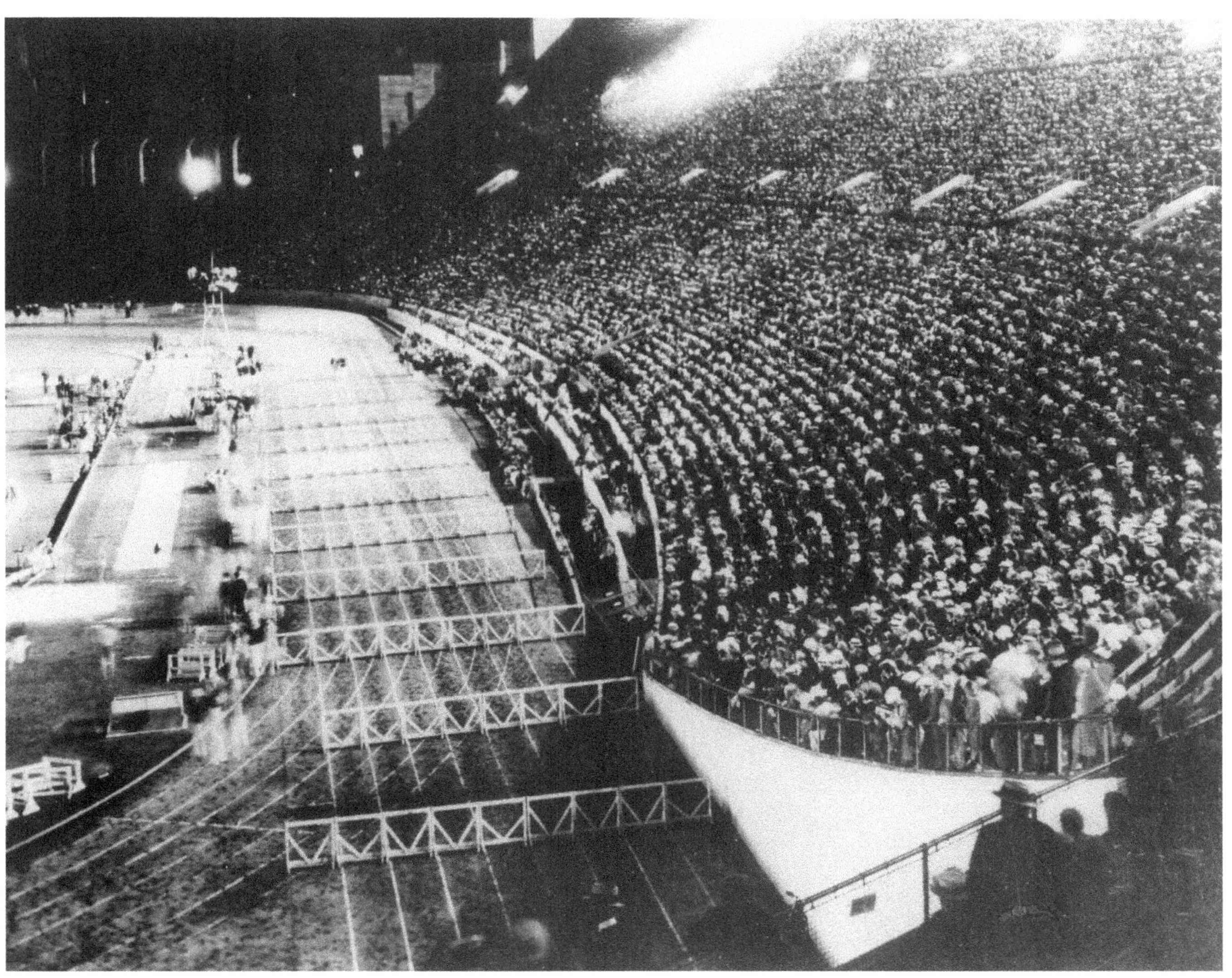

A night event at Olympic Stadium. While mounted on the victory platform during the 1932 Olympic Games, Italian Luigi Beccali, winner of the gold medal in the 1,500-meter race, gave the fascist salute. American Mildred "Babe" Didrikson (1914–1956) made history at the 1932 Olympics. Didrikson won gold medals and set new world records for both the 80-meter hurdles and the javelin, and she won the silver medal in the high jump. Didrikson later became a very successful professional golfer and was considered the greatest woman athlete of modern times.

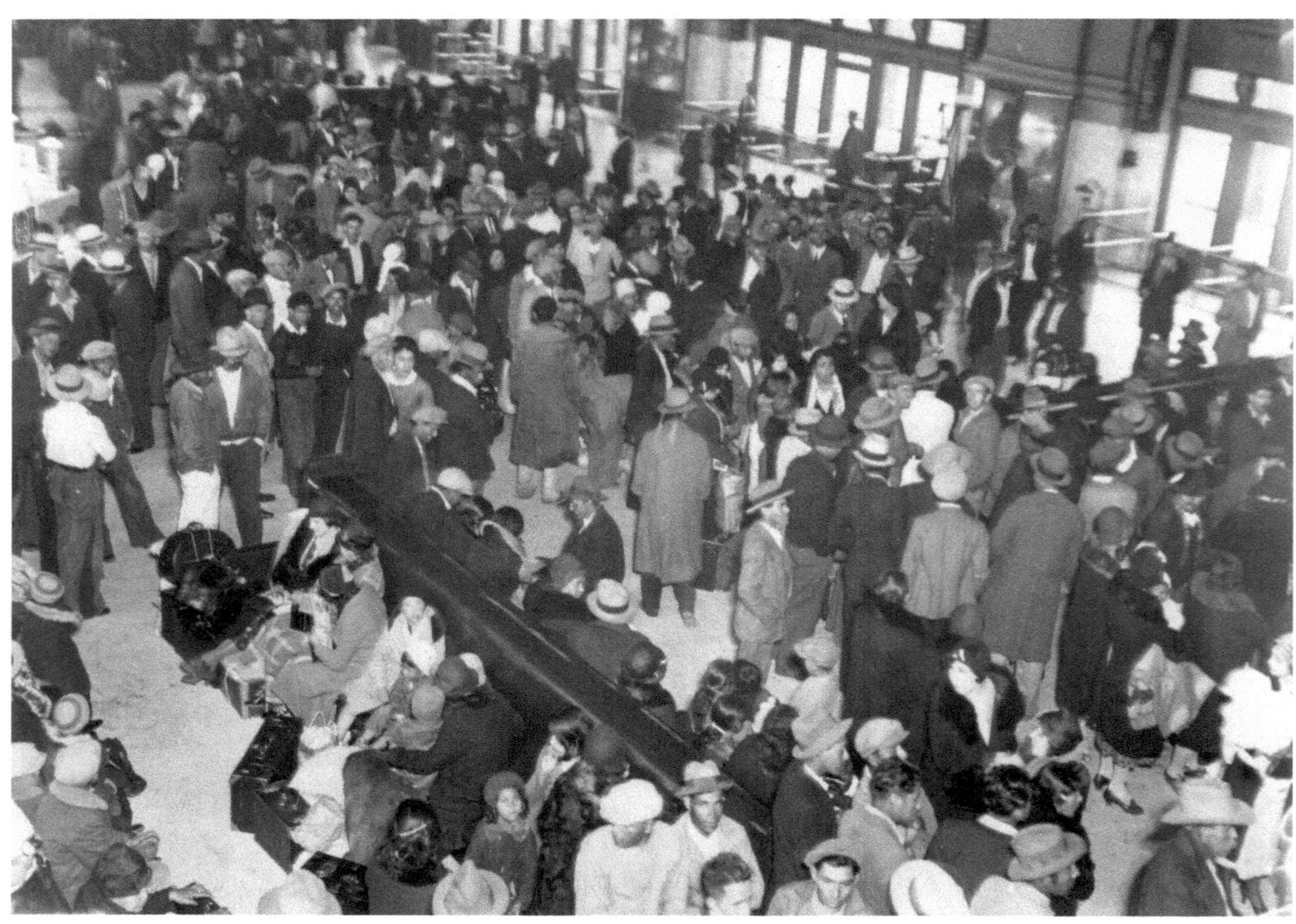

This crowd inside Union Station are some of the Mexican American immigrants deported back to Mexico in 1931-32. Mexicans were exempt from the 1924 Immigration Act that stopped immigration from Europe, and around 900,000 entered the U.S. between 1924 and 1930, some 630,000 illegally. During the Depression, with 25 percent unemployment, the federal government began coercive repatriation. One-third of those living in Los Angeles were encouraged or forced to leave for Mexico.

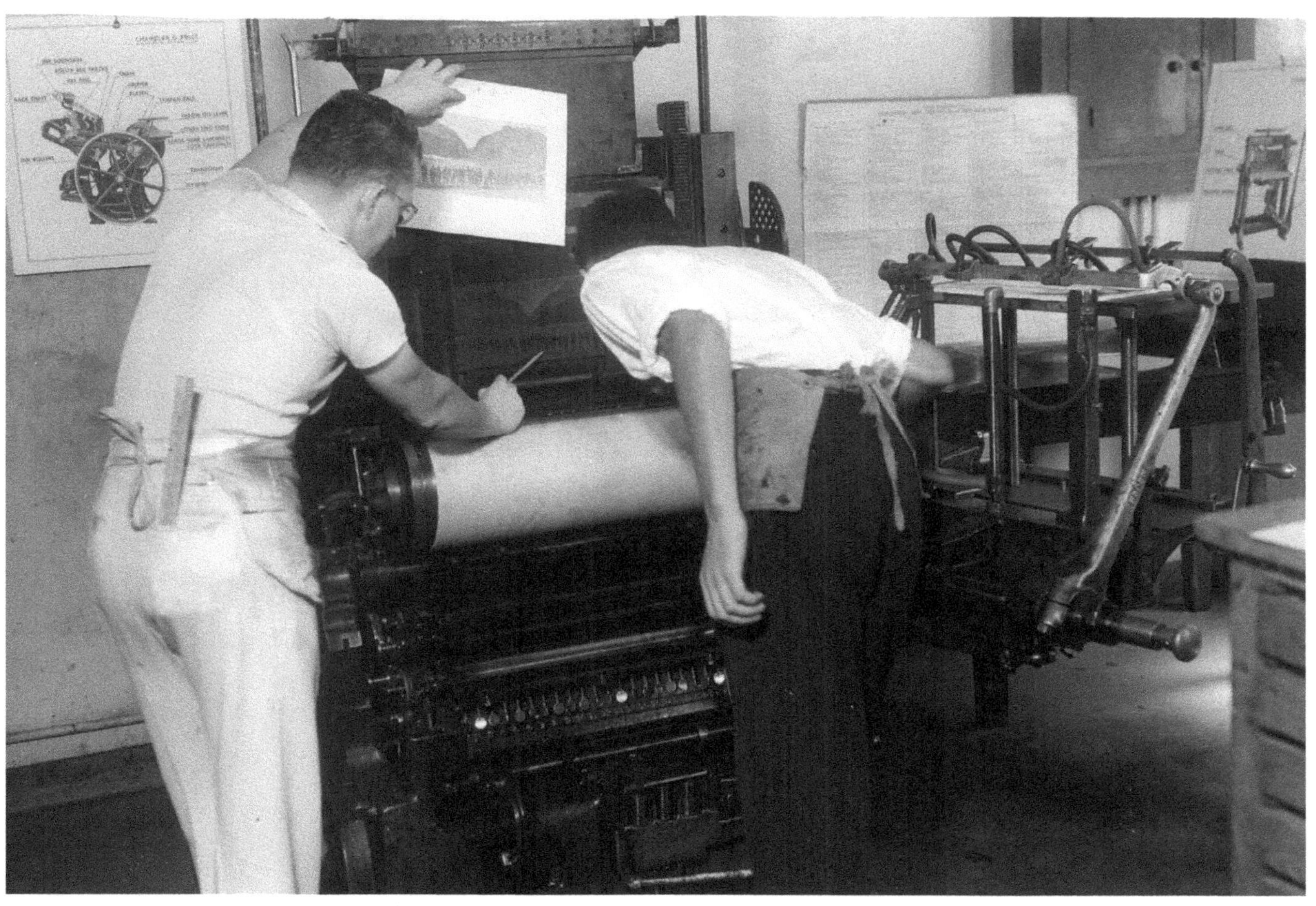

This Los Angeles student received instruction in printing through a Works Progress Administration (Work Projects Administration after 1939) adult education project. The WPA was the largest of President Roosevelt's New Deal agencies, employing millions of people in nearly every part of America. The program was closed down in 1943 during the war production years of World War II.

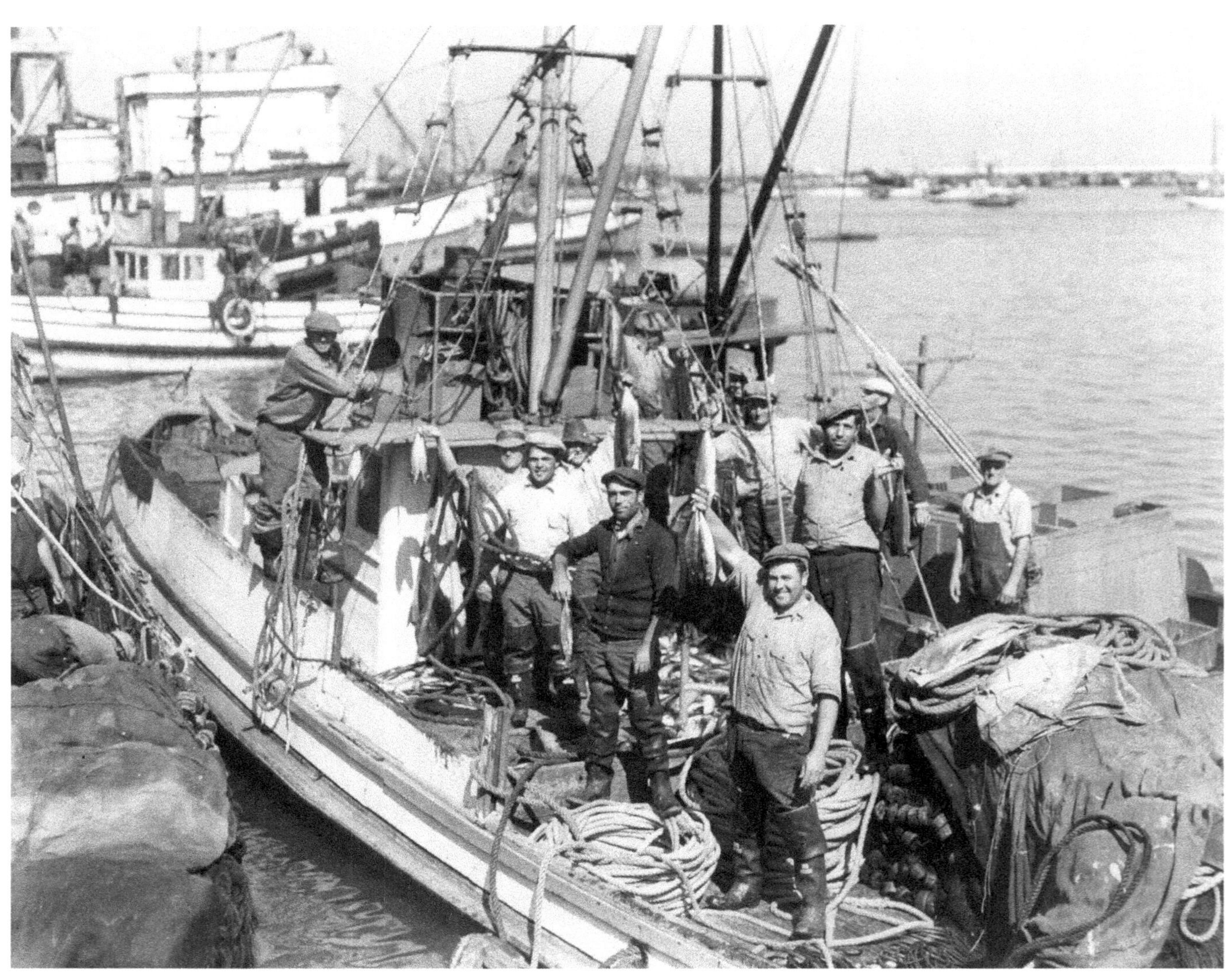

For many decades, Los Angeles harbor was divided into little villages and docks according to ethnic groups or nationalities that spoke little English. Here Russian fishermen proudly display their day's catch.

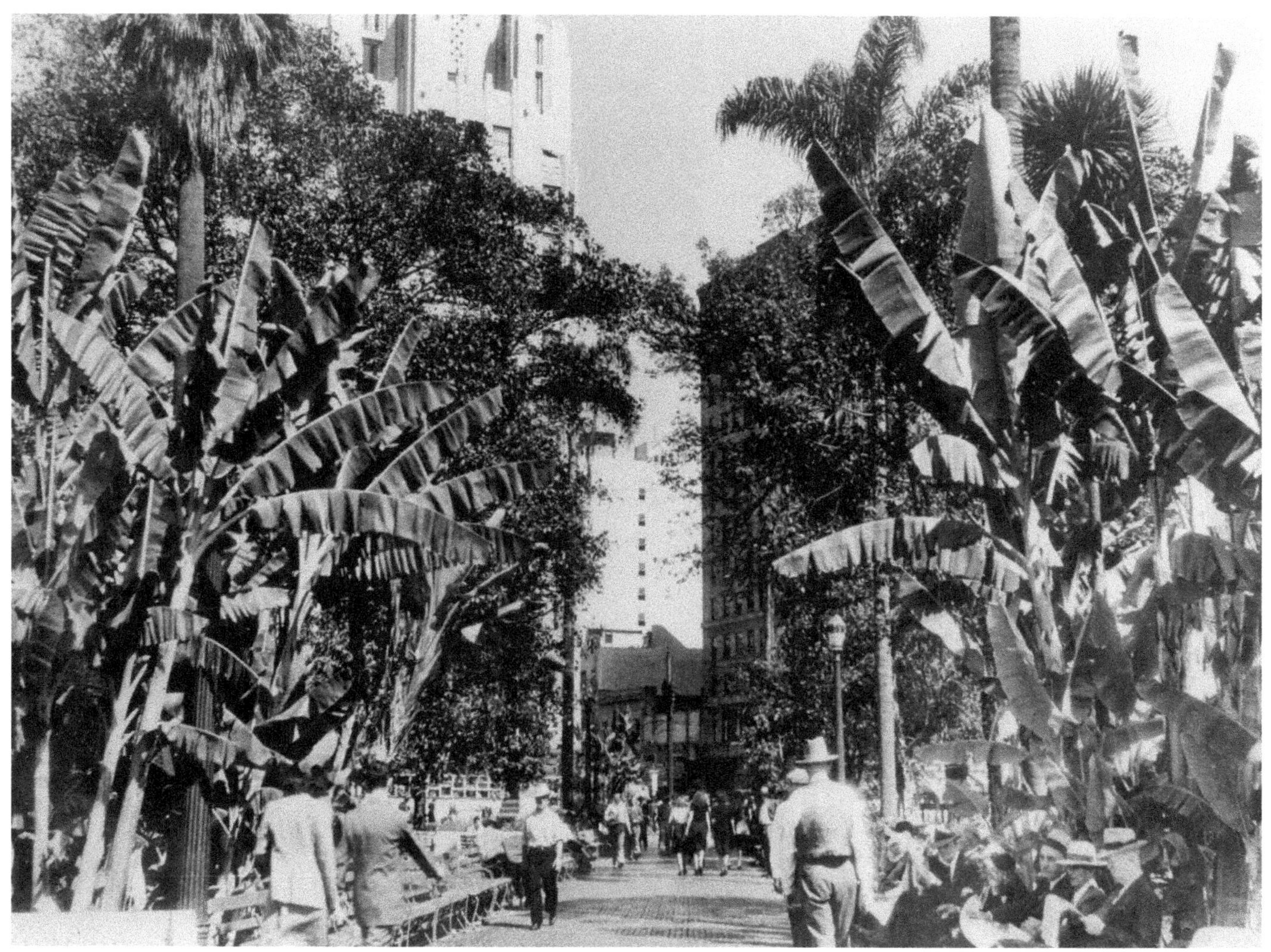

Pershing Place at the center of Los Angeles. Palm and banana trees stand against a background of what would have appeared then as blue sky and white buildings. This is the image of L.A. as utopia. Progressive lawyer and journalist Carey McWilliams (1905–1980) wrote that if this vast metropolitan area could be created by improvisation, propaganda, and boosterism, it did not seem incredible "that a new society might be evoked . . . in which the benefits of the machine age would be shared by all alike."

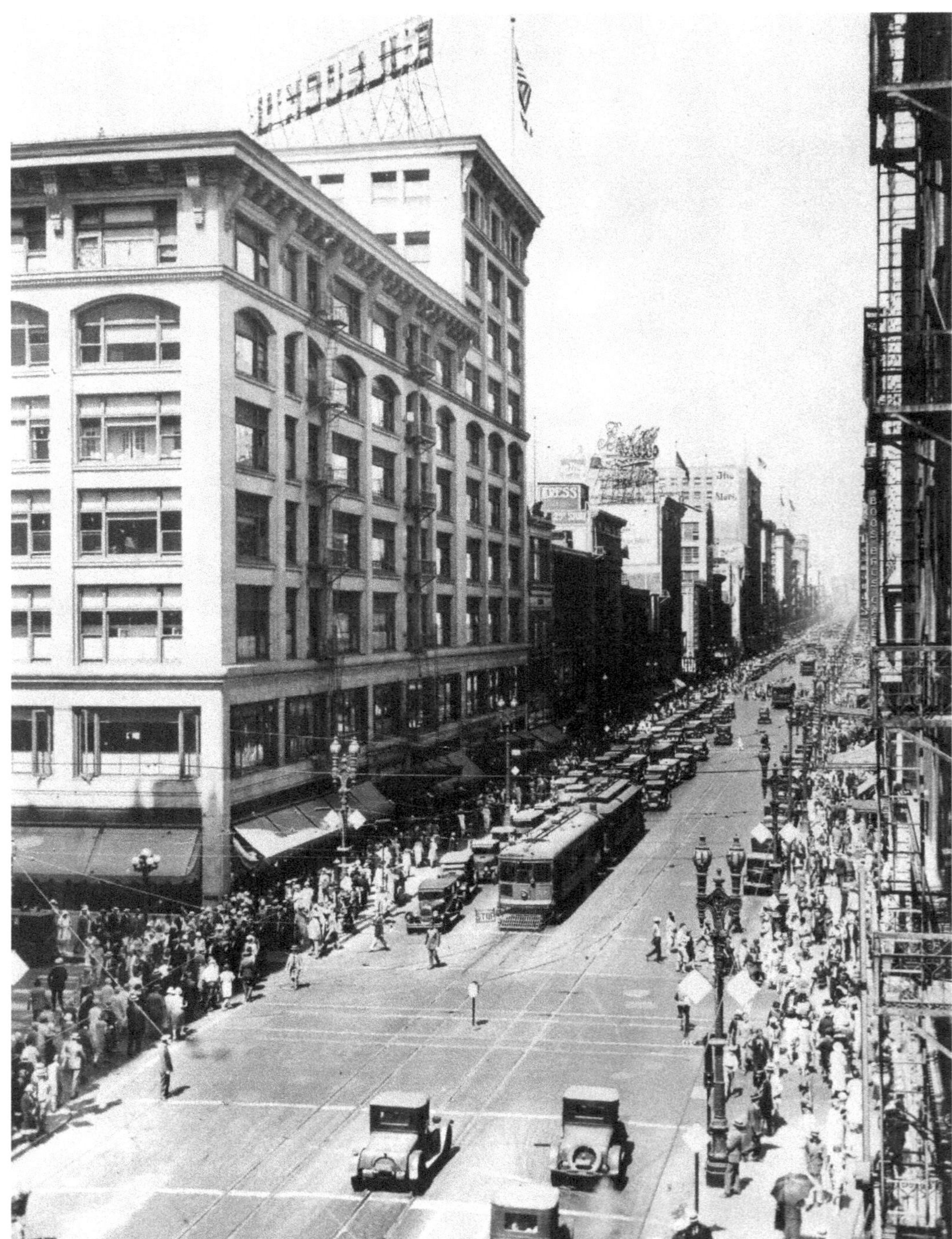

This view of Broadway looking north from West 7th Street shows a major downtown L.A. shopping district. In 1930 the ratio of population in the central metropolitan area to outlying suburbs in most American cities was sixteen to one (as in Pittsburgh) or more. L.A.'s ratio was only three to one, making its structure radically different from other U.S. cities'.

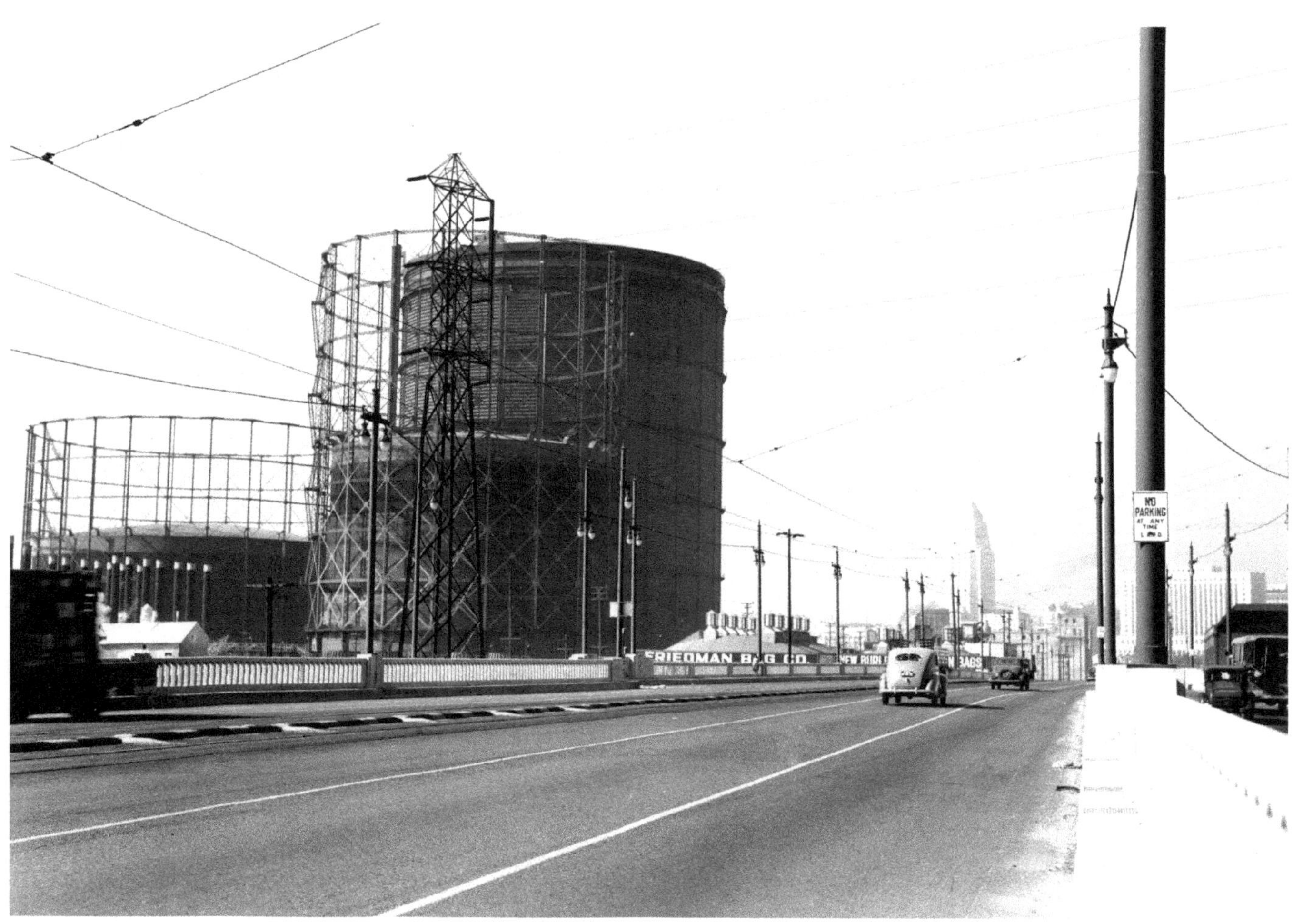

This view toward the center of Los Angeles is from the terminus of Ramona Boulevard. Despite the economic downturn of the Depression, by 1938 nearly 72 percent of the L.A. labor force drove cars to their jobs. Only 20 percent used public transportation, and the remainder walked.

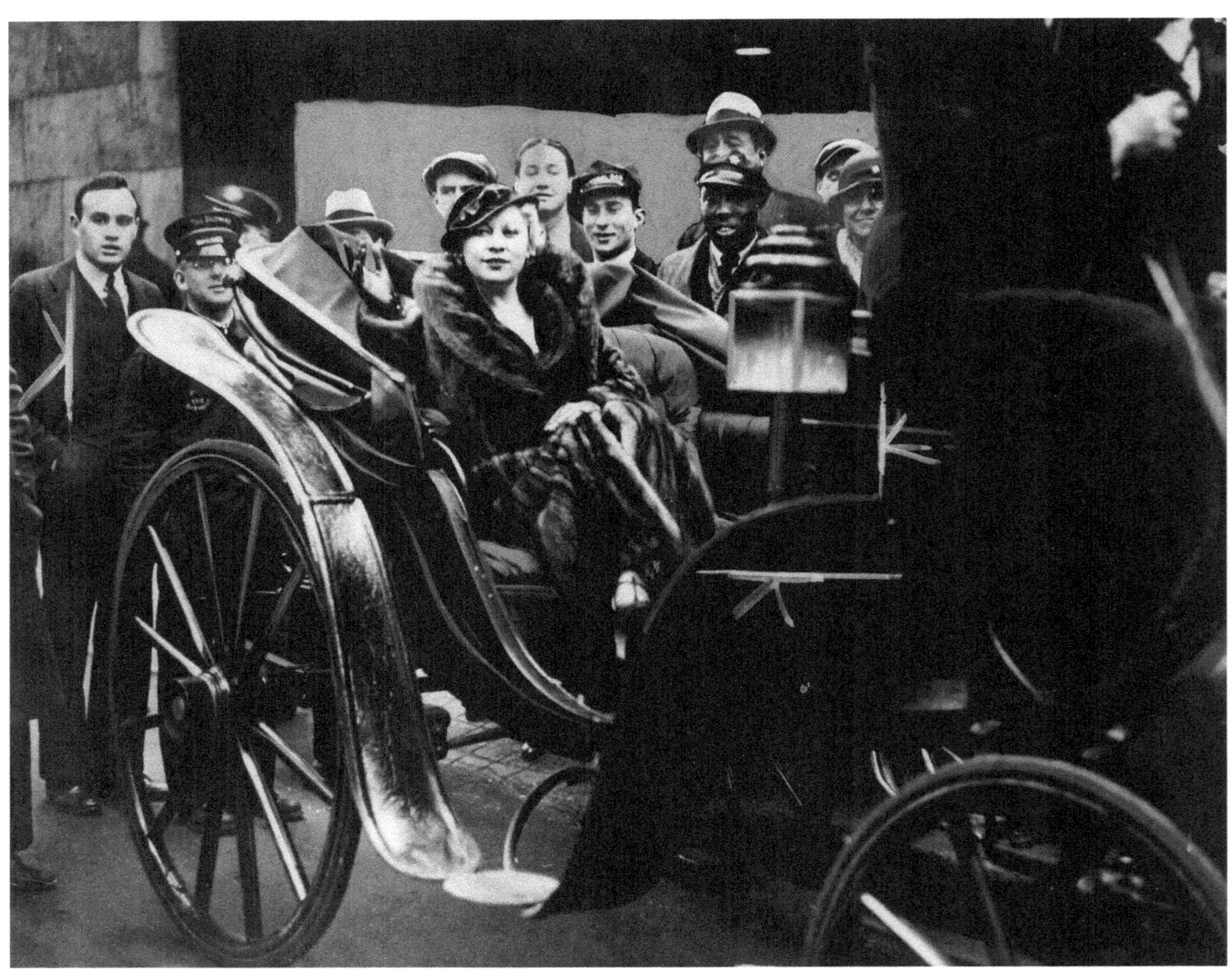

In 1932, comedian, actress, and writer Mae West (1893–1980) started making films. The controversial 38-year-old sex symbol was famous for her outrageous quotes such as "When I'm good, I'm very, very good, but when I'm bad, I'm better." When her cinematic career ended, West continued to perform on stage, radio, and television. "Between two evils, I always pick the one I never tried before."

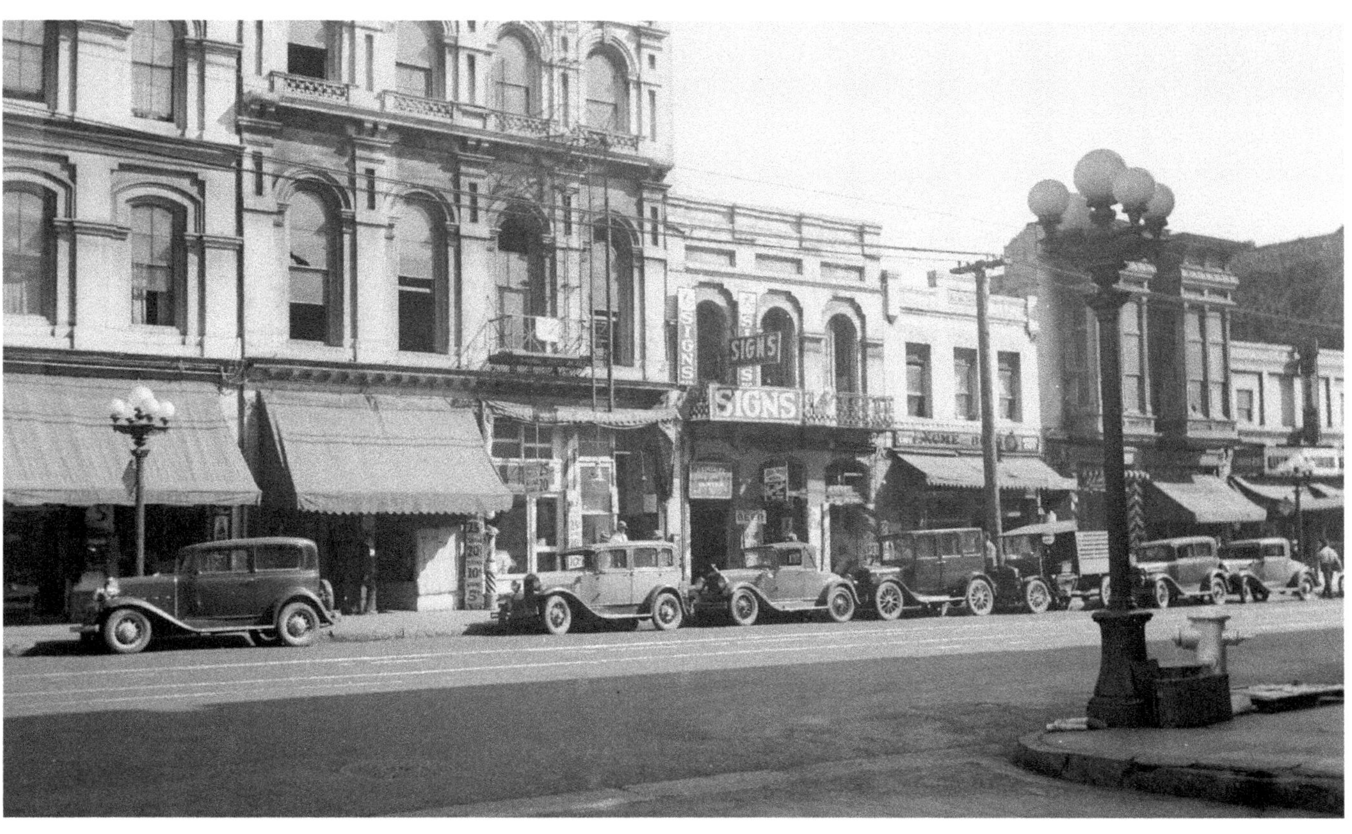

This photo was taken as part of the Historic American Buildings Survey of 1934. The Masonic Temple Number 42 on North Main Street in Los Angeles is the building advertising signs at center. Most Masonic temples in the United States were built between 1870 and 1930 as meeting places for the Freemason fraternal organization. The origins and early development of Freemasonry are a matter of some debate and conjecture. Famous members include presidents George Washington and Franklin Roosevelt.

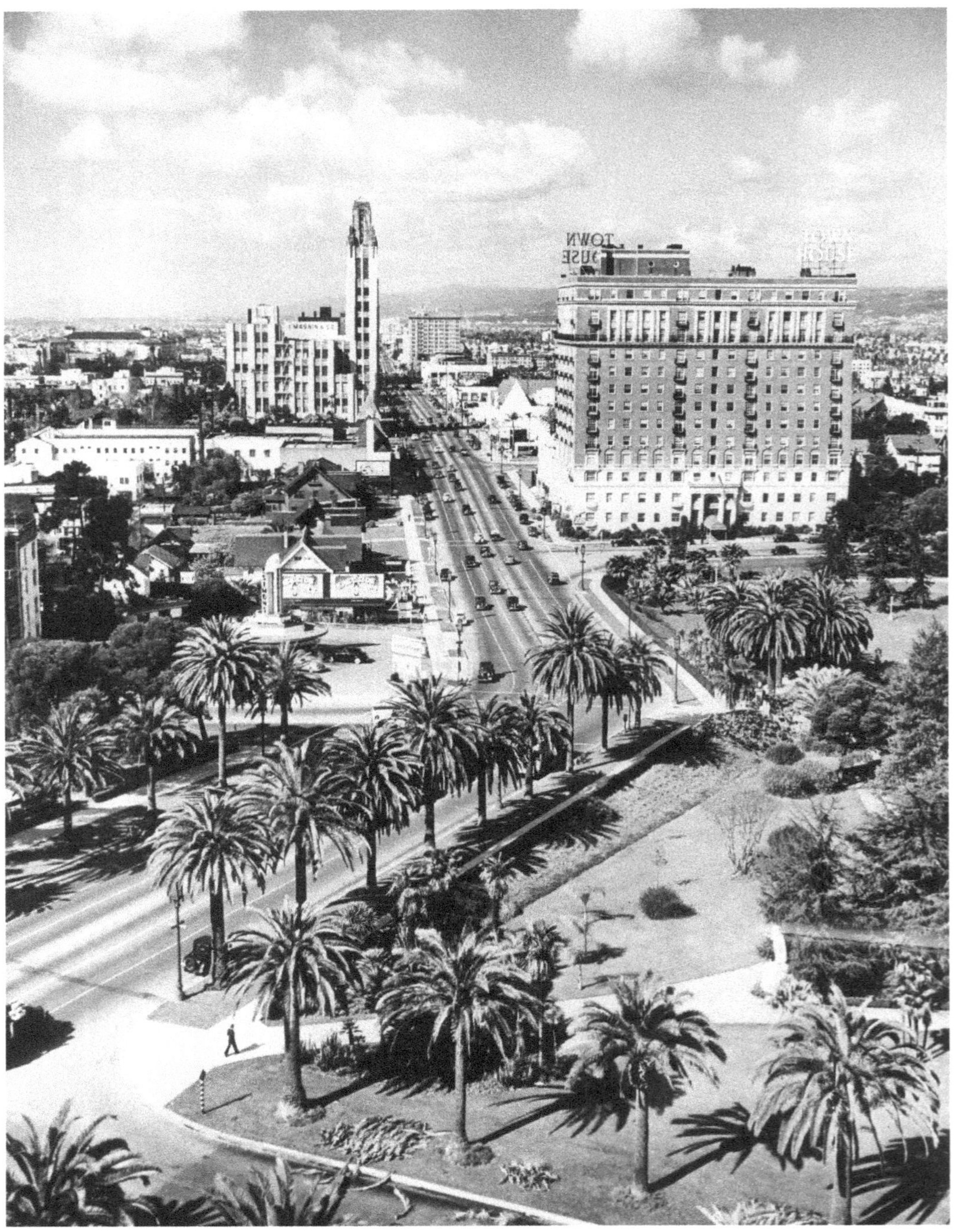

Wilshire Boulevard, looking toward Beverly Hills and Santa Monica, where many famous Hollywood screen stars lived in the 1930s and today. Wilshire was designed to accommodate six cars at a time, as were most of the major Southern California thoroughfares back then.

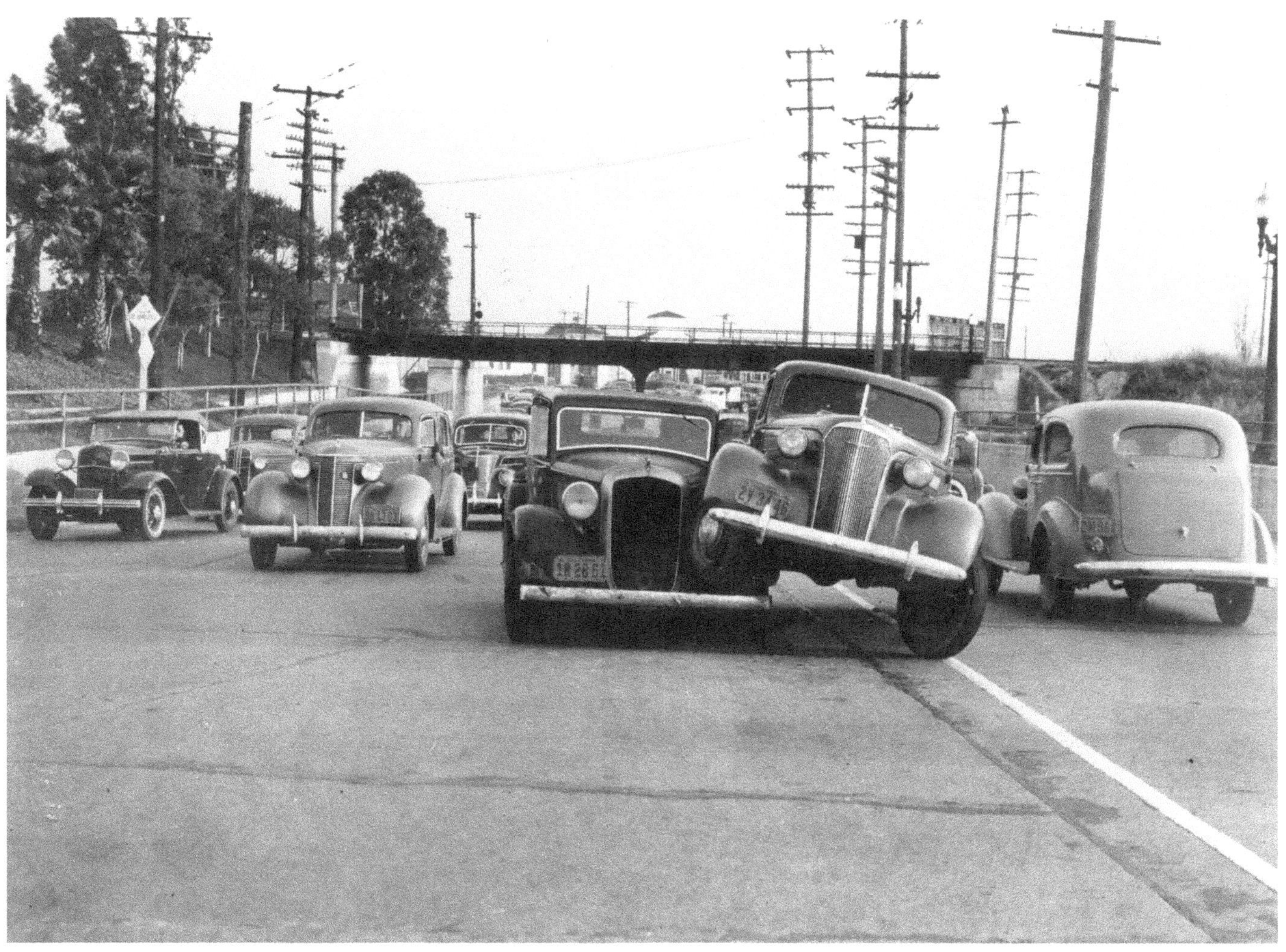

Bandini Underpass in Los Angeles. The Major Traffic Street Plan instituted in the previous decade improved traffic flow for a few years, but it proved inadequate by the early 1930s. The city was unable to decide whether to finance a rapid-transit system, so Angelenos continued to jam the roads with their cars. This congestion led to the rise of suburbs and the decentralization of retail businesses.

This was the Los Angeles Stock Exchange home office at 639 South Spring Street as it appeared in 1937. The stock market crash of 1929 was not the fundamental cause of the Great Depression of the 1930s, but the stock market collapse and subsequent panic did trigger and mark the start of the economic disaster.

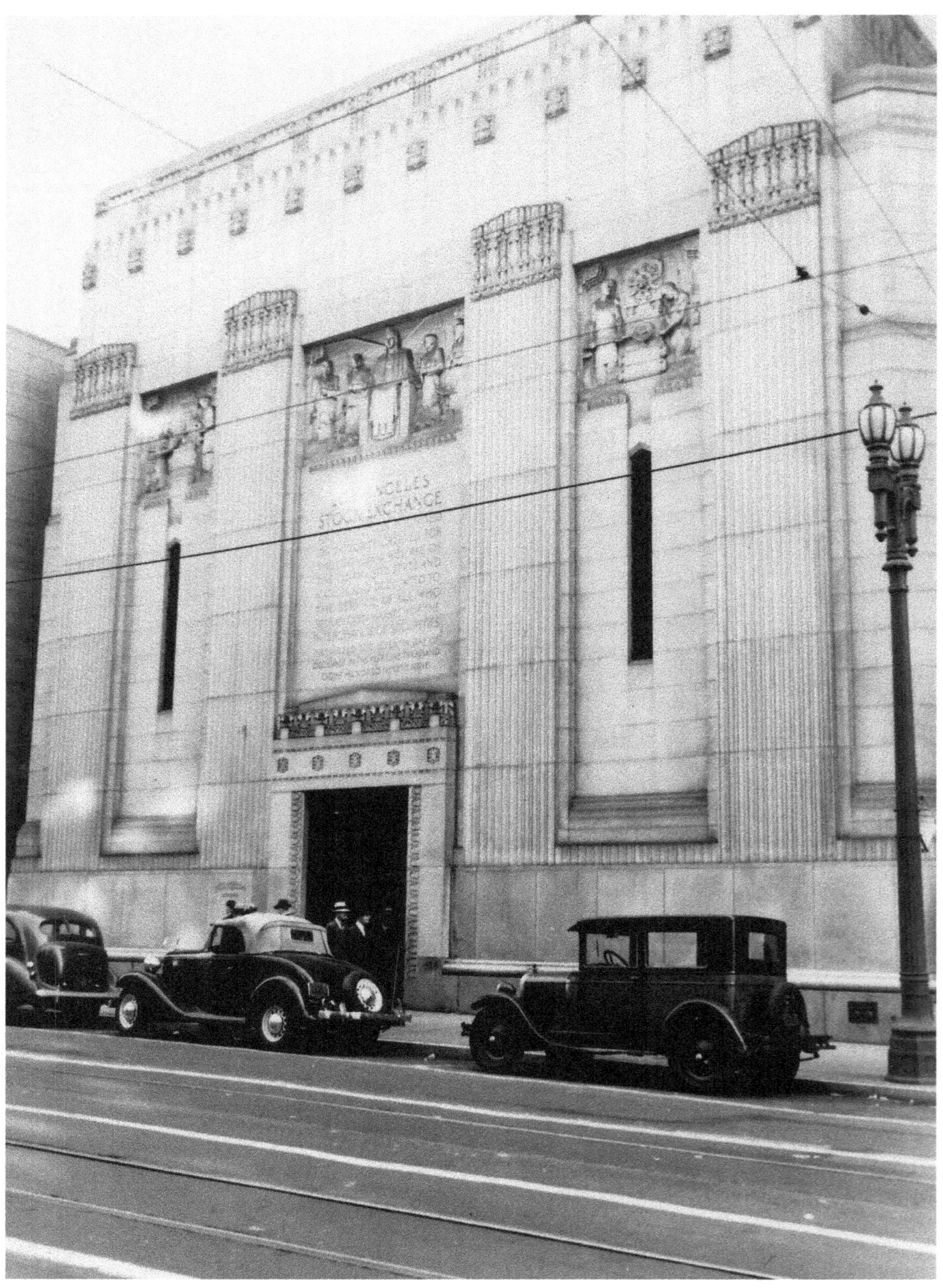

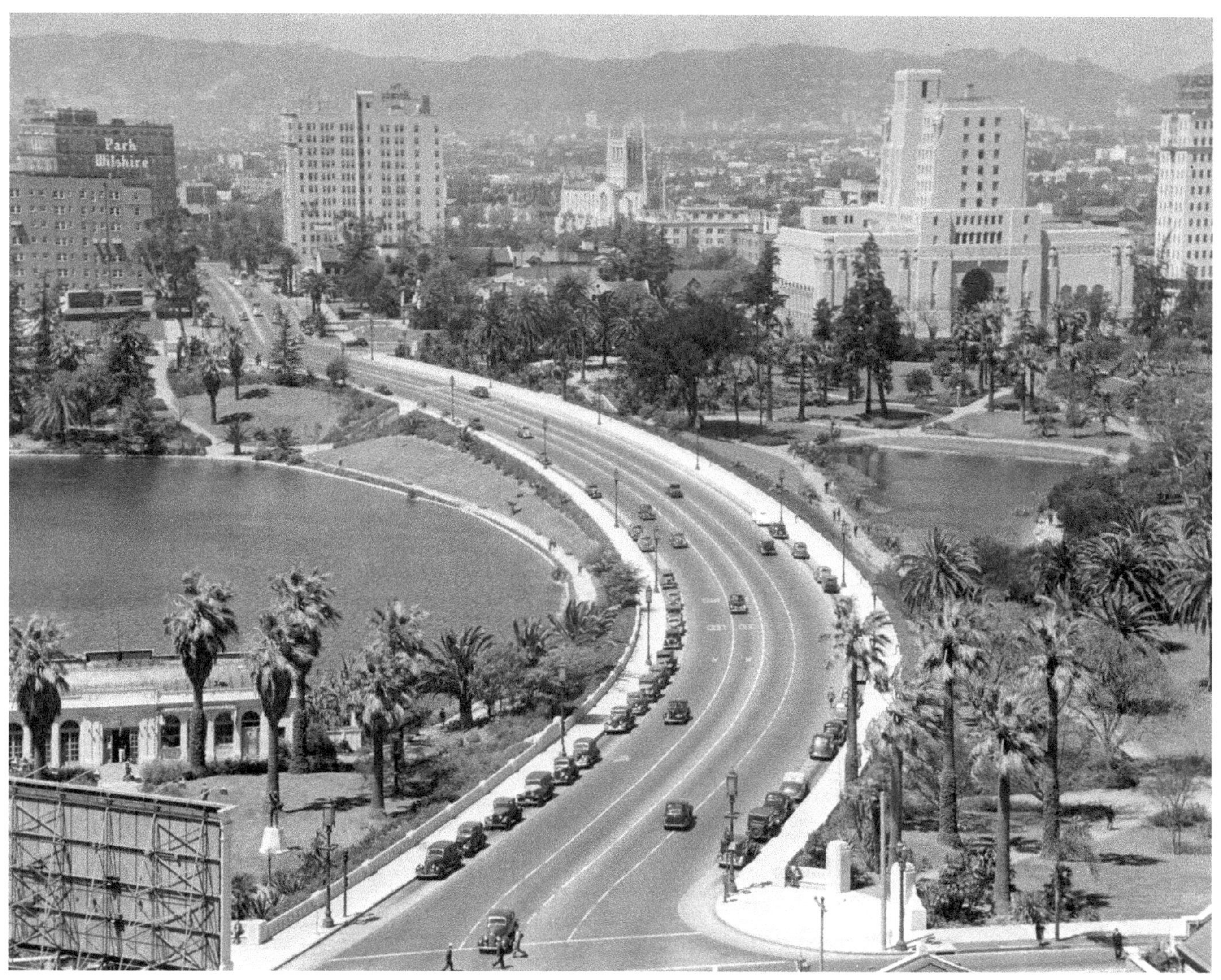

Built in the 1880s, MacArthur Park, crossed here by Wilshire Boulevard, was originally named Westlake Park but was renamed shortly after the end of World War II. Prior to 1930, Los Angeles lacked an adequate number of streets leading into the downtown area. The city therefore built this bridge across the lake and turned Wilshire into one of L.A.'s most important traffic arteries.

A promotional photograph from the Federal Theater Project stage production *Run Little Chillun* with Jess Lee Brooks (1894–1944) and Ruby Elzy (1908–1943).An African American thespian regarded as an exceptional actor, Brooks worked in 24 movies, including *Dark Manhattan* (1937) and *Gang War* (1940). His co-star Elzy was a pioneer black opera singer who appeared on stage, radio, and film. Her most prominent screen role was in the 1941 *Birth of the Blues* with Bing Crosby.

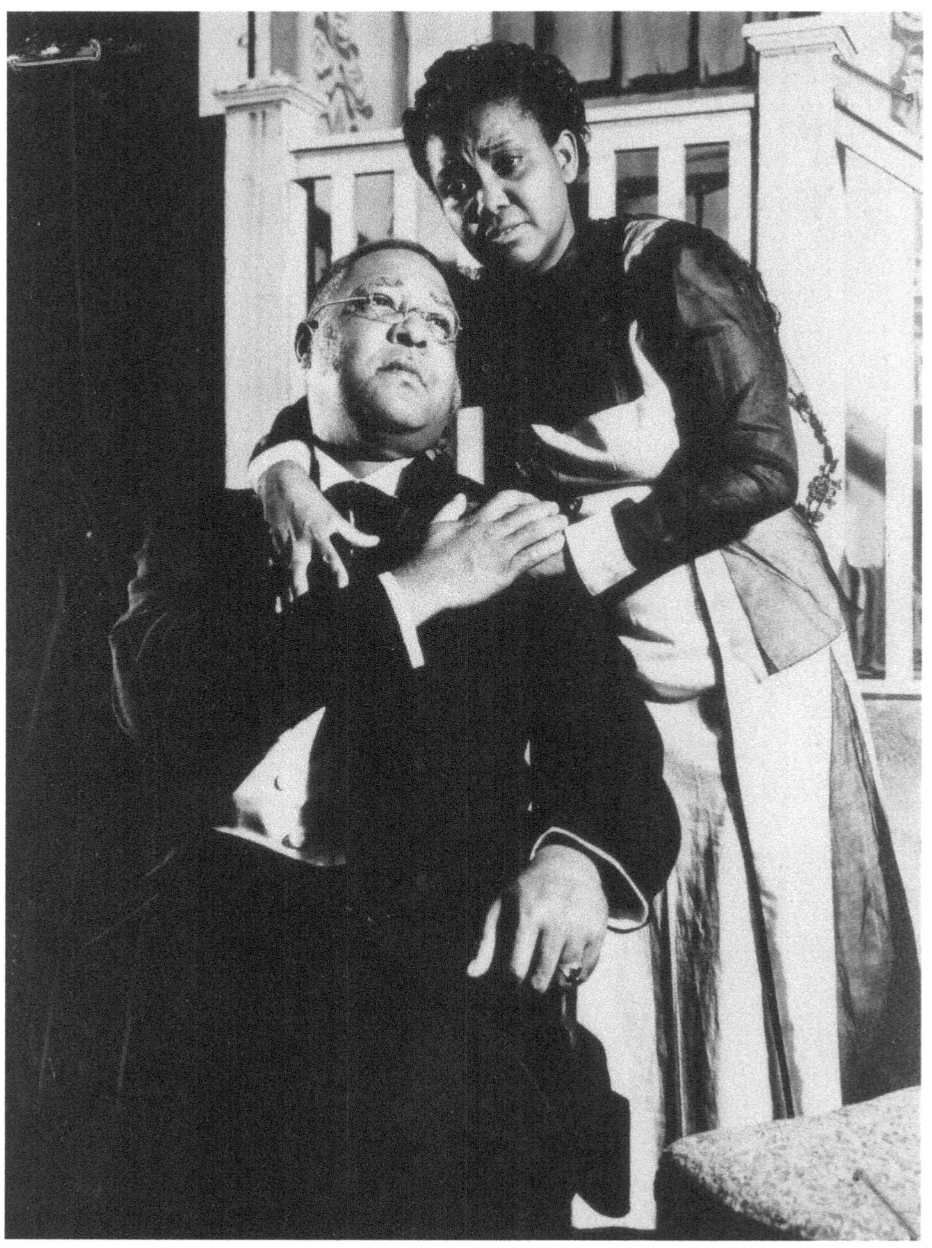

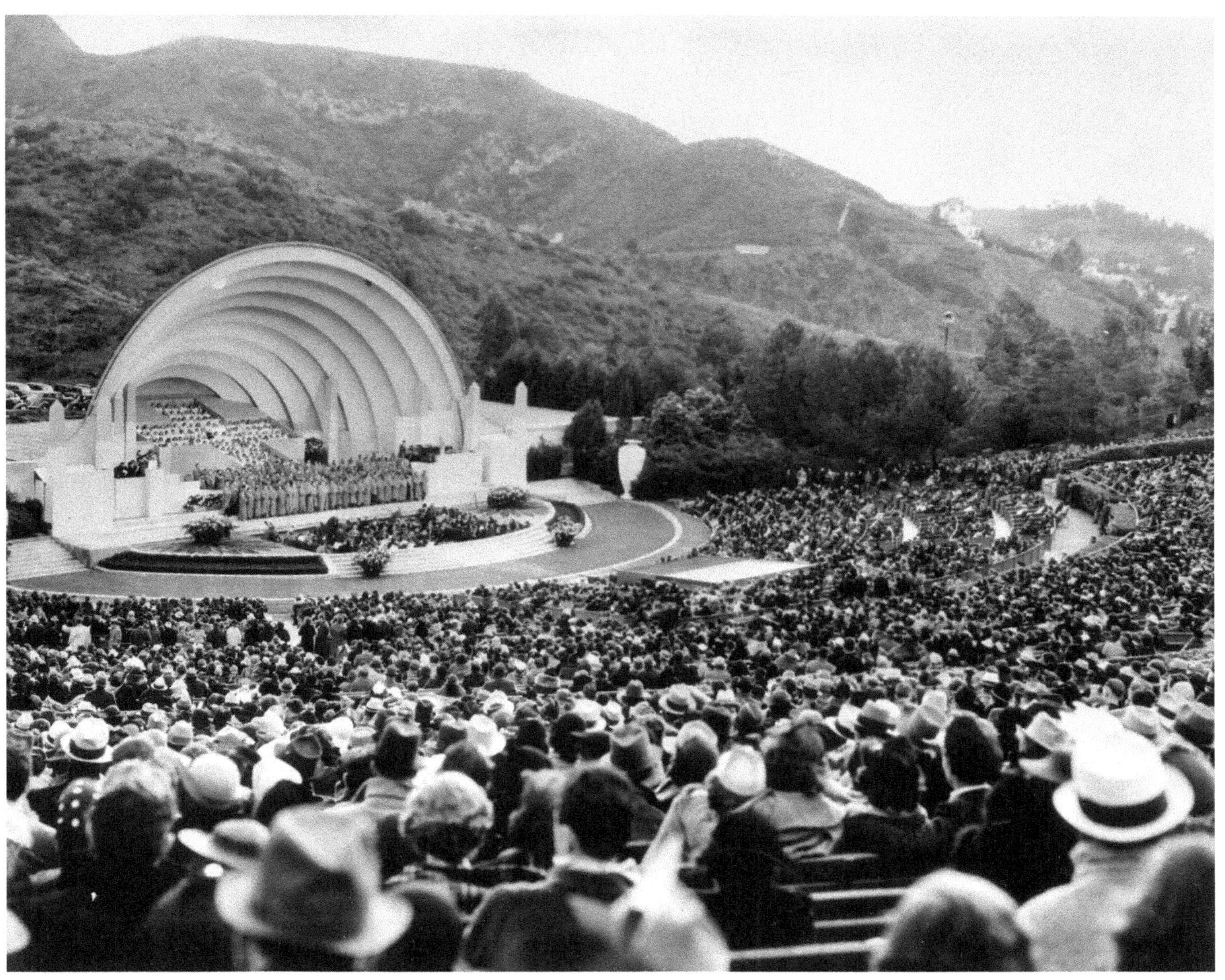

Hollywood Bowl was rebuilt in 1929 with its distinctive set of concentric arches known as the band shell. The Technocracy Movement, advocating a form of society where the welfare of human beings is optimized by widespread use of technology, and other organizations held public events in the Bowl during the 1930s. This is an Easter Sunrise Service featuring WPA Orchestra and Singers.

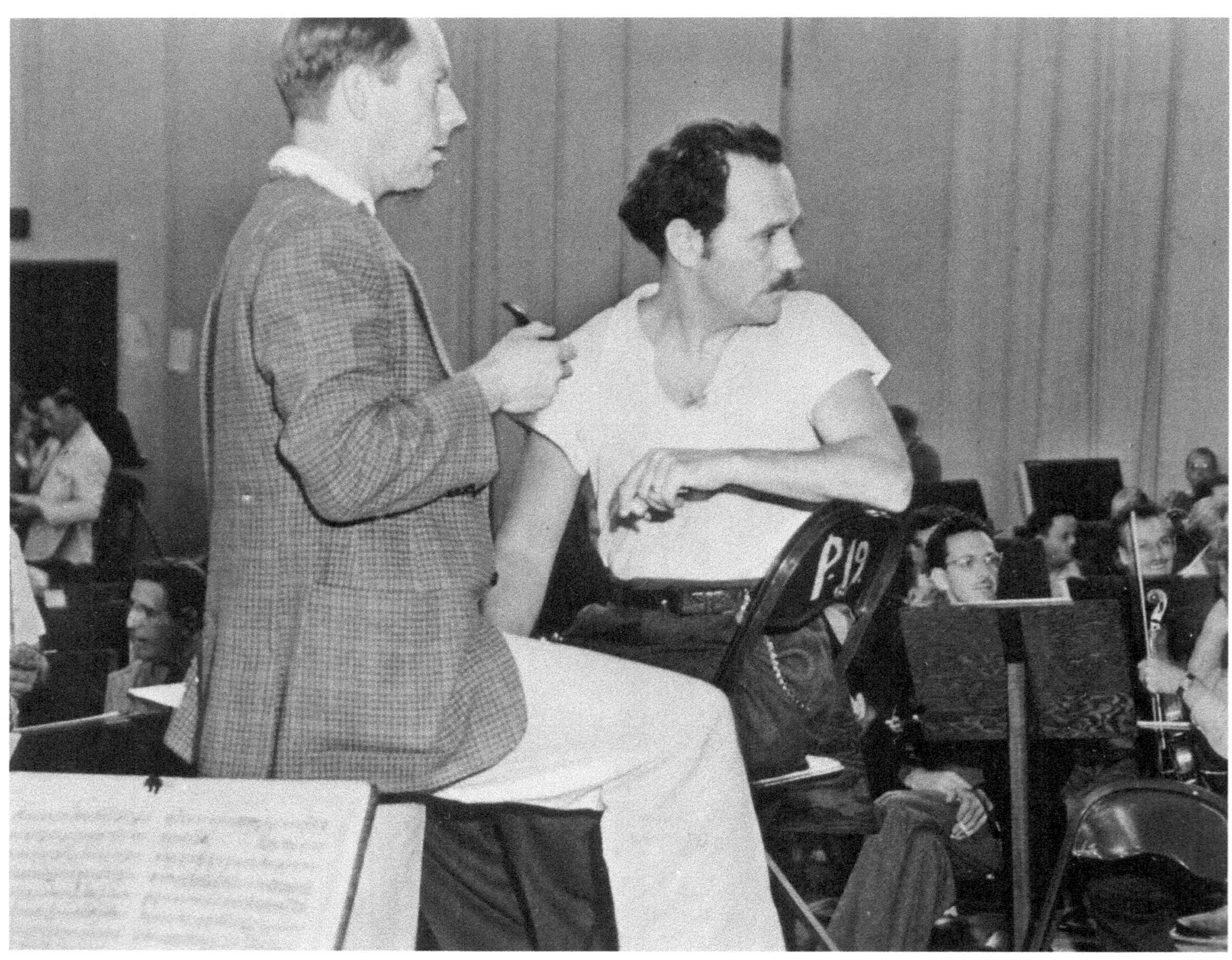

The two men working with the orchestra are Morris Hutchins Ruger, composer, and Gastone Usigli, conductor and general director of the opera *Gettysburg* that premiered at the Hollywood Bowl, September 23, 1938. Ruger (1902–1974) was a composer, concert singer, and music teacher. His works included sonatas, chamber music, chorales, and this opera.

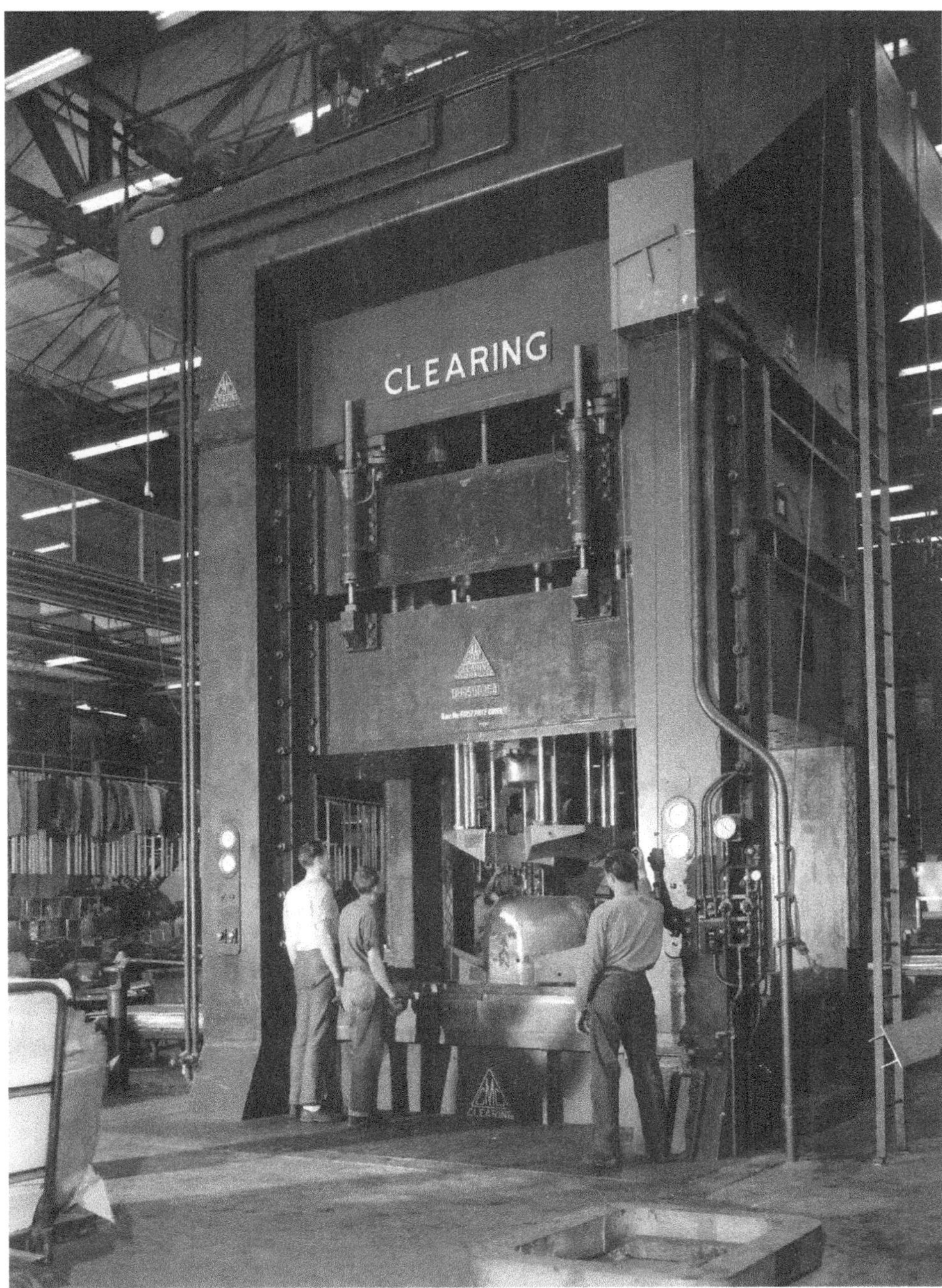

Inside the Vega Aircraft Corporation in Burbank, around the late 1930s. The Vega Aircraft Corporation was a subsidiary of the Lockheed Aircraft Company and was responsible for much of the parent company's production in World War II. The Vega company was first formed in August 1937 as the AiRover Company to produce a new light plane design. It was soon renamed Vega to honor Lockheed's first aircraft design.

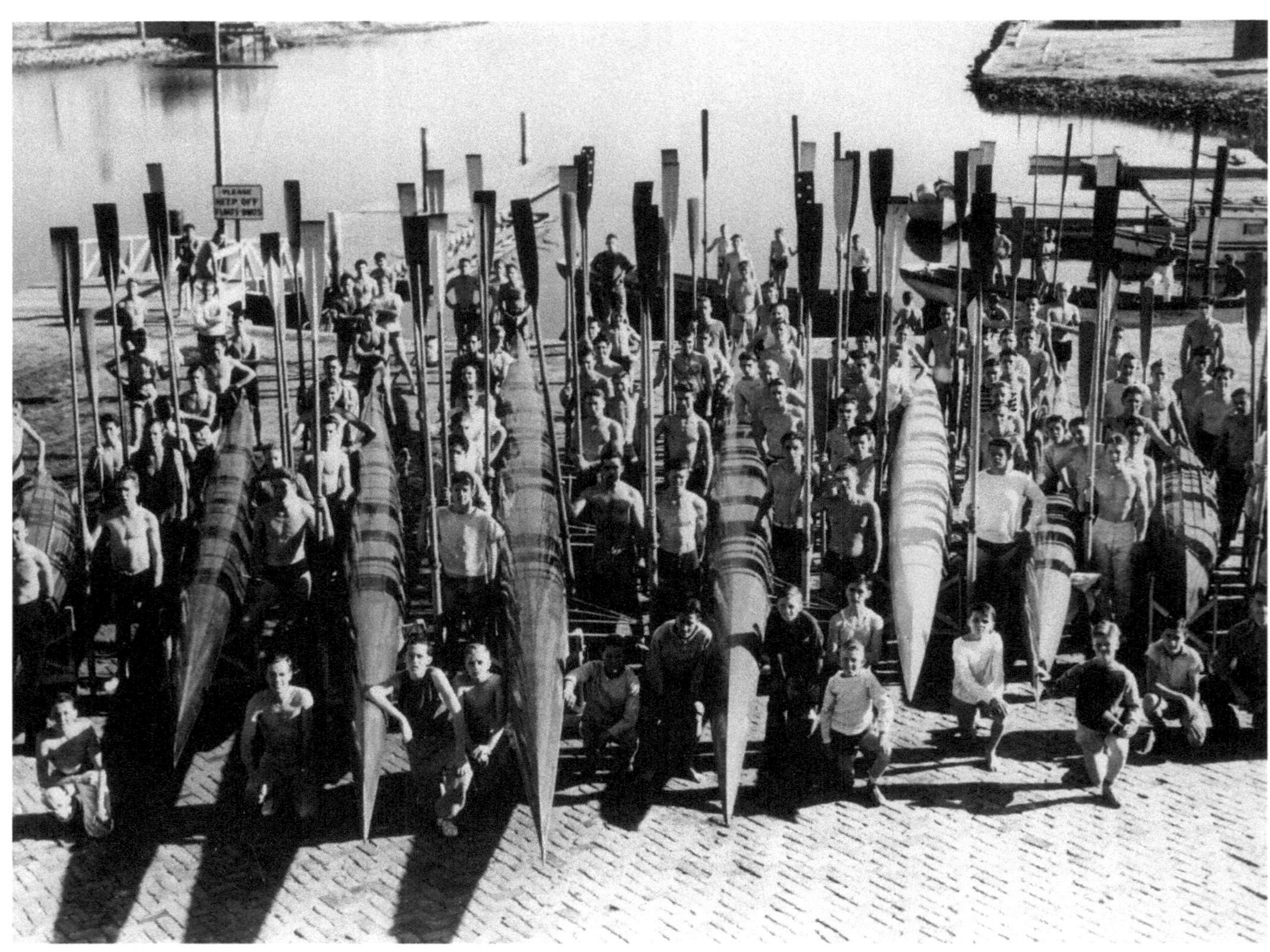

The Long Beach Recreation Commission offered boating activities with the aid of the Works Progress Administration. These high school and junior college students are part of crew groups at Long Beach Marine Stadium in 1936. The young men received instruction and practice in rowing and handling of gigs, navy-type cutters, whale boats, canoes, crew boats, barges, and many other types of boats.

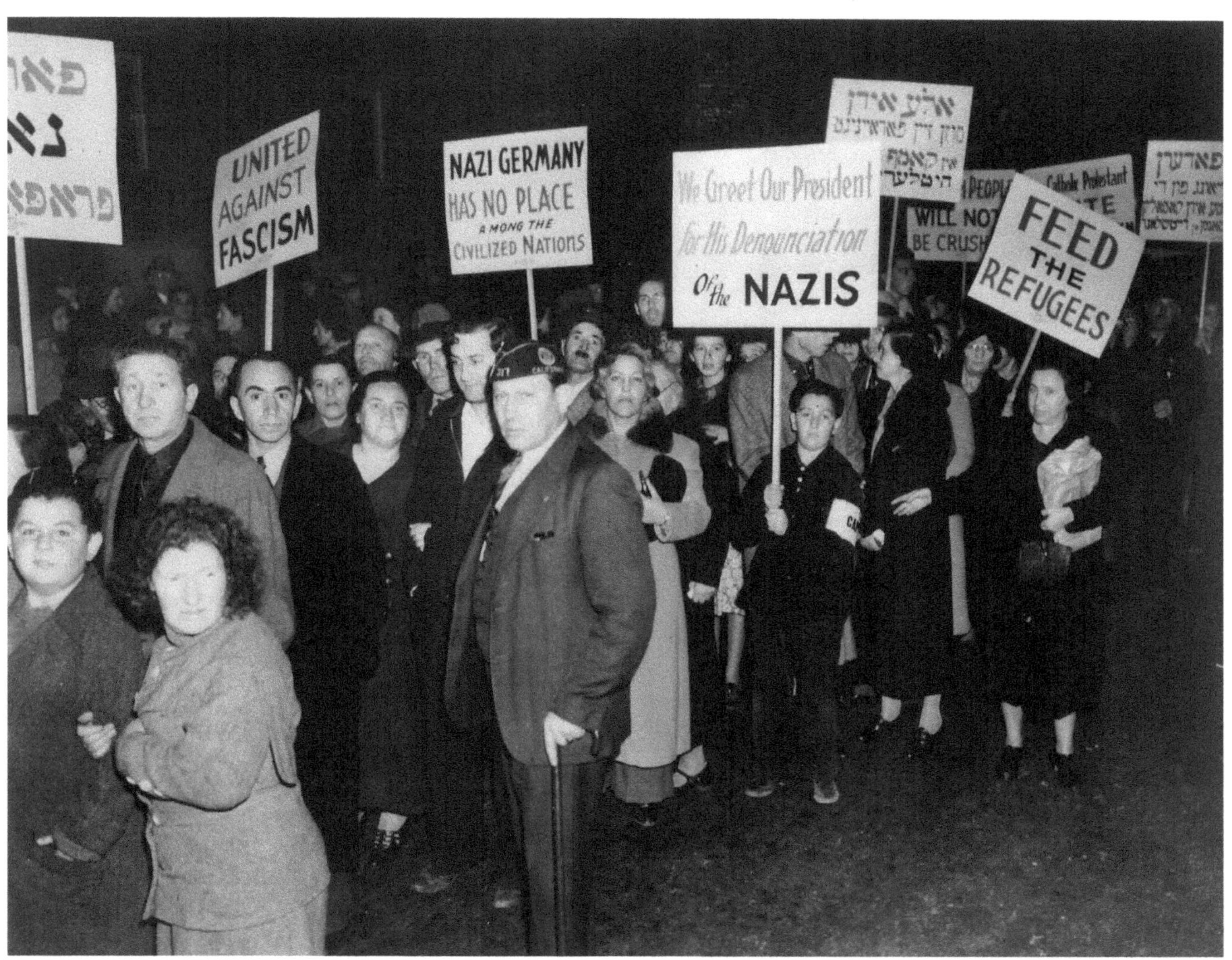

Los Angeles marchers in 1938 carry signs that urge the United States to boycott German imports to protest Nazi Germany's repressive policies toward its Jewish citizens. Worse was yet to come. The terms "Holocaust" and "Shoah" are used to describe the methodical extermination of more than six million Jews killed during World War II as a deliberate ideological policy of genocide by the Nazis.

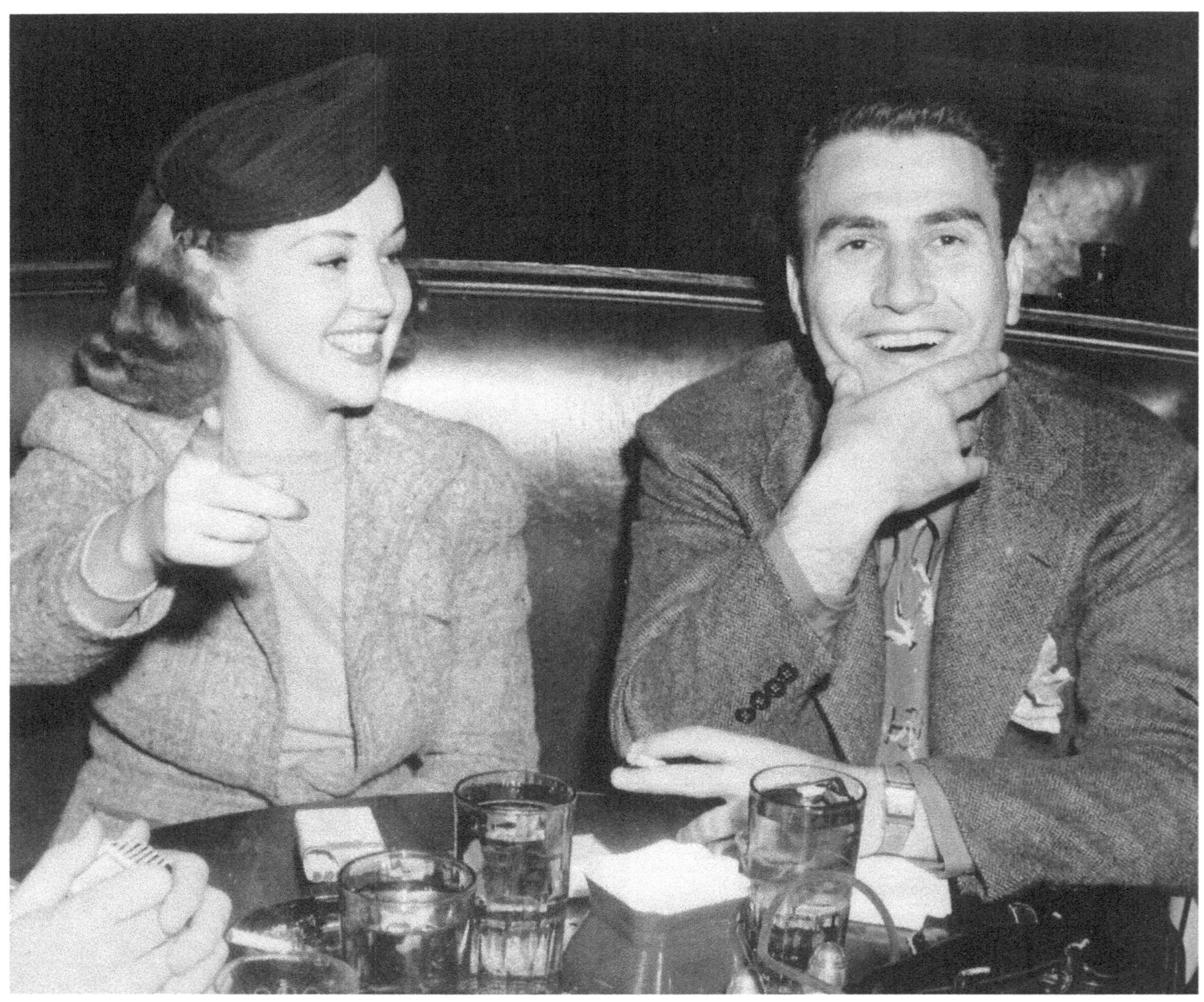

Movie star Betty Grable (1916–1973) and jazz musician Artie Shaw (1910–2004) enjoy each other's company at a Hollywood restaurant in 1939. That year was a watershed for both Hollywood film and Los Angeles writing. *Gone with the Wind* premiered as one of the most profitable films of all time. *The Big Sleep* by Raymond Chandler (1888–1959), his first crime fiction to feature protagonist Philip Marlowe, was published, as was *The Day of the Locust* by Nathanael West (1903–1940), a novelization of West's experiences living in a hotel on Hollywood Boulevard. On September 1, Nazi Germany invaded Poland.

The Second World War and a New Expansion

(1940–1949)

The walls of Alexander Hamilton Junior High School at Long Beach crumbled in the earthquake of 1933. The school was rebuilt as it appears here in 1940, with earthquake-proof windows, constructed by the Public Works Administration. The architecture style is known as Art Deco, a popular international design movement in the 1920s and 1930s that also affected interior and industrial design, as well as fashion, painting, graphic arts, and film.

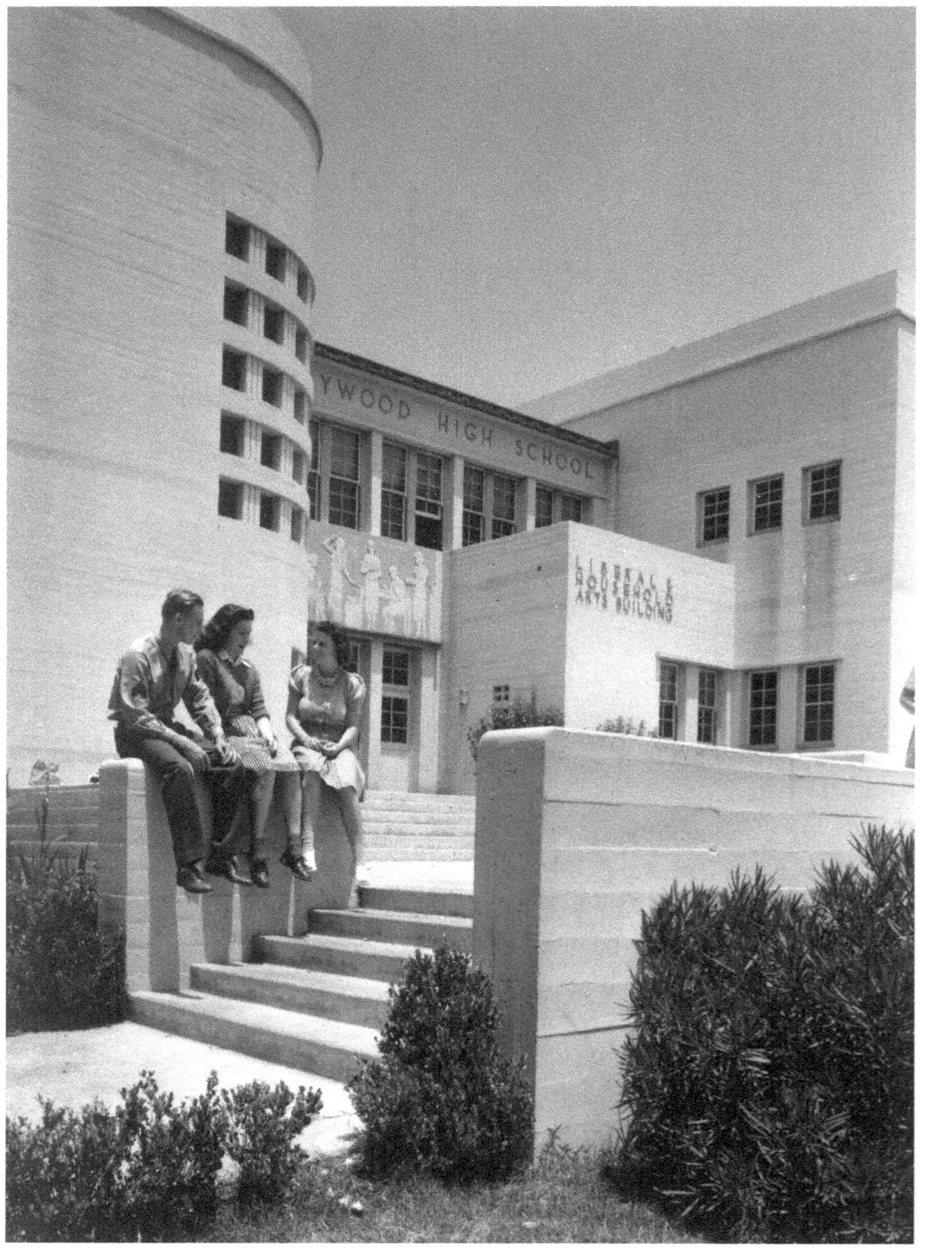

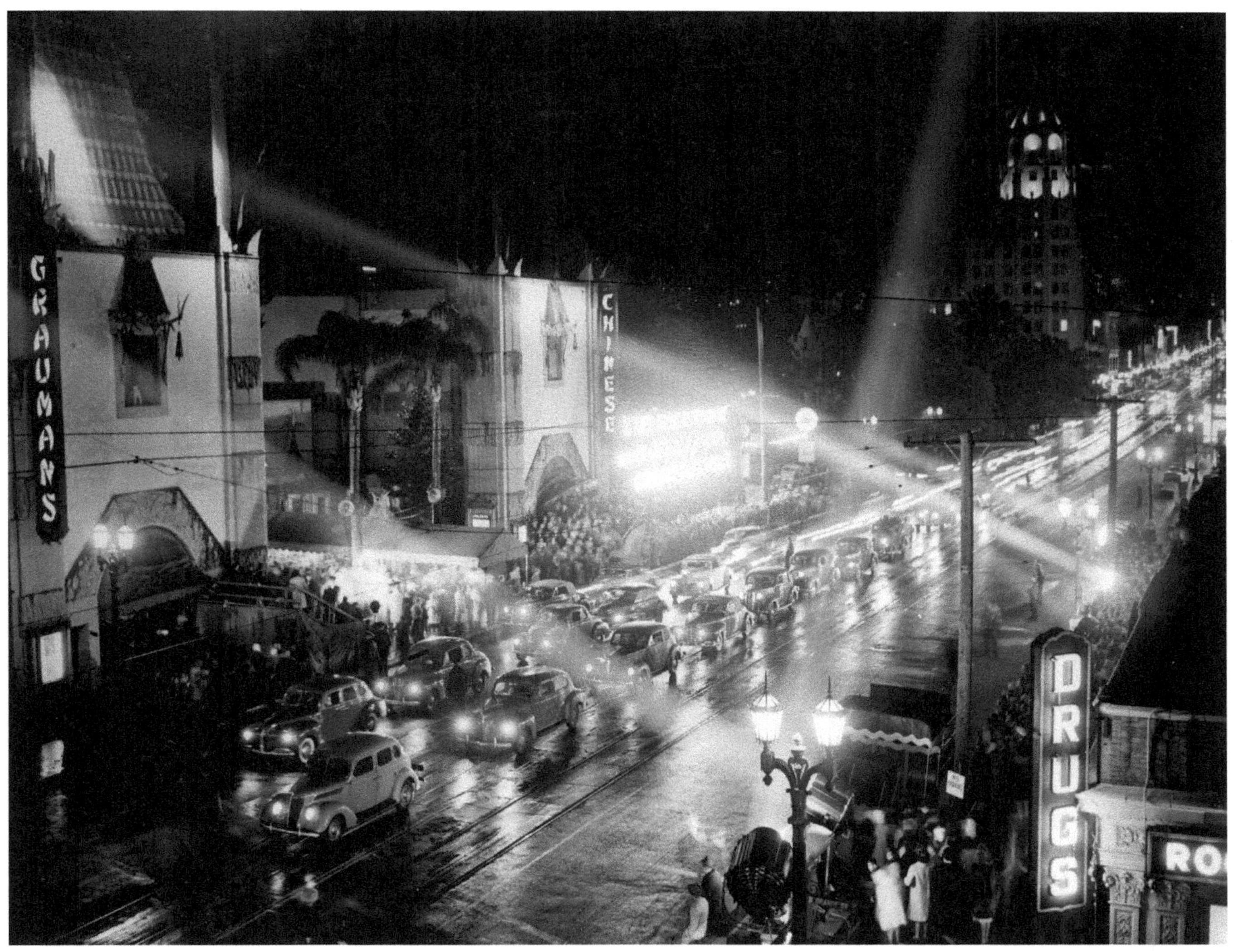

The crowds and traffic at a Grauman's Chinese Theatre premiere attest to Hollywood's continued influence. More than 7,500 movies—95 percent of all American films—were released by the eight leading studios between 1930 and 1945. This period is remembered as Hollywood's golden age, when new genres were formed, the Production Code and B-films were introduced, the first animated feature *Snow White* appeared, and the studio system rose to mammoth status.

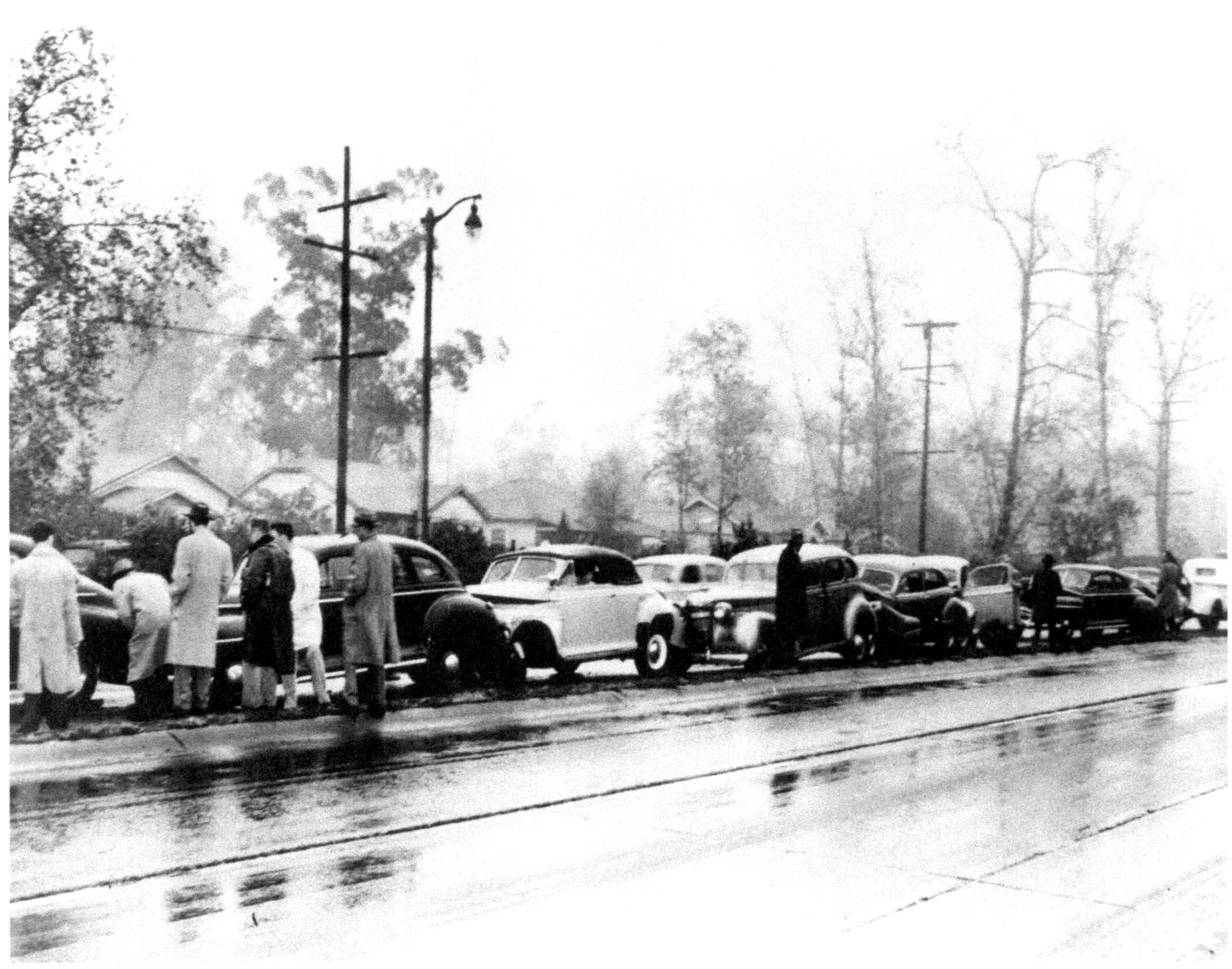

With so many cars, traffic accidents became routine occurrences in Los Angeles. Here, rain-wet Arroyo Seco Parkway (now called the Pasadena Freeway) caused a pileup in which seven people were injured. Arroyo Seco was the first freeway in the West. Because of its engineering significance, it was designated a historic engineering landmark by the American Society of Civil Engineers in 1999.

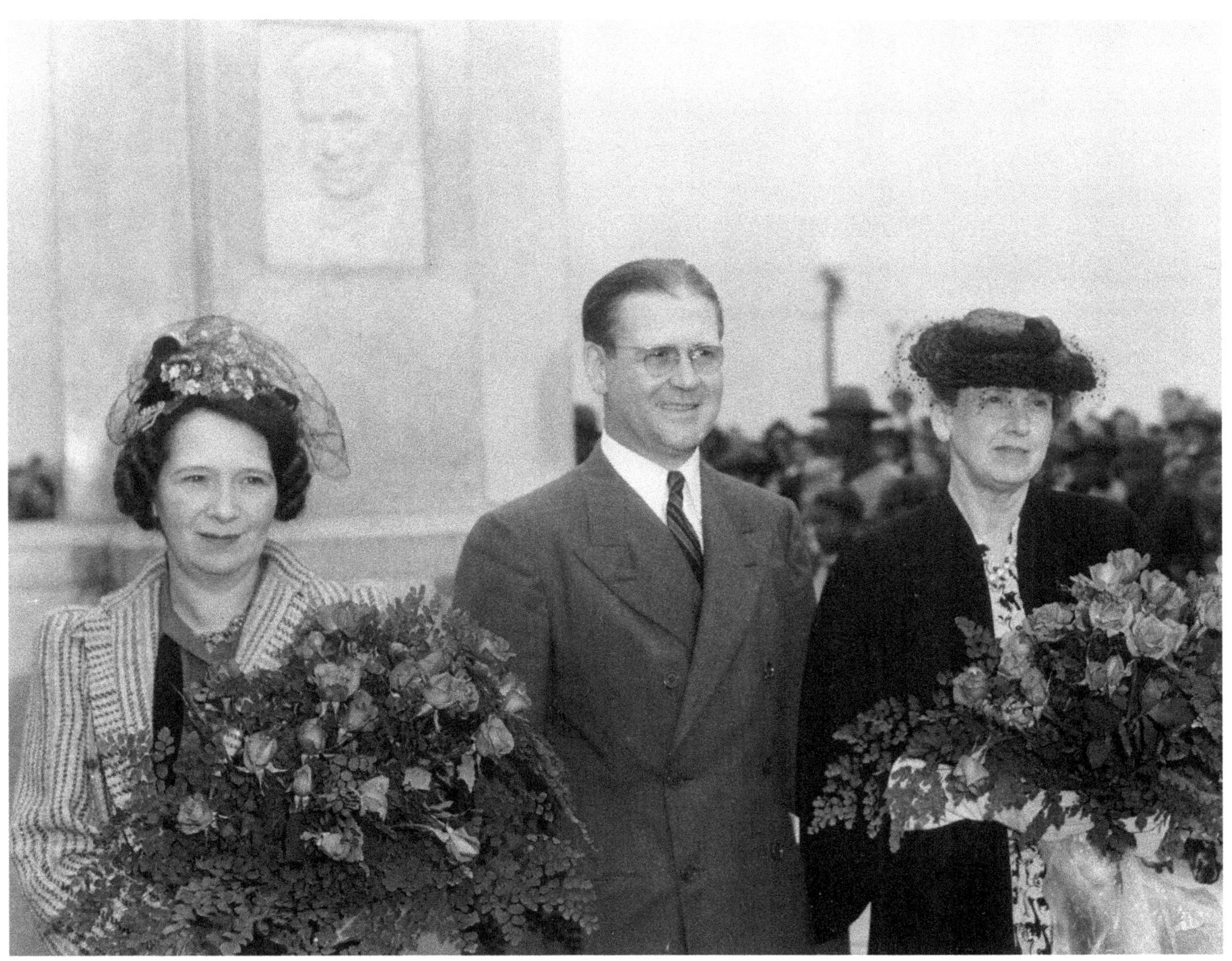

Not quite six years after Will Rogers (1879–1935) died in a plane crash, the Will Rogers Memorial Park and Playground in Southwest Los Angeles was formally dedicated on June 14, 1941. The new play center honoring the popular humorist and actor was sponsored by the County of Los Angeles. The photo shows (left to right) Betty Blake Rogers, widow of the late actor; Gordon McDonough of the County Board of Supervisors; and Mrs. McDonough.

This is the First Street viaduct, west approach, under construction in Los Angeles in 1941. A viaduct is a type of bridge that spans the gap between two high points of land and does not cross any water.

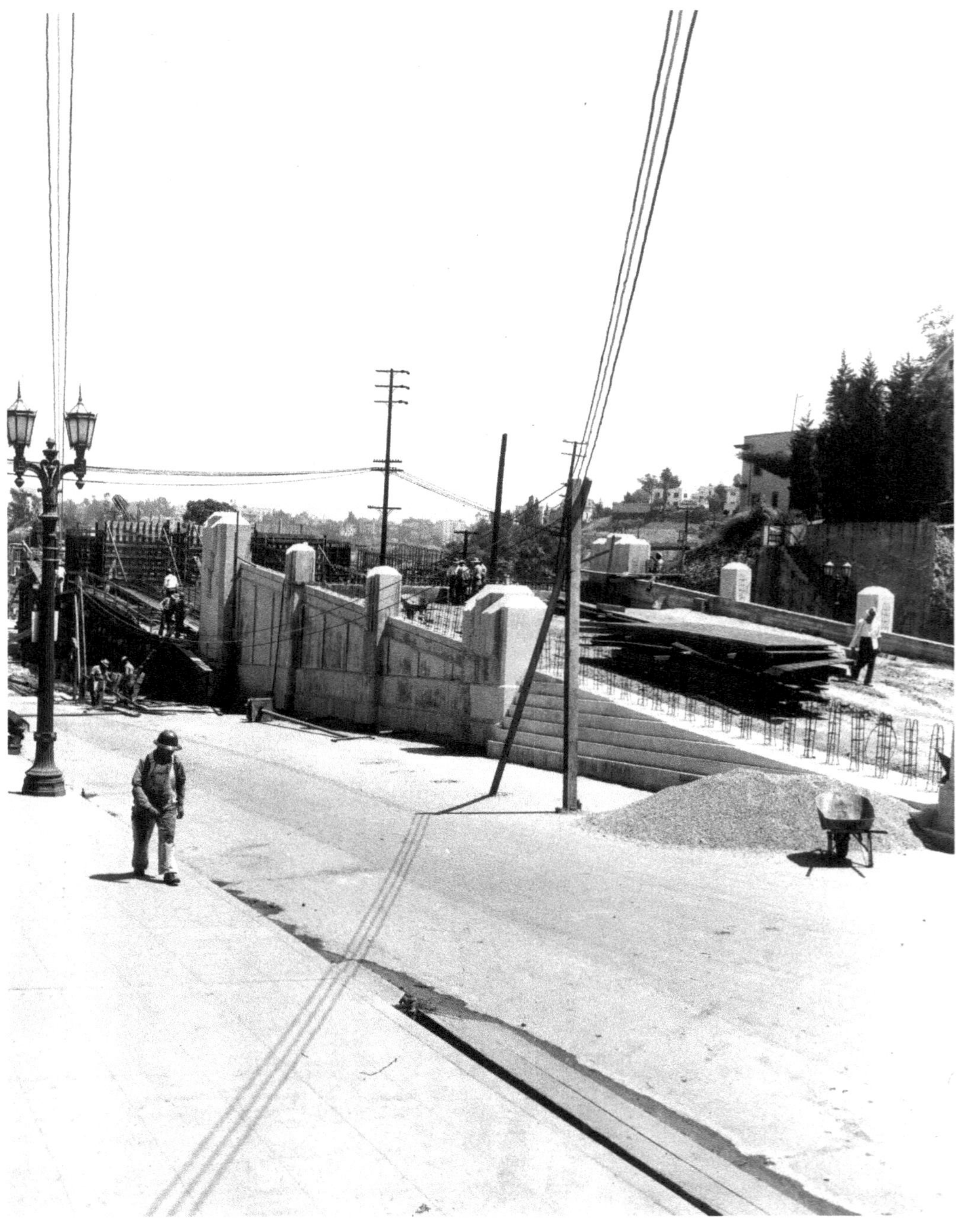

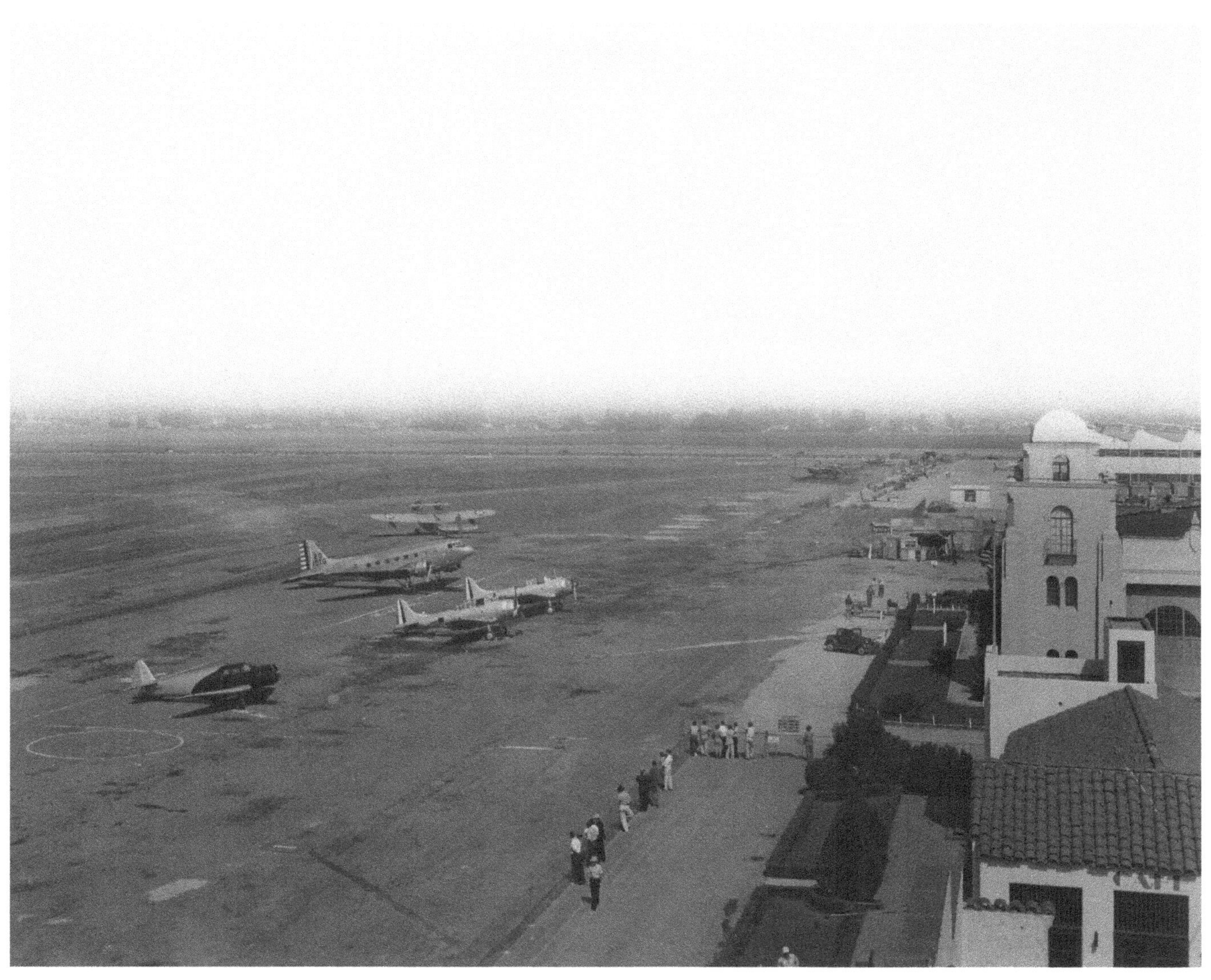

Formerly known as Mines Field, the Los Angeles Municipal Airport was converted into one of the major airports on the Pacific Coast in 1940 as the Work Projects Administration provided 1,600 workers to make improvements. When the National Defense Program was launched, the Mines Field conversion became a priority project. The photo is shot from the central tower.

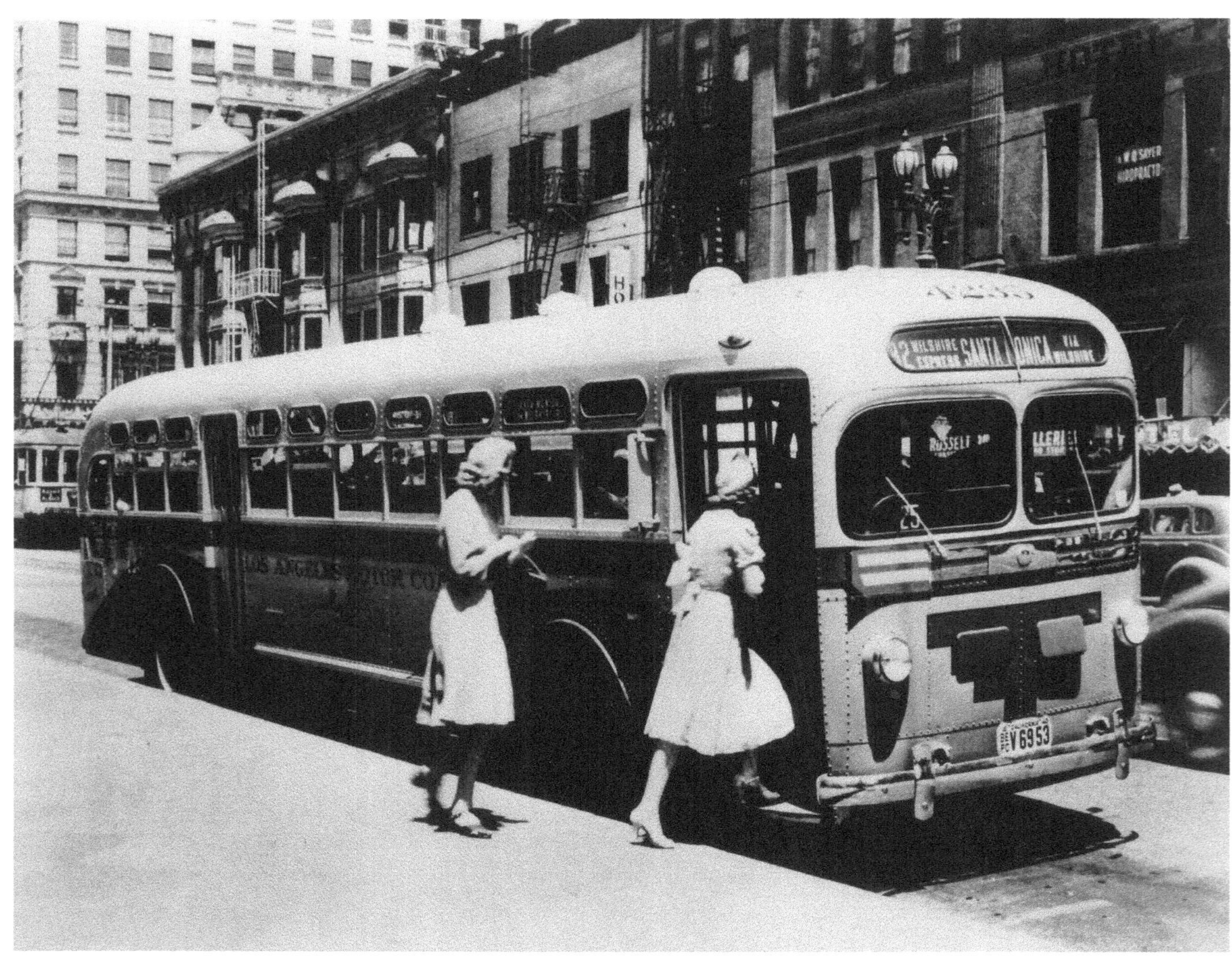

Young women board a bus in Los Angeles. Unlike streetcar lines that required rails, bus routes could be adjusted easily and quickly. World War II halted construction on the parkways and freeways, and gasoline was rationed. For many workers, buses provided a viable transportation alternative to automobiles on L.A.'s crowded roadways.

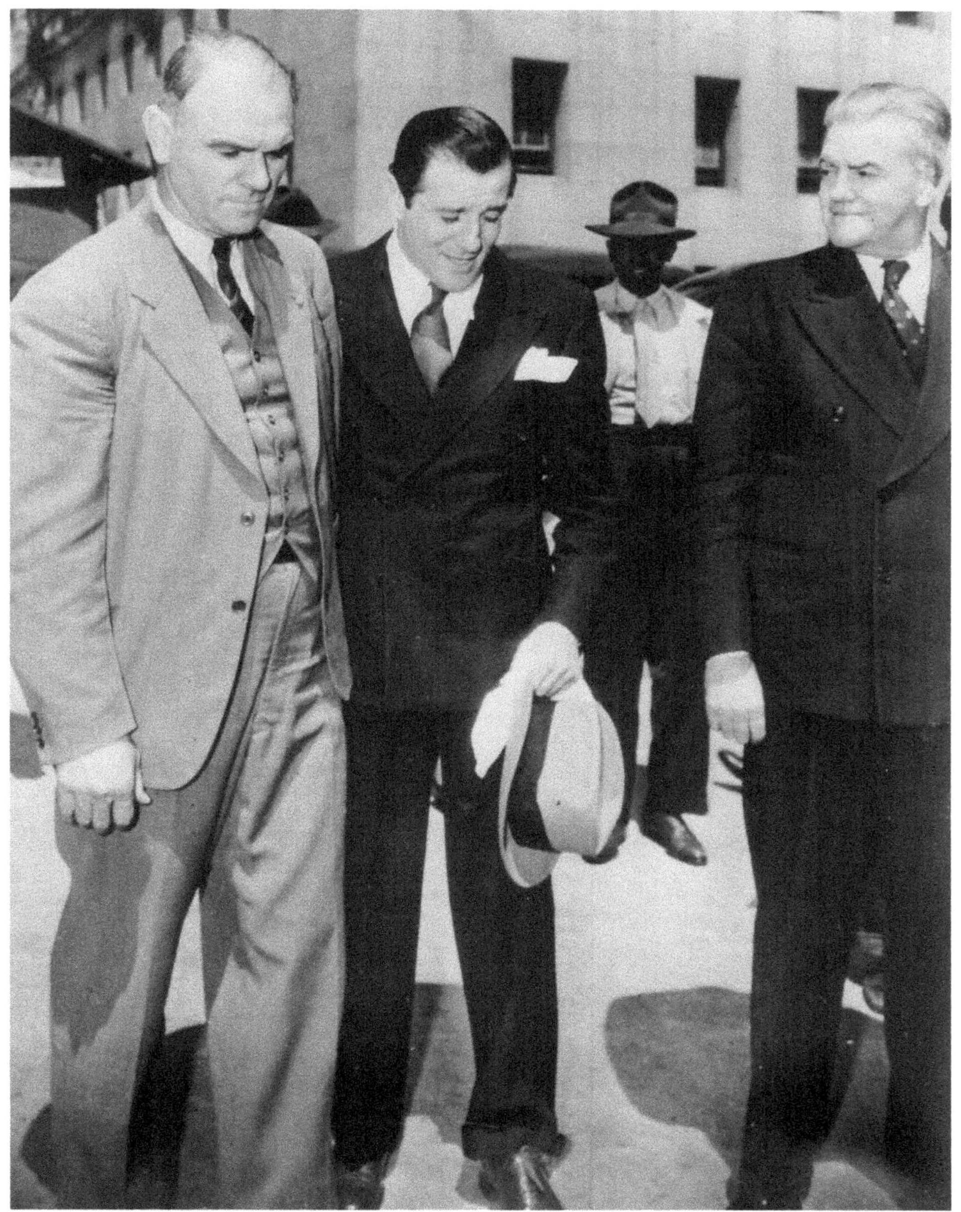

Benjamin "Bugsy" Siegel is led away by U.S. Marshals in Los Angeles in 1941. Siegel (1906–1947) was famous for his affairs with female Hollywood personalities and for building Las Vegas. In California he ran the illegal transcontinental race wire service and giant prostitution rings, and he also smuggled narcotics across the Mexican border.

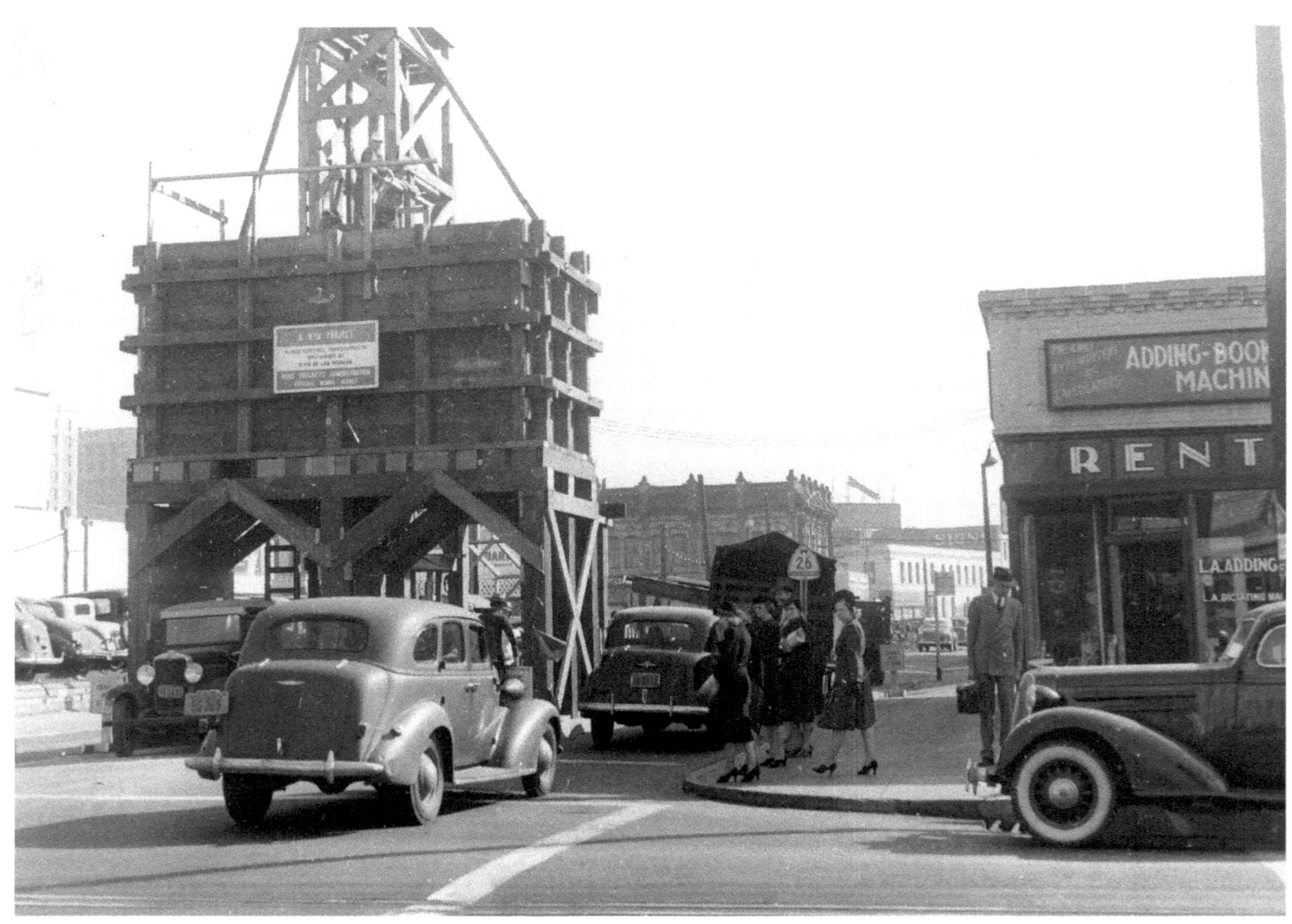

When bad weather did occasionally hit Los Angeles, the city as originally designed was not able to accommodate the sudden influx of water. A 1940 WPA project, the Olympic Boulevard storm drain, shown here, was part of a citywide storm drain system underneath the streets. Its basic structure was a tapered, reinforced-concrete main line with dozens of connecting laterals and catch-basins, making it one of the largest in the West.

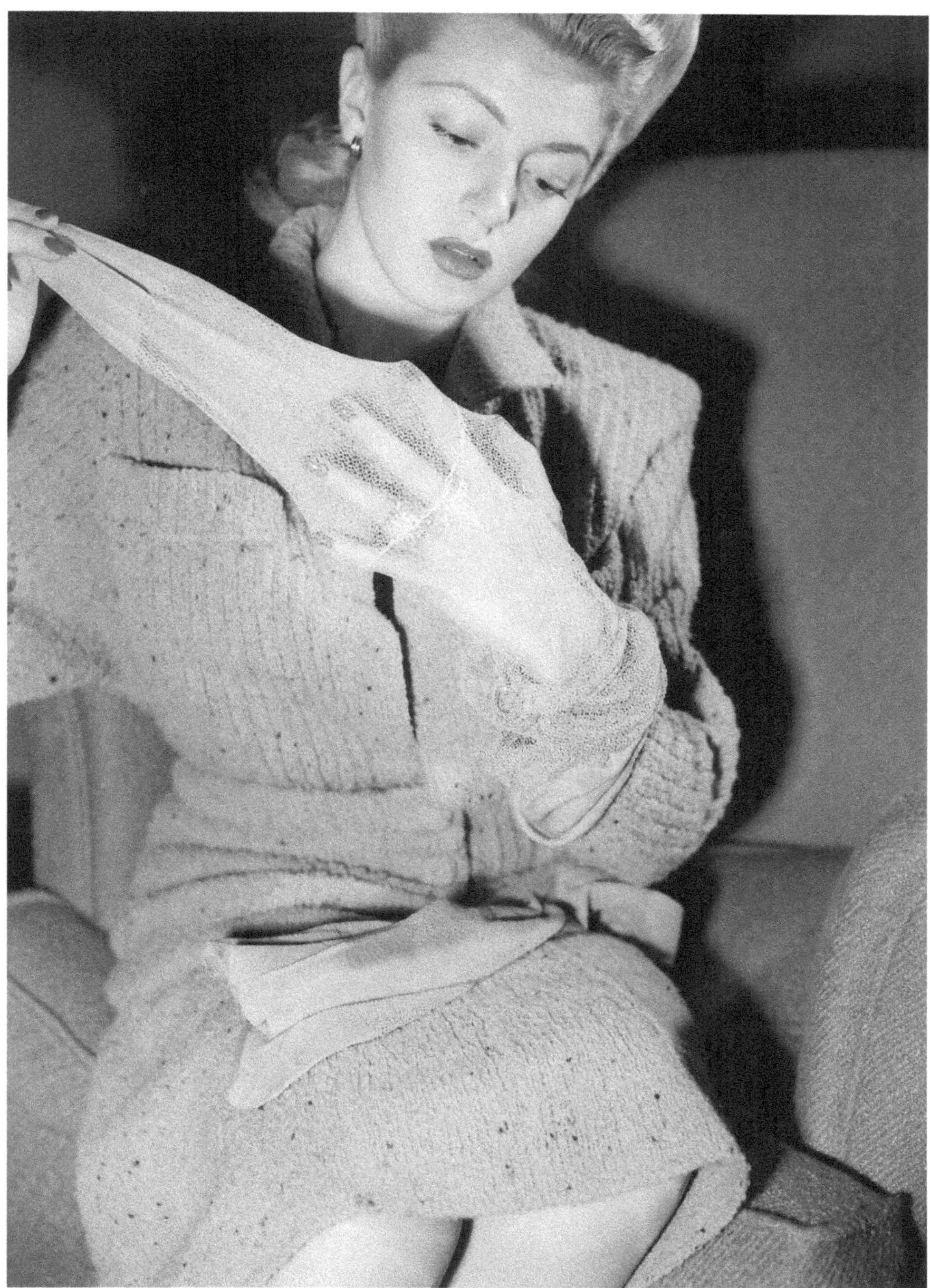

Lana Turner (1921–1995), the popular movie femme fatale, shown here just two months before the Japanese attack on Pearl Harbor, inspects the bracelet design embroidered on dressy, lisle cotton mesh hose. During World War II, Turner made tours selling War Bonds. She wrote her own speeches and promised "a sweet kiss" to any man who purchased a bond worth $50,000 or more. "I'm told I increased the defense budget by several million dollars," she said.

Hollywood and Vine Streets looking north on Vine. This was one of L.A.'s main thoroughfares before the Hollywood Freeway and other superhighways became the primary automobile conveyance. During the 1940s the Pacific Electric Railway "Red Cars" still served the area, but they would disappear during the next decade.

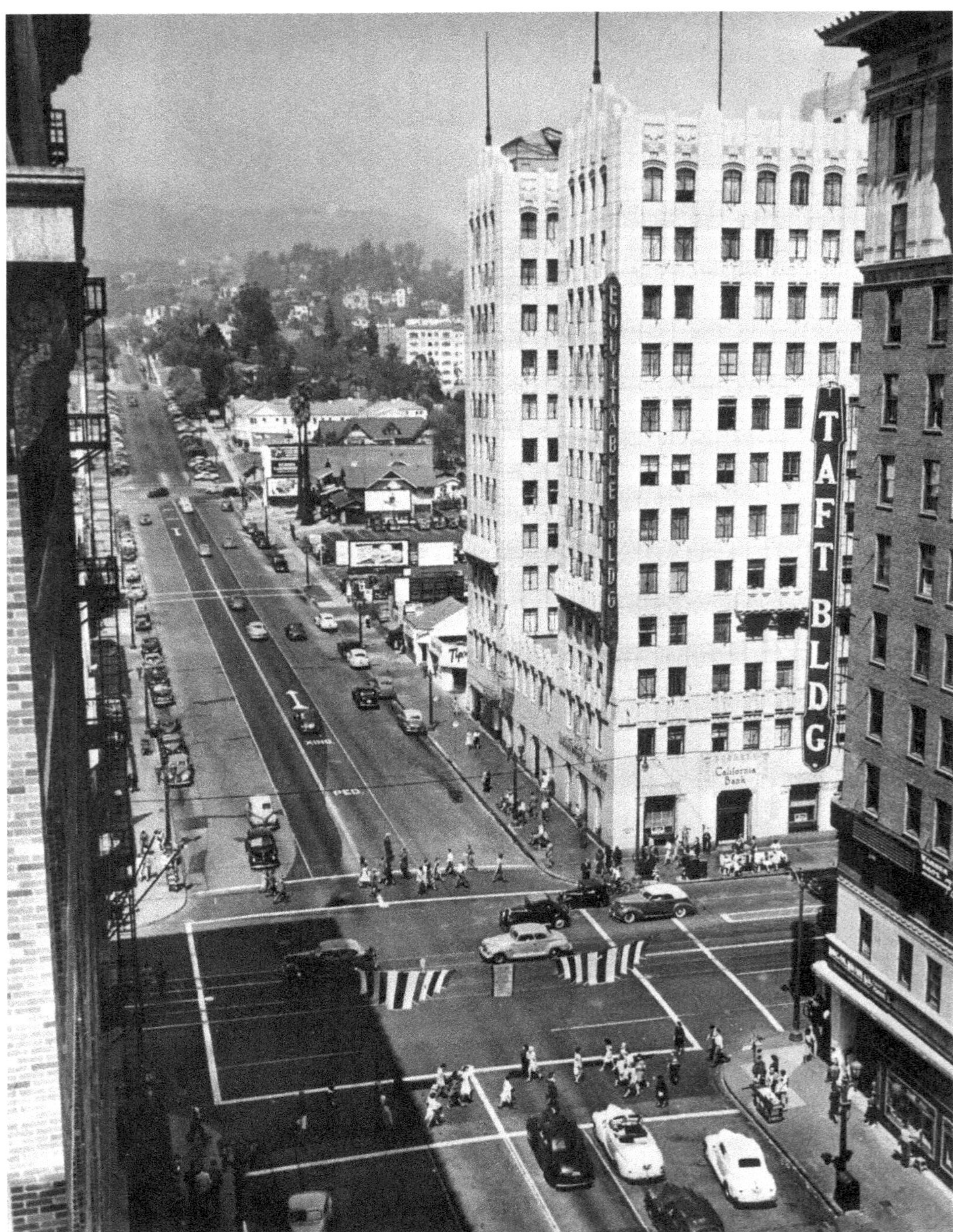

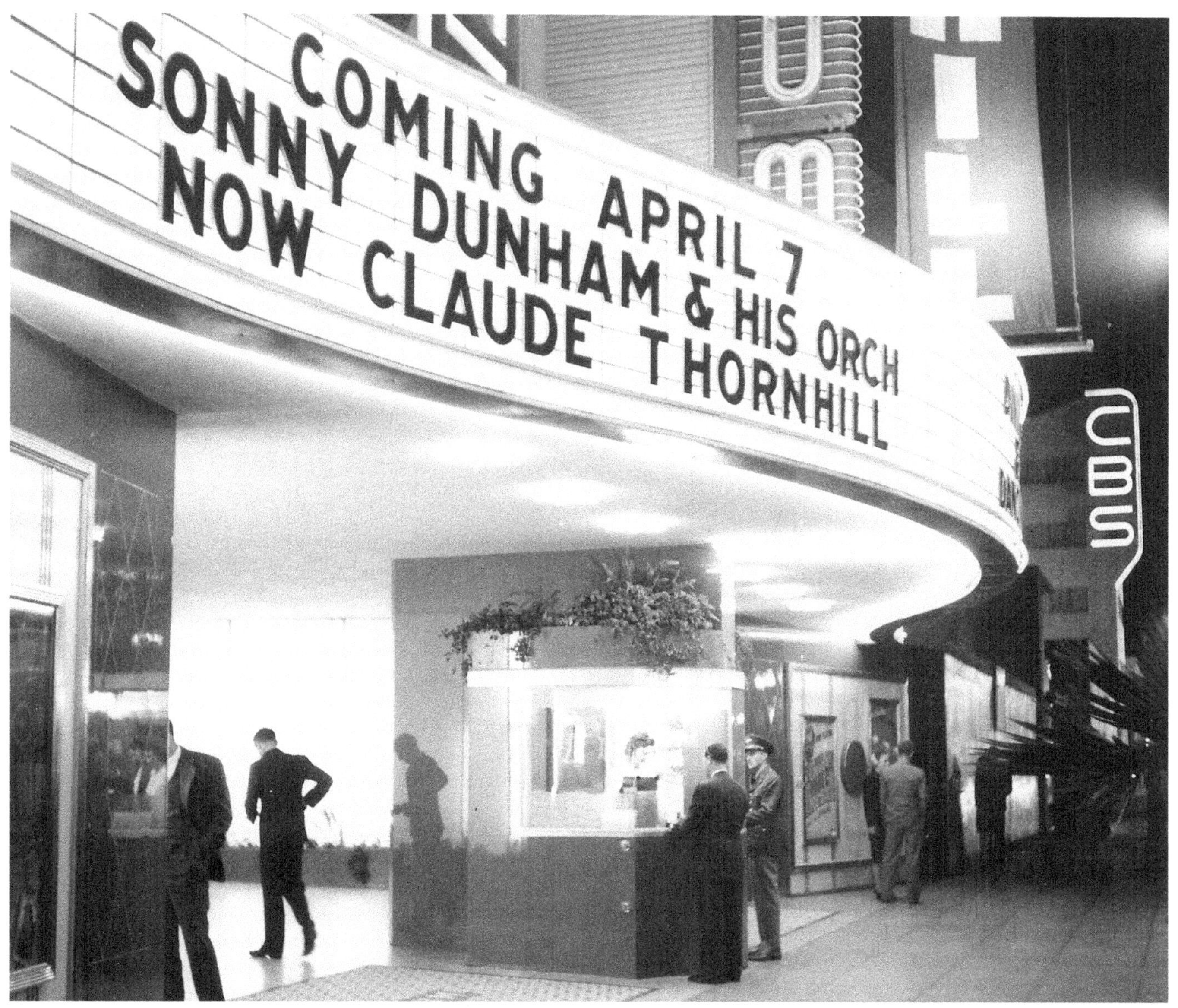

Dance halls existed in American cities since the early 1800s. This sign and ticket window of a large dance palace in Hollywood in April 1942 marks the height of the Swing Era, when big-band swing music was the most popular music in America. Trumpet player Elmer "Sonny" Dunham (1911–1990) was one of the preeminent bandleaders of the 1940s. His band was featured in the 1942 Universal picture *Behind the Eight Ball.*

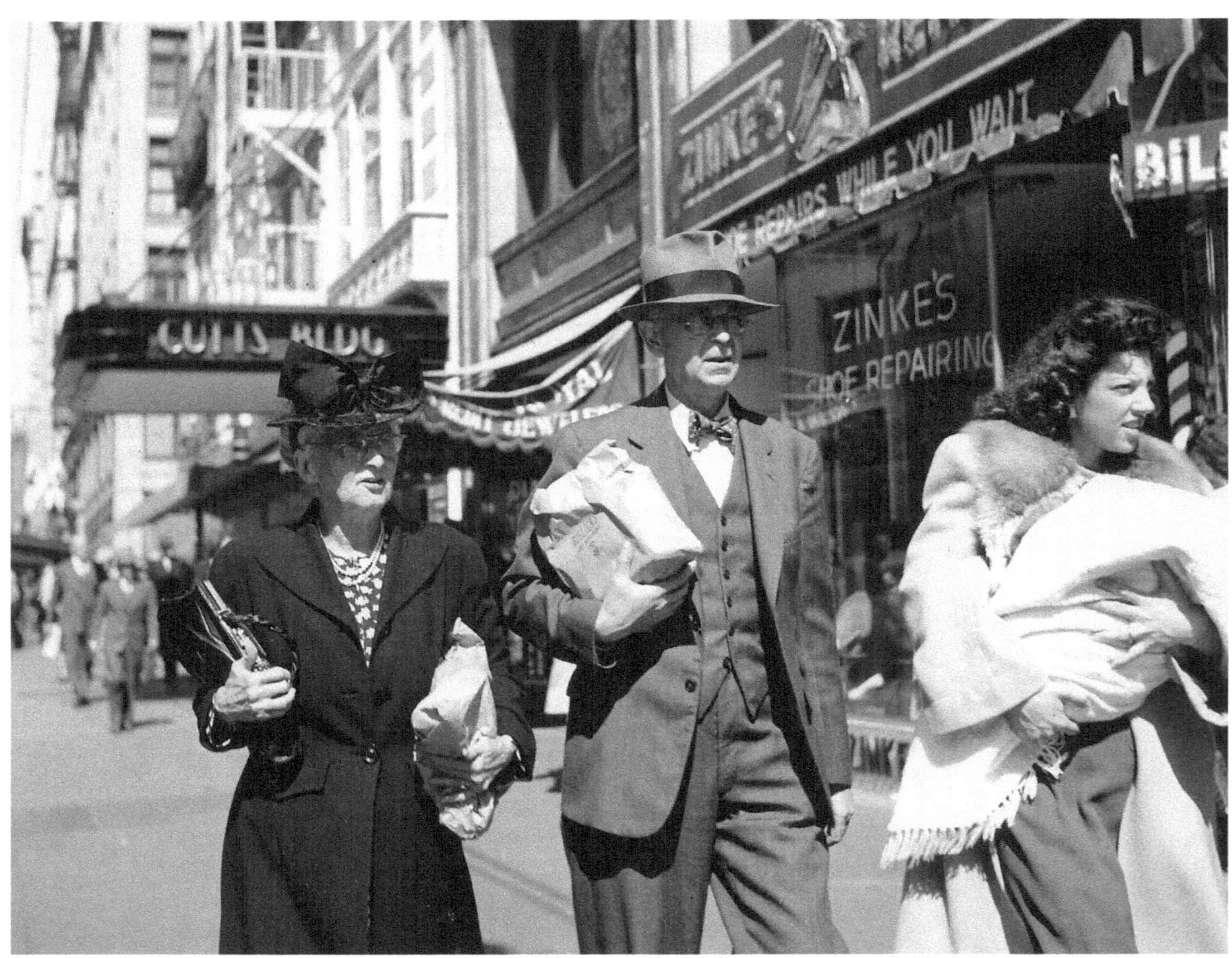

In the spring of 1942, Los Angeles shoppers like these people had to start living with government rationing of food, fuel, and even clothing. Americans were asked to conserve on everything for the duration of the war. The Food Rationing Program provided each citizen with a certain amount of points weekly, using food stamps to purchase meats, butter, oils, etc., and processed foods such as soups, baby food, and catsup. By 1945, about 40 percent of America's vegetables were produced in private "Victory Gardens."

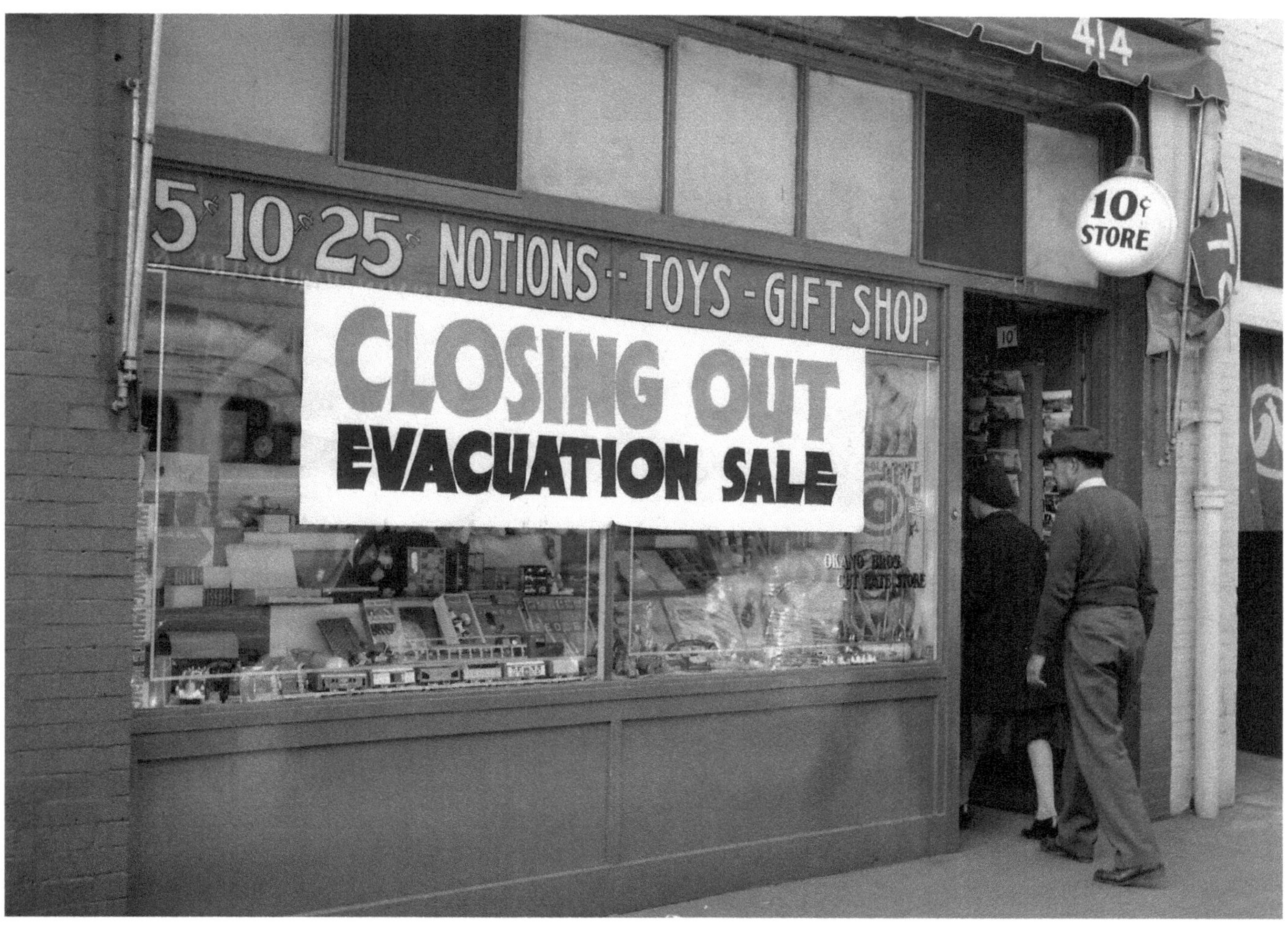

The Japanese surprise attack on Pearl Harbor and rapid conquest of a large portion of Asia and the Pacific caused American civil and military leaders to worry about the loyalty of the more than 100,000 people of Japanese descent living on the West Coast of the United States. Fear of espionage and sabotage, plus racial bias, resulted in President Roosevelt ordering their forced removal to internment camps in April 1942. Here is one of many businesses in L.A.'s Little Tokyo required to close due to the evacuation.

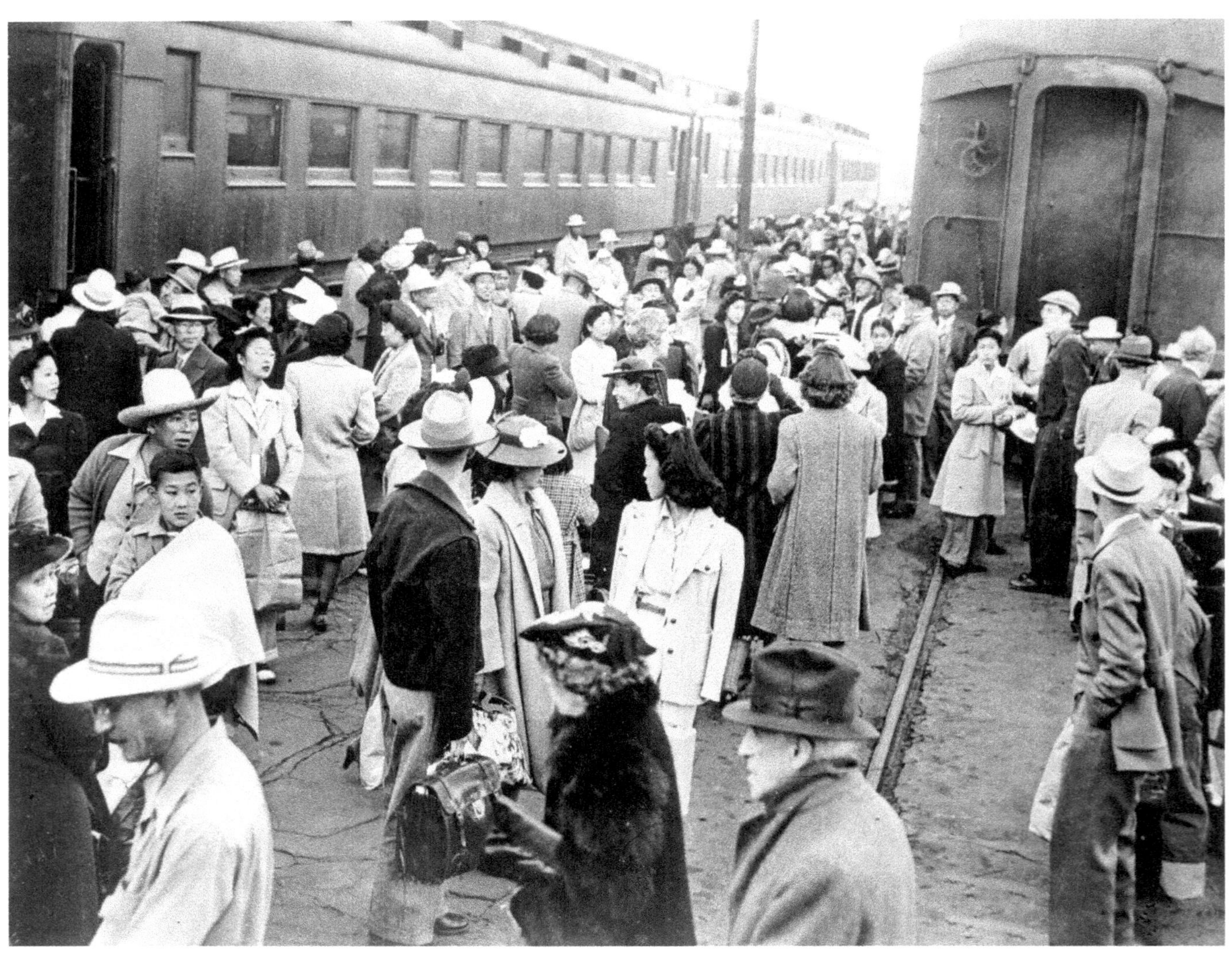

In 1942, 110,000 men, women, and children of Japanese ancestry were sent to camps called "War Relocation Centers" in remote areas of the U.S. Almost two-thirds of them were American citizens, but in 1944, the Supreme Court upheld the constitutionality of the removal and detention, ruling that civil rights of a racial group may be curtailed when there is a "pressing public necessity." These evacuees at a Los Angeles railroad station are waiting to board a train destined for the Santa Anita Assembly Center.

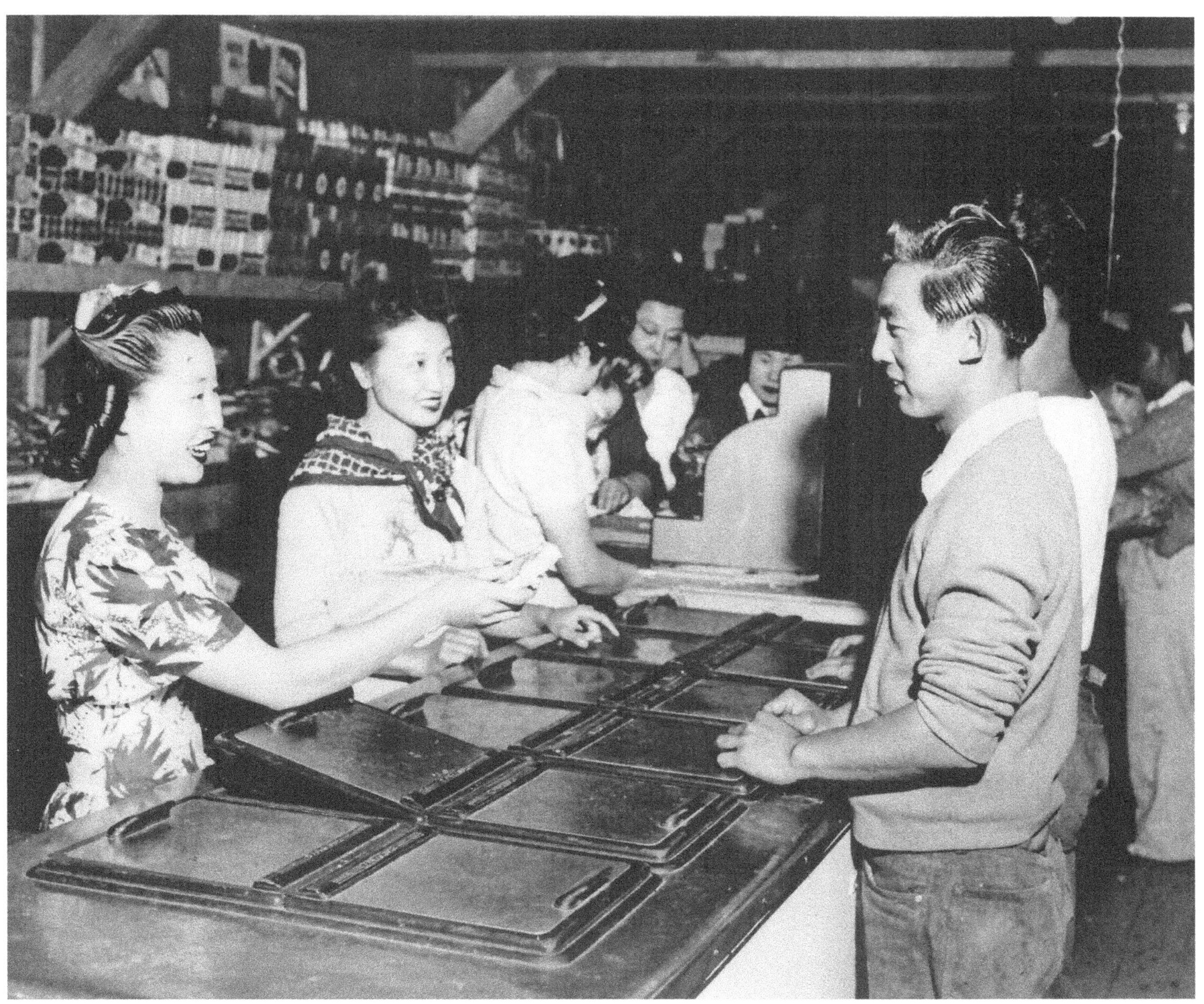

In May 1942, young Japanese American women are shown serving ice cream in a relocation center's community store in Manzanar, California. Some compensation for property losses was paid in 1948, but reparations to surviving internees did not occur until 1990. In 1988, President Ronald Reagan signed legislation that apologized for the internment noting that government actions were based on "race prejudice, war hysteria, and a failure of political leadership."

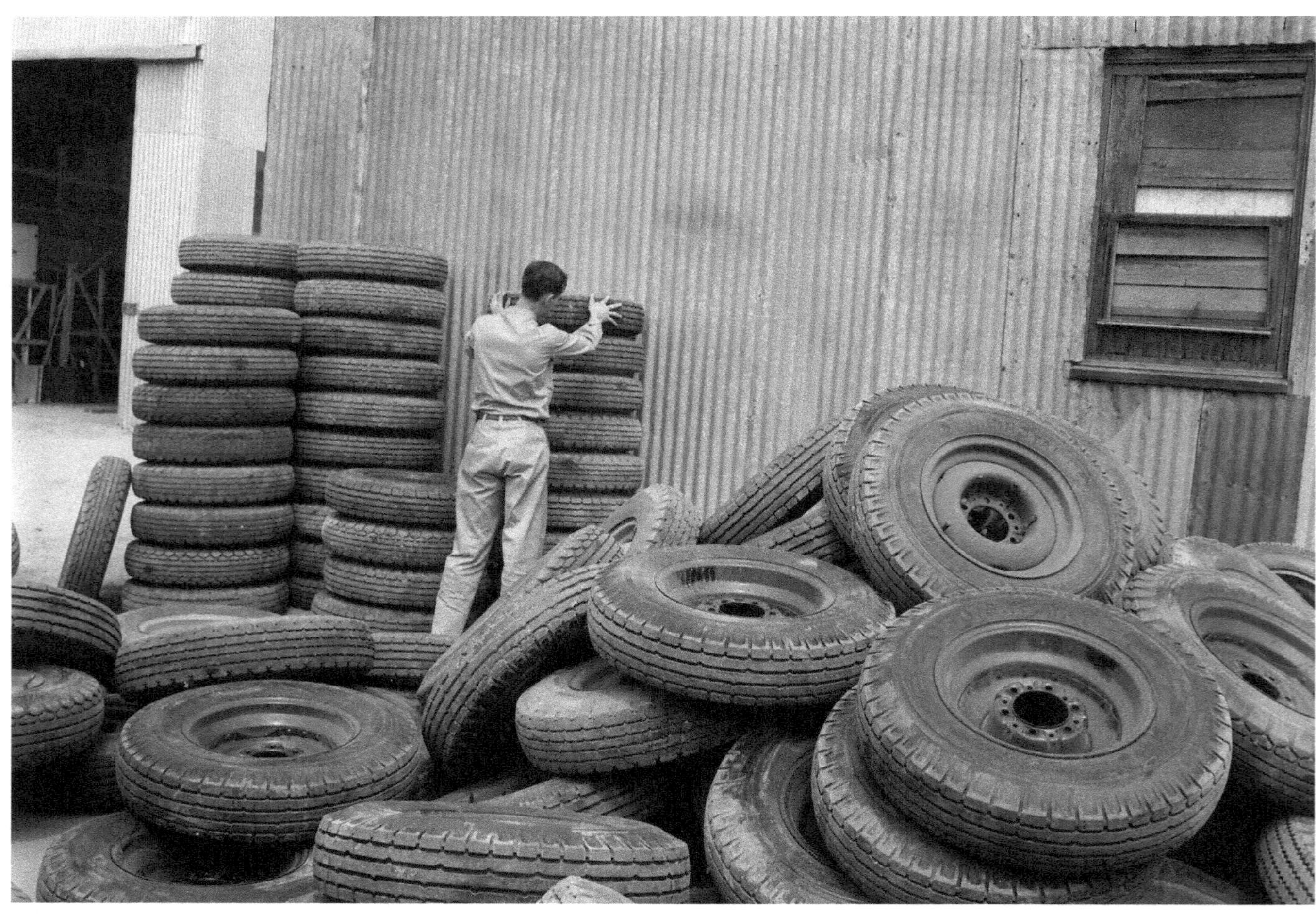

During World War II, Americans were urged to conserve and recycle metal, paper, and rubber. This batch of tires, or "shoes," were removed from trailers that had been delivered from the Los Angeles plant of the Western Trailer Company to war housing areas. Such tires would be registered and recycled for use in other trailers.

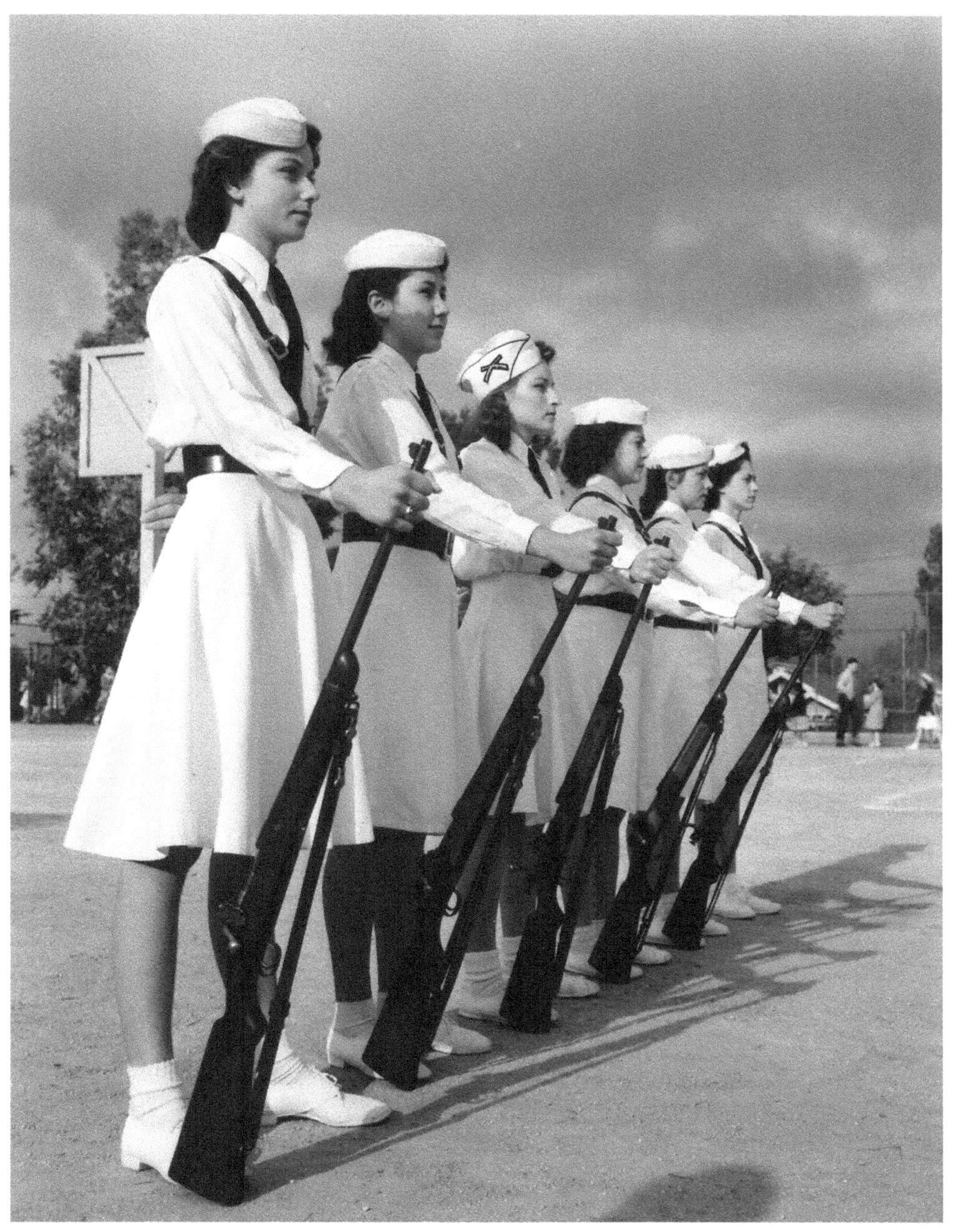

In late 1942, the Victory Corps was created to allow high school students to aid in the war effort. A member needed to participate in a physical fitness program and volunteer for at least one extracurricular wartime activity. These are students at Roosevelt High School in Los Angeles. In 1945, activists at Roosevelt H.S. organized hundreds of other students from local schools to protest against the Board of Education's granting white supremacist Gerald L. K. Smith (1898-1976) a permit to speak at Polytechnic High School.

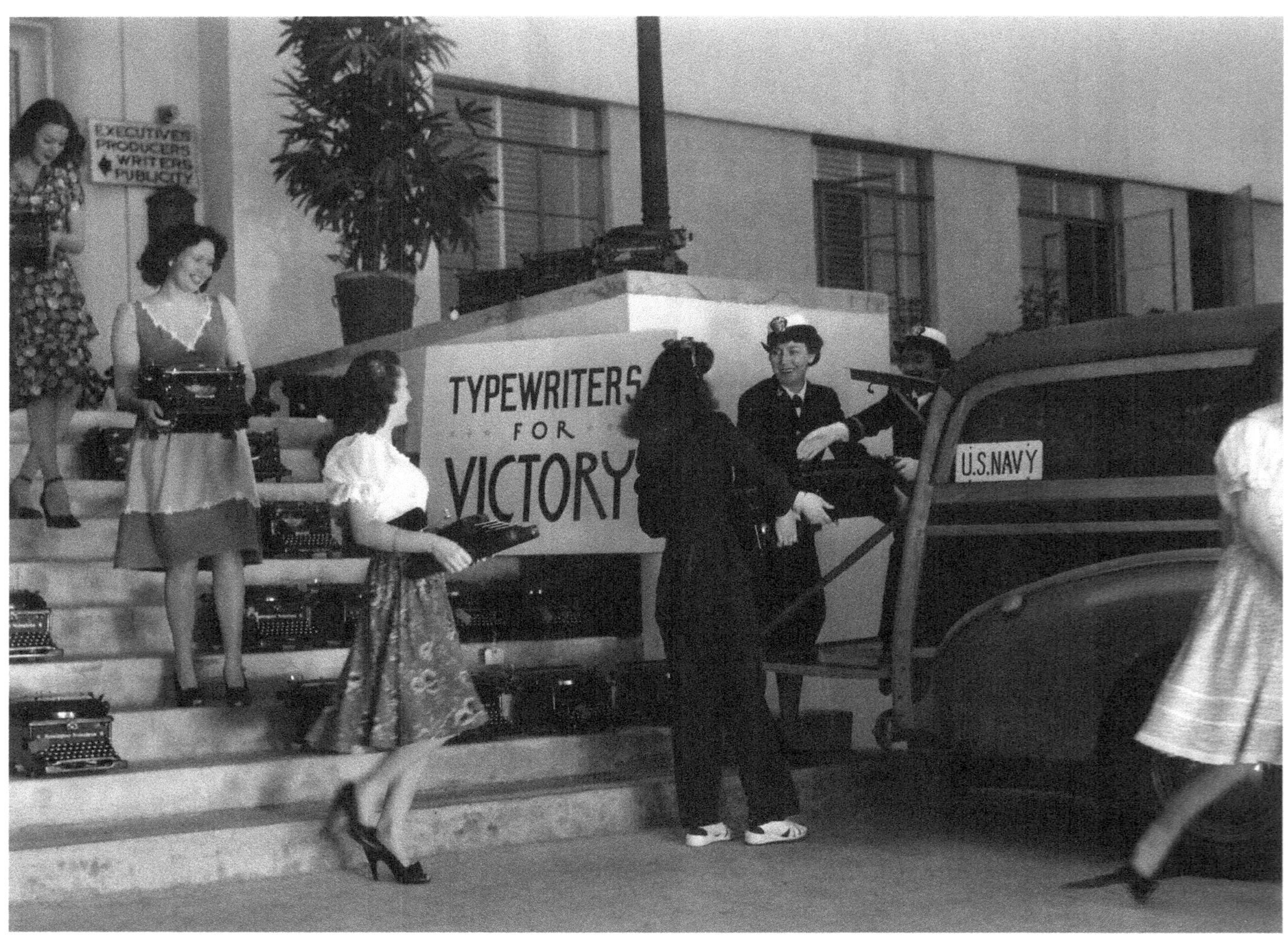

This Office of War Information photo was titled "Hollywood enlists its typewriters for war." In 1942, Hollywood studios responded to the government's urgent call for 600,000 typewriters for the armed services. These machines provided by 20th Century Fox studios were handed off to two U.S. Navy Waves ("Women Accepted for Volunteer Emergency Service"). Women also served with the U.S. Army and Army Air Corps ("Wacs" for Women's Army Corps), and in the Marines Corps as a Women's Reserve.

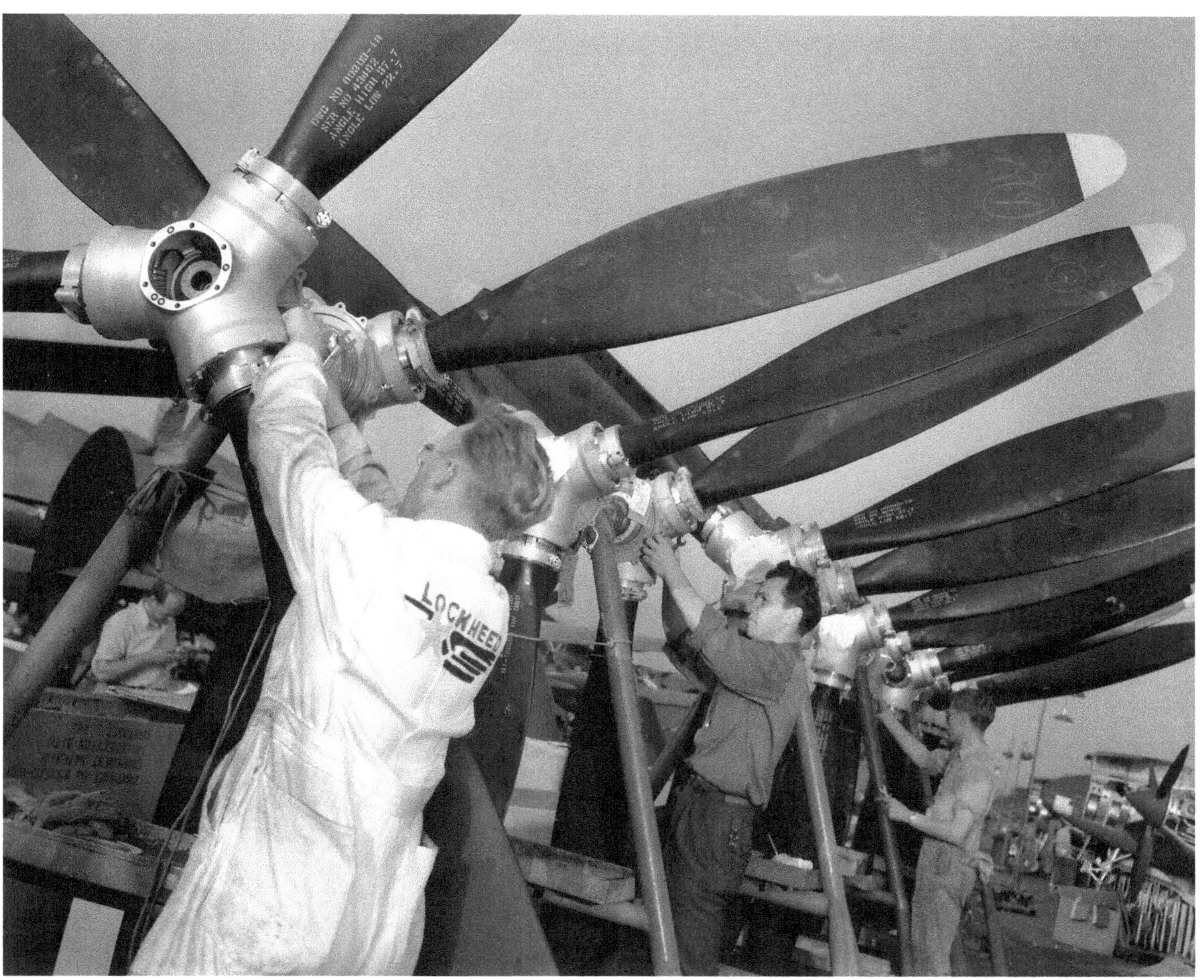

Three-blade, variable-pitch propellers are prepared for installation on Lockheed P-38 pursuit planes at a large Los Angeles aircraft plant in July 1942. That year a unit of eighteen P-38s, outfitted with special long-range fuel tanks, intercepted and shot down the bomber carrying Admiral Isoroku Yamamoto, commander of the Combined Fleet of the Imperial Japanese Navy.

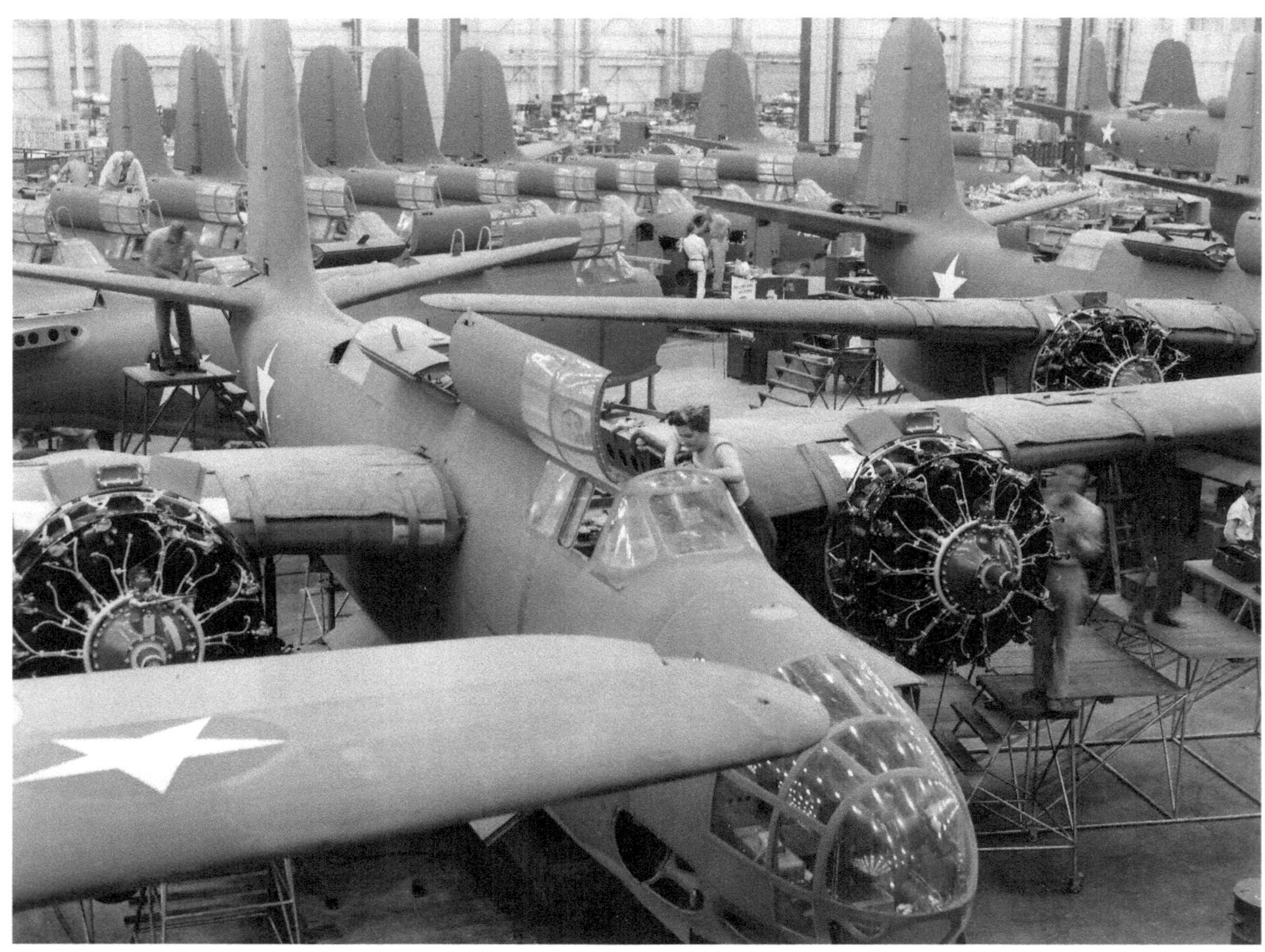

Defense workers at the Douglas Aircraft Company plant in Long Beach in October 1942 assemble DB-7/A-20 "Havoc" medium bombers. The model was called the "Boston" when it was built for England's Royal Air Force. The U.S. produced a staggering 303,713 airplanes during World War II, more than any other nation, and almost more than double that of Germany and Japan combined.

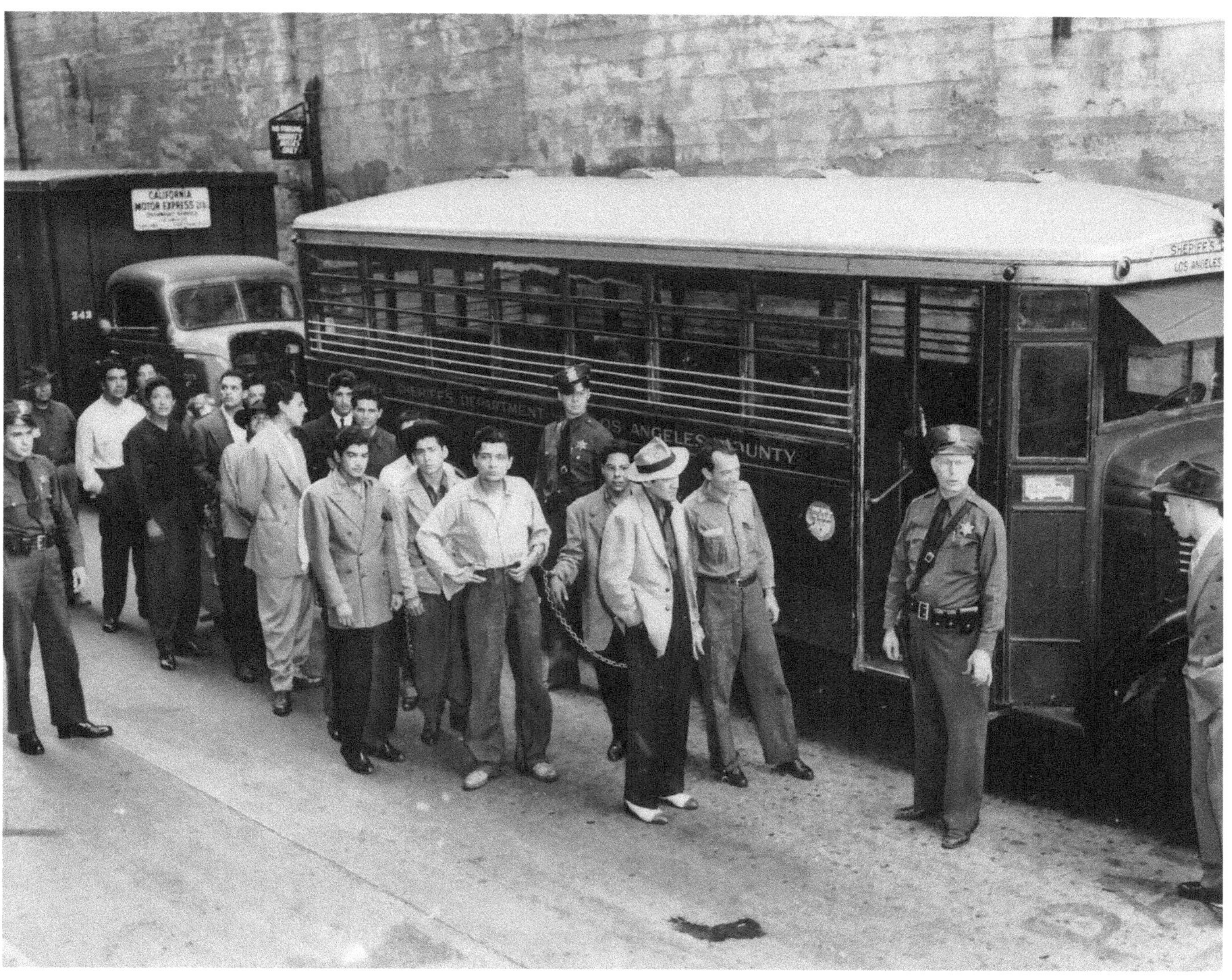

Zoot suiters en route to court after a brawl with sailors that was part of the sporadic anti-Latino "zoot suit riots" in 1942 and 1943. The zoot suit was a style of clothing popularized by African Americans, Mexican Americans, and Italian Americans during the 1930s and 1940s. The violence only subsided when military authorities declared Los Angeles off-limits to all military personnel on June 7, 1943. Of the riots, First Lady Eleanor Roosevelt commented, "The question goes deeper than just [zoot] suits. It is a racial protest."

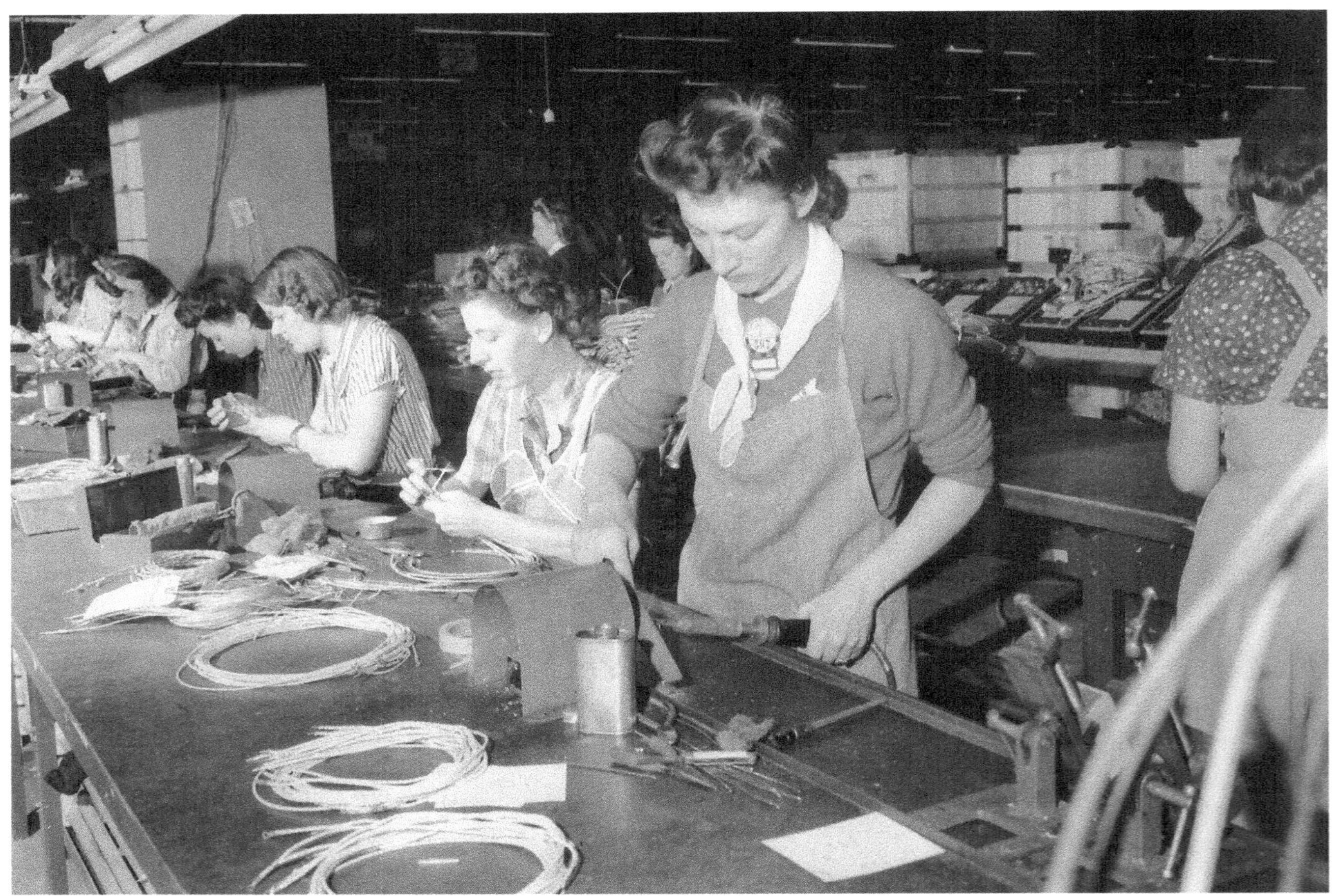

Six million women worked in manufacturing plants that produced munitions and materiel during World War II, such as this assembly line crew making electrical sub-assemblies at an L.A. airplane factory in 1942. Rosie the Riveter symbolized the women who took the places of male workers who were serving in the military. Rosie was a cultural icon of the United States then, and later became a feminist icon for women's economic power.

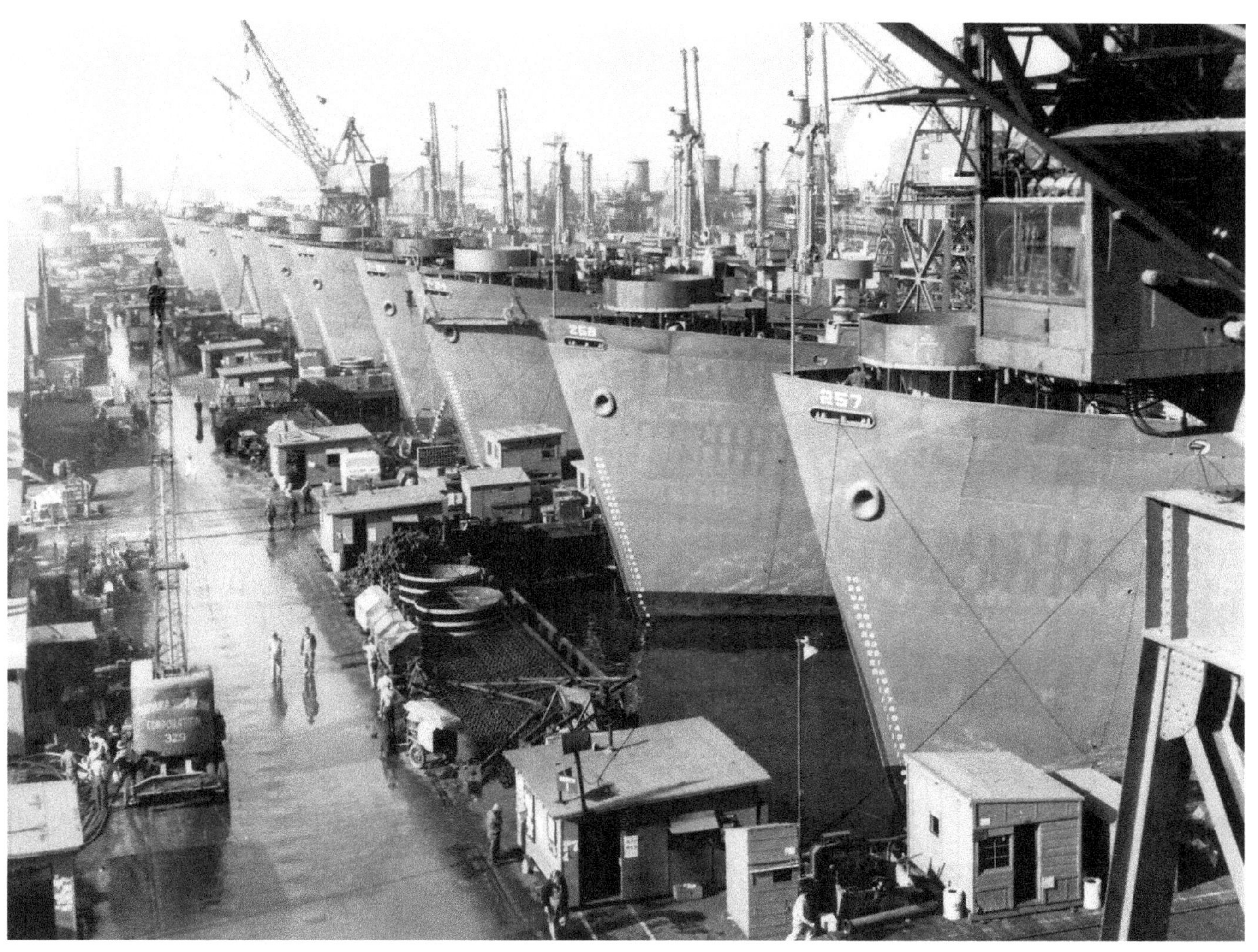

Nine Liberty cargo ships are shown at the docks of the Los Angeles California Shipbuilding Corporation at the end of 1943. During the war, eighteen American shipyards built 2,751 Liberty ships, the most of any single type of vessel in history. It took only 42 days, on average, to build a Liberty ship, using prefabricated sections and welding instead of rivets. The ship came to symbolize America's incredible wartime industrial output.

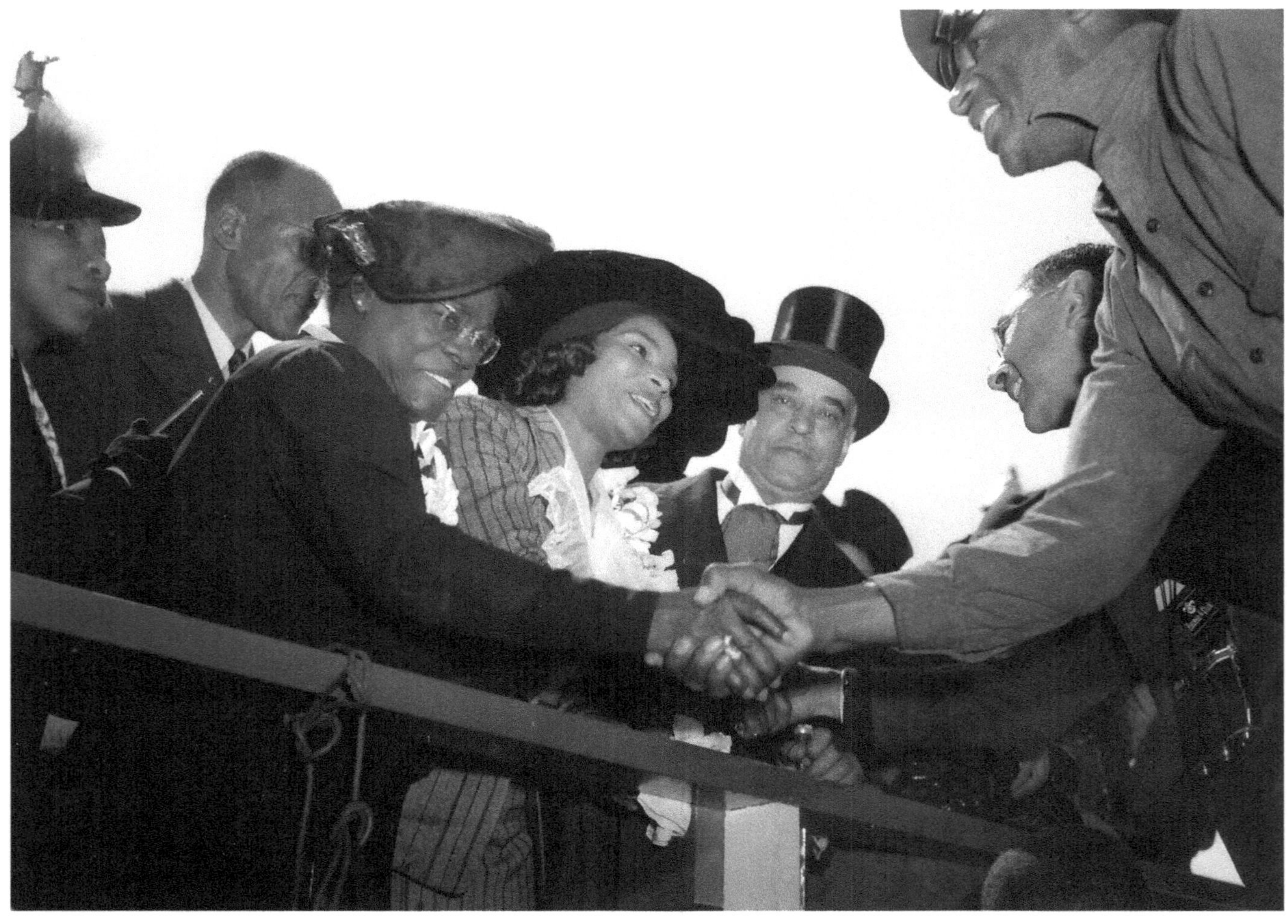

Launched in September 1942, the SS *Booker T. Washington* was the first Liberty ship to be commanded by and named after an African American. Here, Mary McLeod Bethune, Director of Negro Affairs, National Youth Administration; acclaimed singer Marian Anderson; and Dr. William J. Thompkins, Recorder of Deeds, greet workers who helped build the ship.

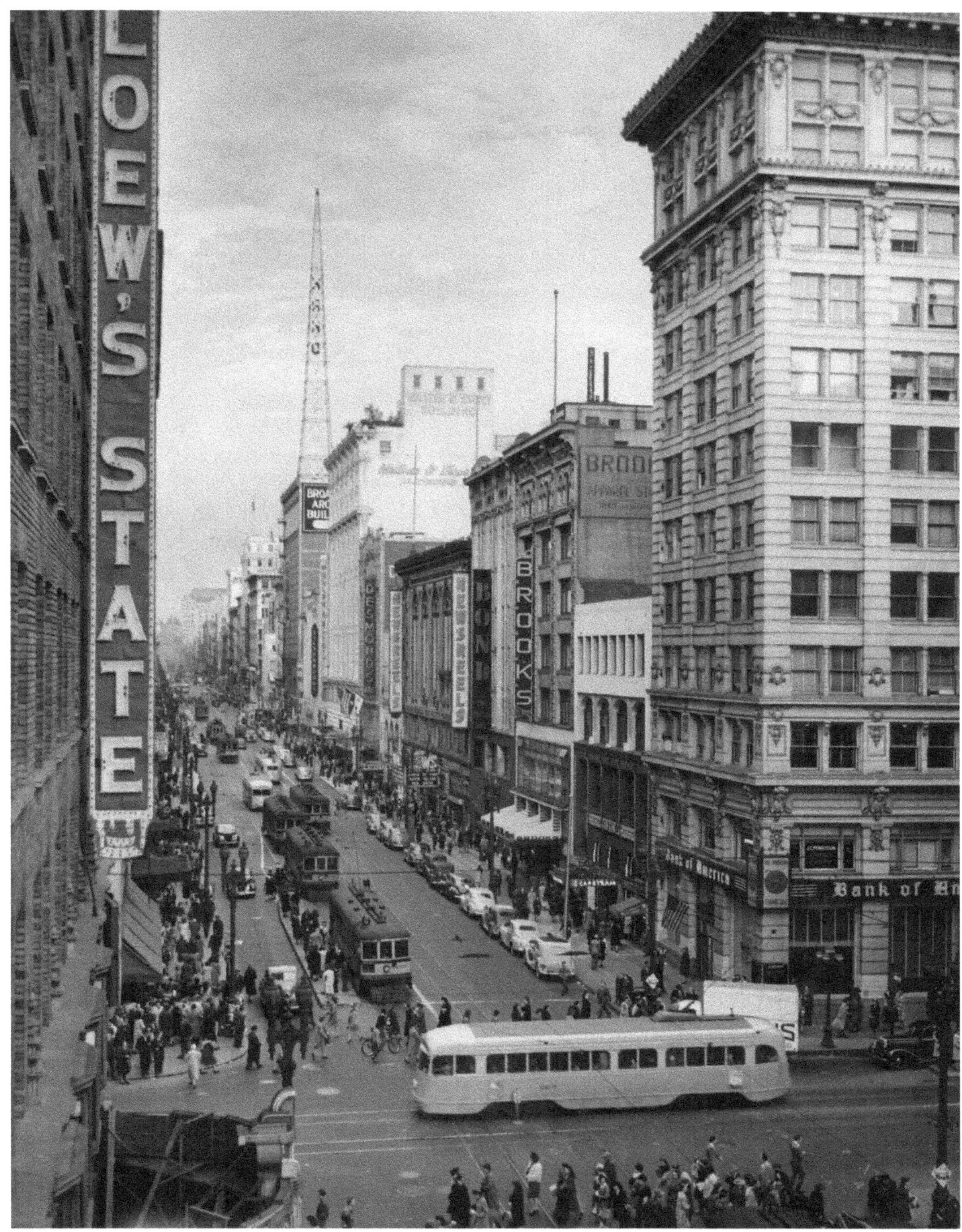

This Spring Street view shows the 1940s financial center of L.A., which held the stock exchange and numerous national business front offices. In addition to the pull of money, many talented writers and artists were lured to Los Angeles by its bohemian lifestyle and other attractions. One of the many British emigrés was Aldous Huxley (1894–1963), who moved to Los Angeles in 1937.

Although war news dominated at this 1942 Los Angeles newsstand, there was plenty of local gossip as well. Budd Schulberg (1914–) summed up all the classic Hollywood stereotypes—the overbearing producer, the naive ingenue, the scheming writer—in his 1941 story "A Table at Ciro's." Schulberg's scathing 1941 book *What Makes Sammy Run?* outraged the film establishment.

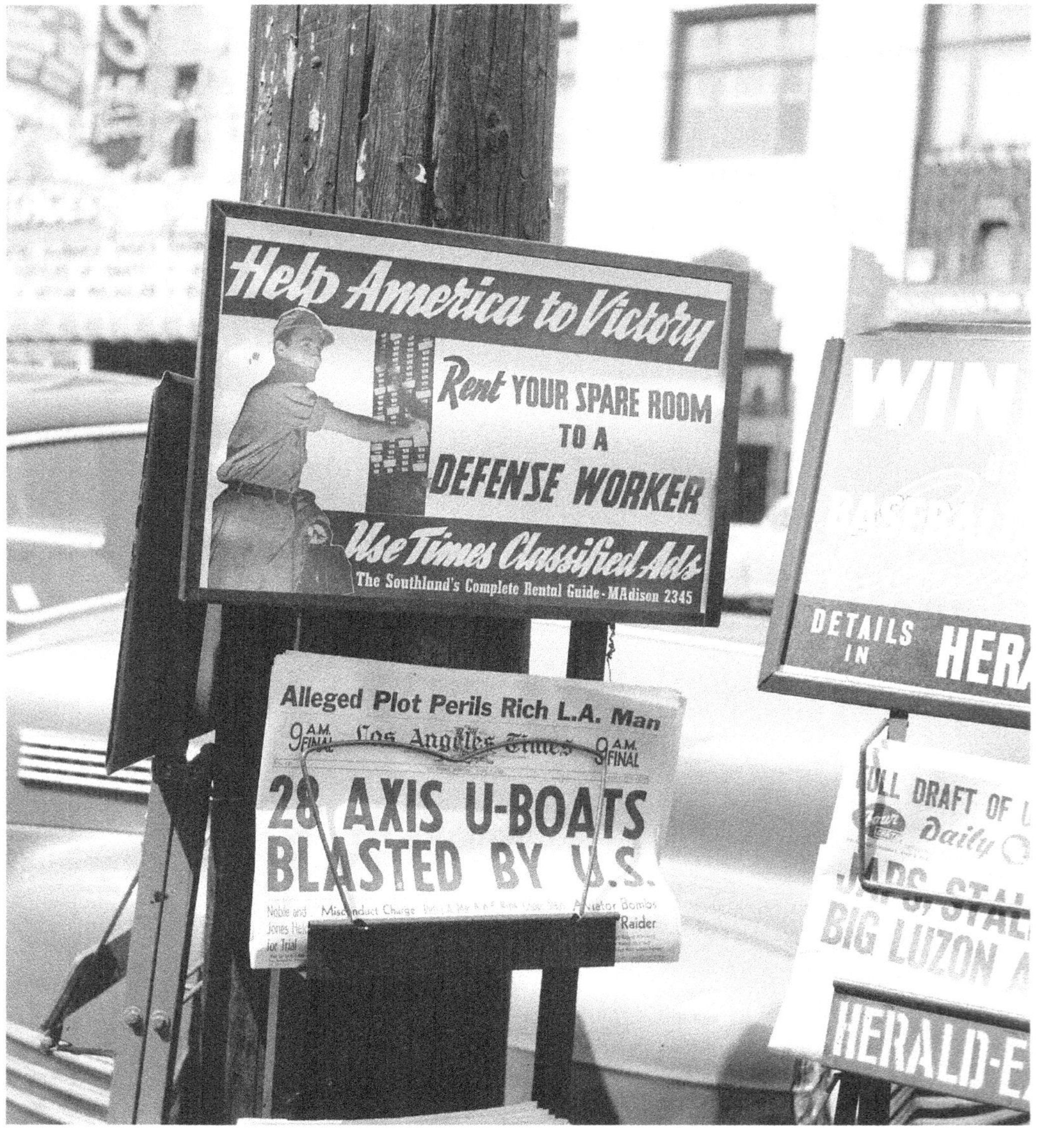

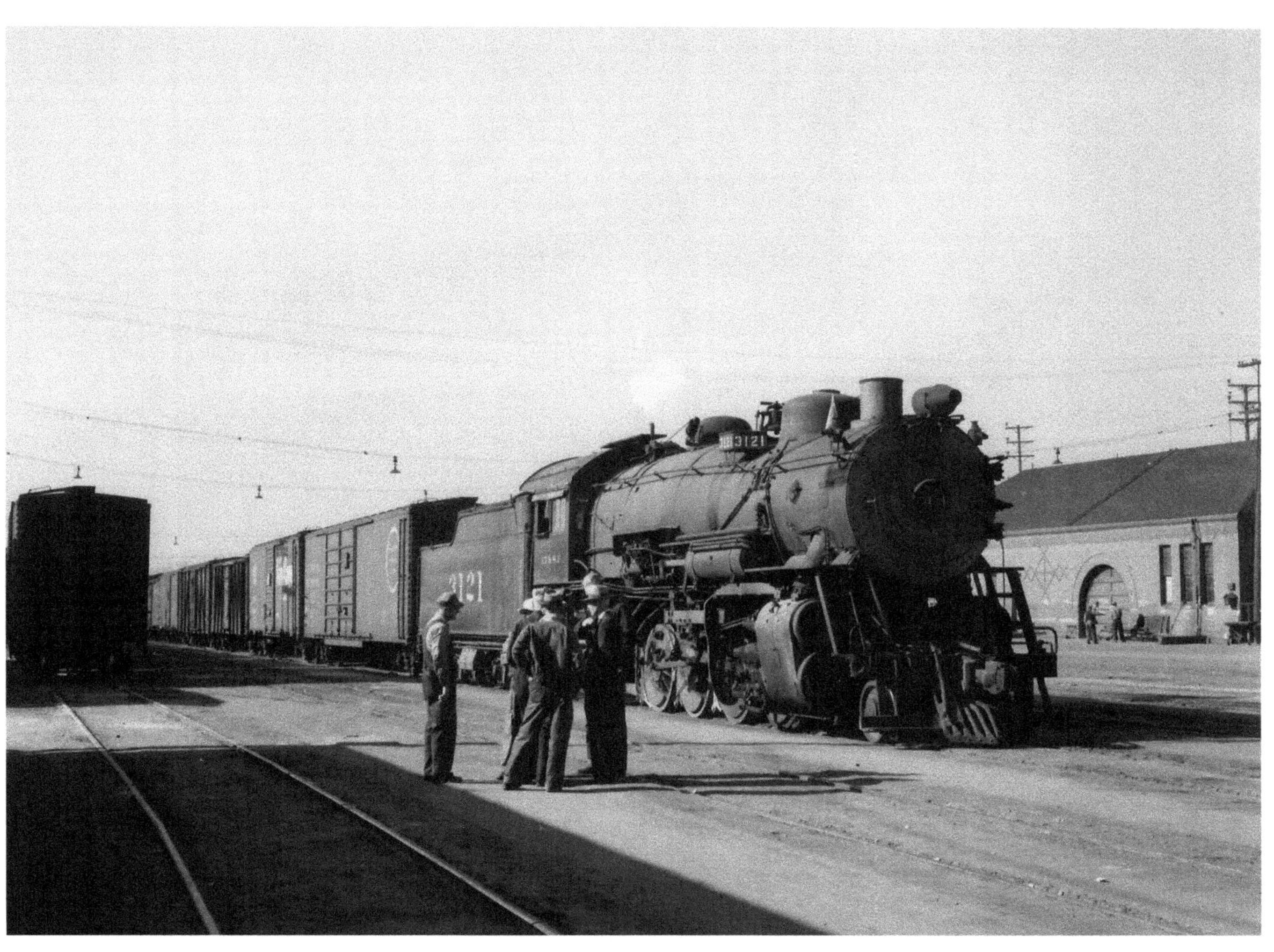

An Atchison, Topeka and Santa Fe freight train prepares to leave the yard in Los Angeles in March 1943. Novelist, poet, and screenwriter William Faulkner (1897–1962) worked in Hollywood but took the train home to Mississippi as often as he could. In a 1945 letter he commented, "I don't like this damn place [L.A.] any better that I ever did." Unlike other Hollywood writers, Faulkner used California as a setting only once, in *Golden Land*, a tale of insidious corruption.

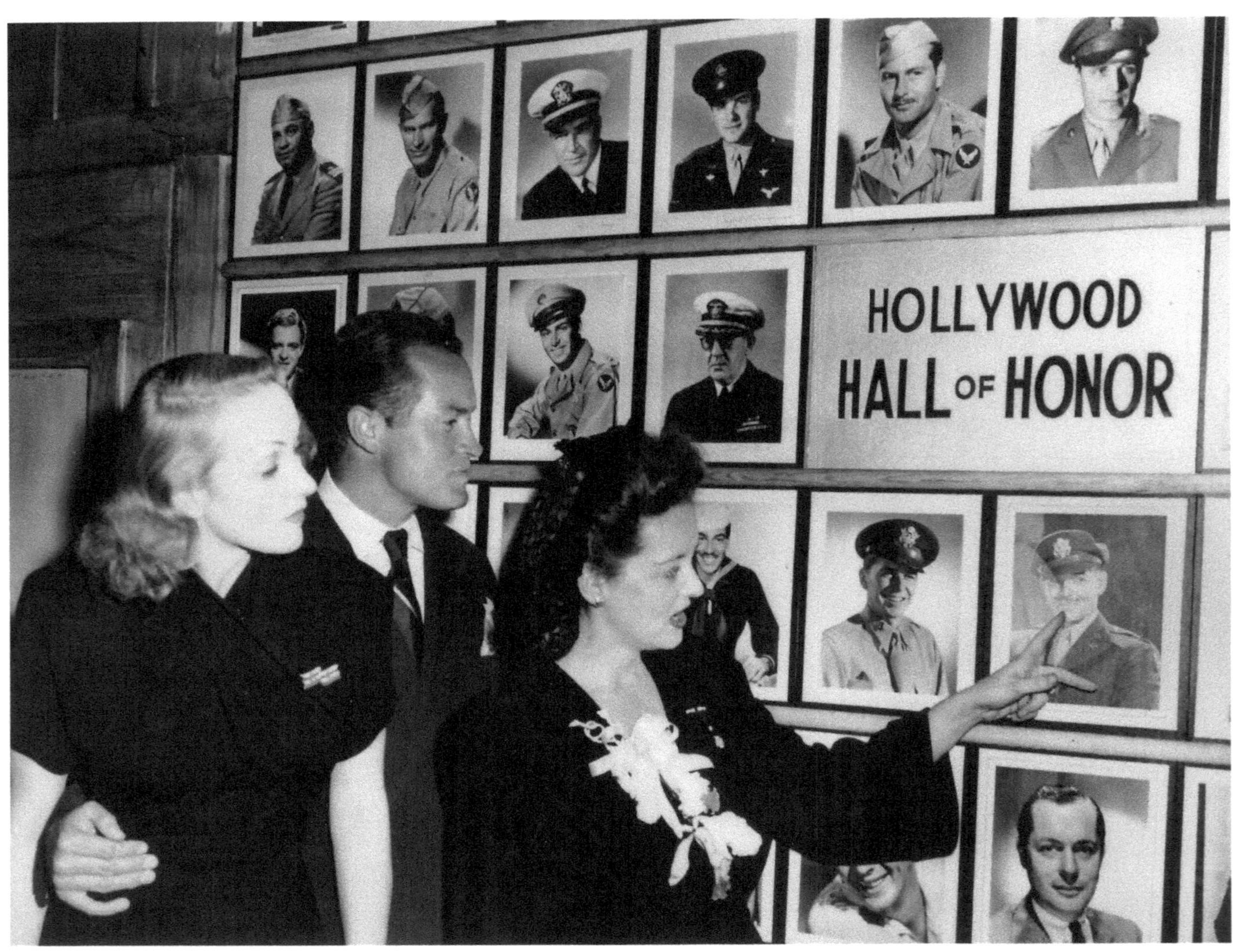

At the Hollywood Canteen in 1943, film star Bette Davis (1908–1989) points out pictures of movie servicemen to German-born singer and actress Marlene Dietrich (1901–1992) and comedian Bob Hope (1903–2003). Hope is most notable for his famous United Service Organizations (USO) tours for American troops overseas. Hope always convinced a handful of talented performers and celebrities to accompany him on these tours that began in 1941 and continued through nearly all of America's conflicts thereafter.

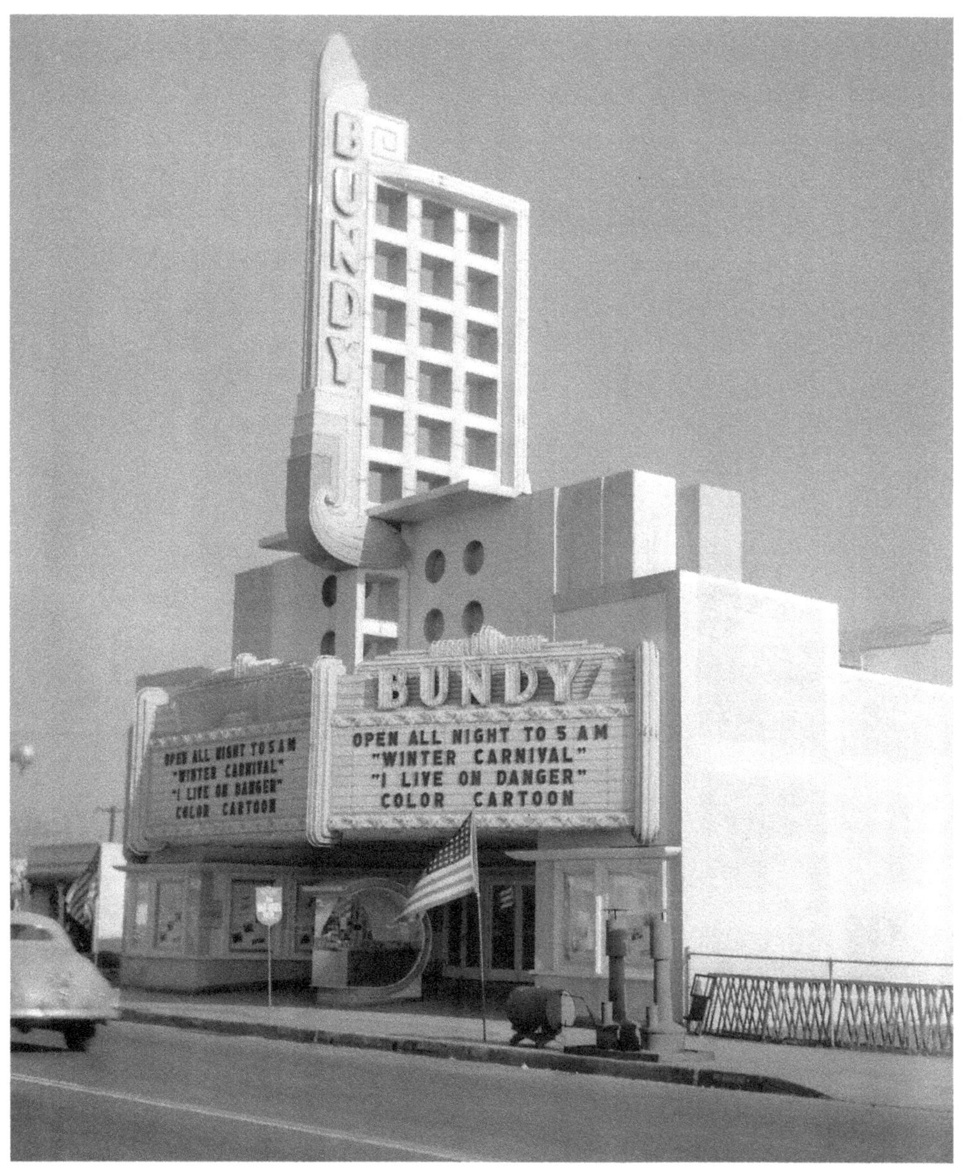

A movie theater on the highway between Los Angeles and Santa Monica in 1943 stayed open past midnight to cater to the swing shift workers from the nearby aircraft plants. Theater owners decided they could attract more customers and also save on costs if they offered two movies for the price of one. A typical double bill included trailers, a newsreel, a cartoon and/or a short film, a low-budget second feature (the B-movie), and the high-budget main feature (the A-movie).

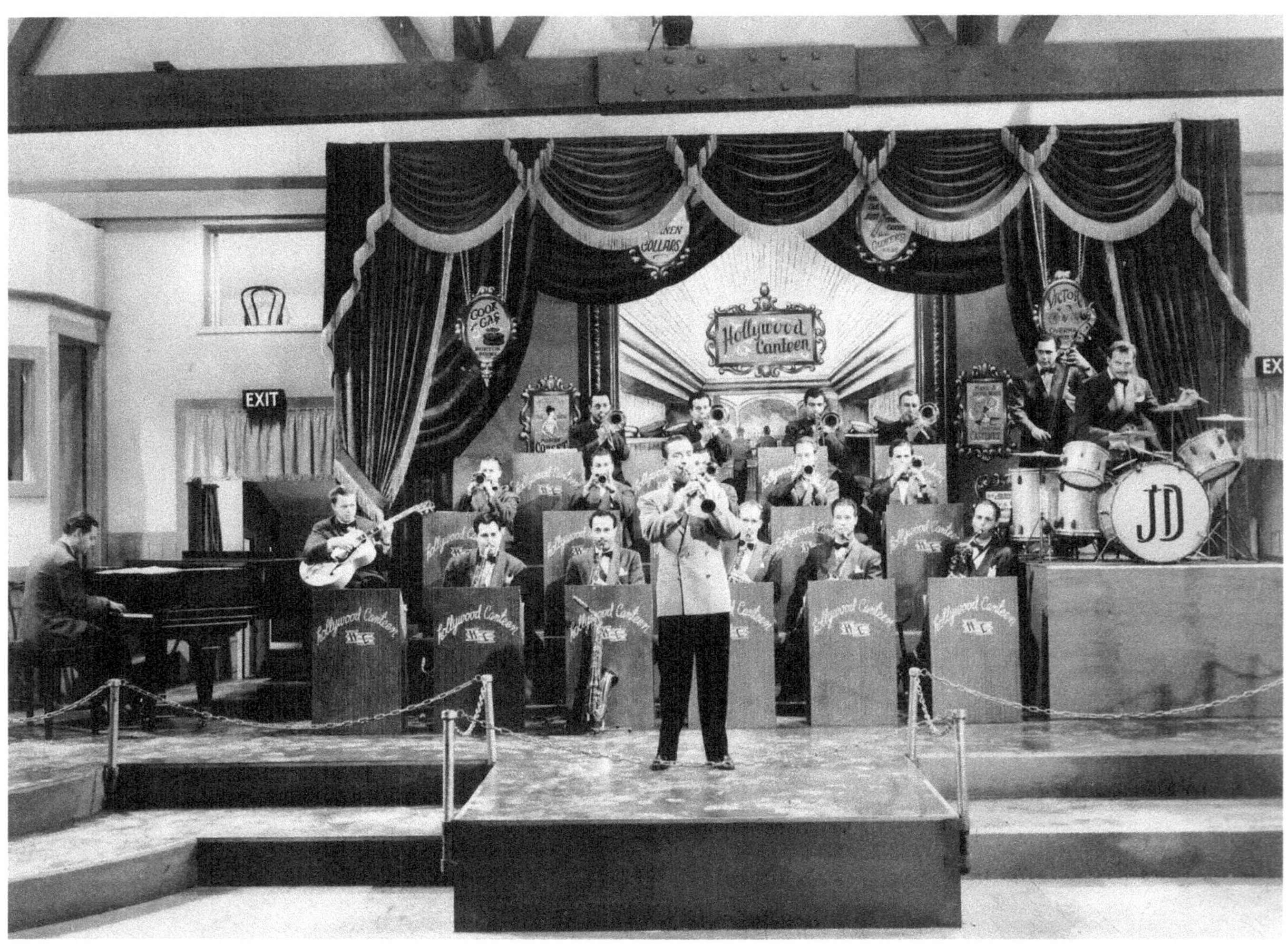

Hollywood was not shy about making movies about itself. Here, big-band leader Jimmy Dorsey (1904–1957) and his orchestra are on stage in a scene from the 1944 film *Hollywood Canteen*, one of several movies in which he appeared. Dorsey is considered one of the outstanding musicians of the pre-bebop jazz era.

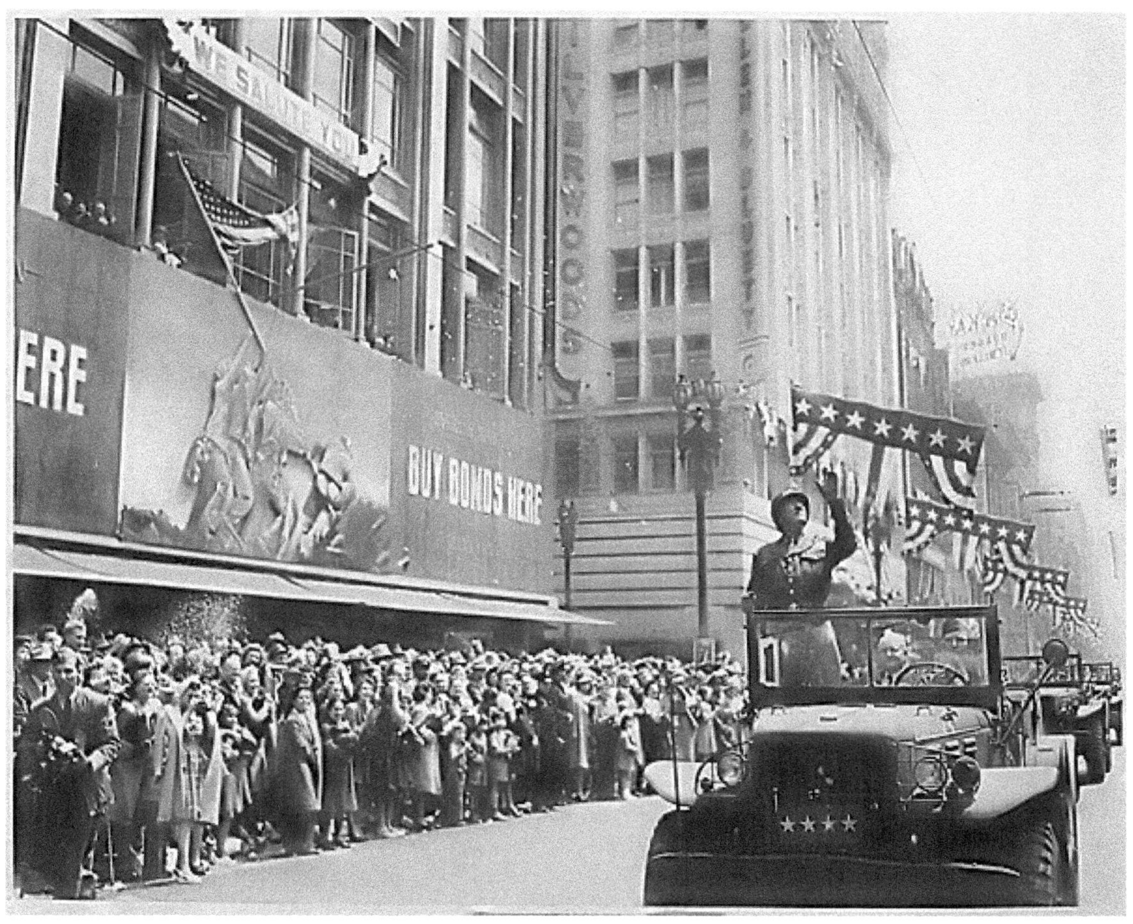

A crowd lining a Los Angeles street cheers for General George S. Patton as he passes by during a visit June 9, 1945, a month after Germany surrendered. The controversial Patton was acknowledged as an outstanding field commander. His Third Army inflicted nearly nine casualties on the German forces for every one it suffered, the best of any Allied army in Northwest Europe during 1944–1945. Hitler called Patton "that crazy cowboy general." Patton died six months after this victory parade as a result of a traffic accident in Germany.

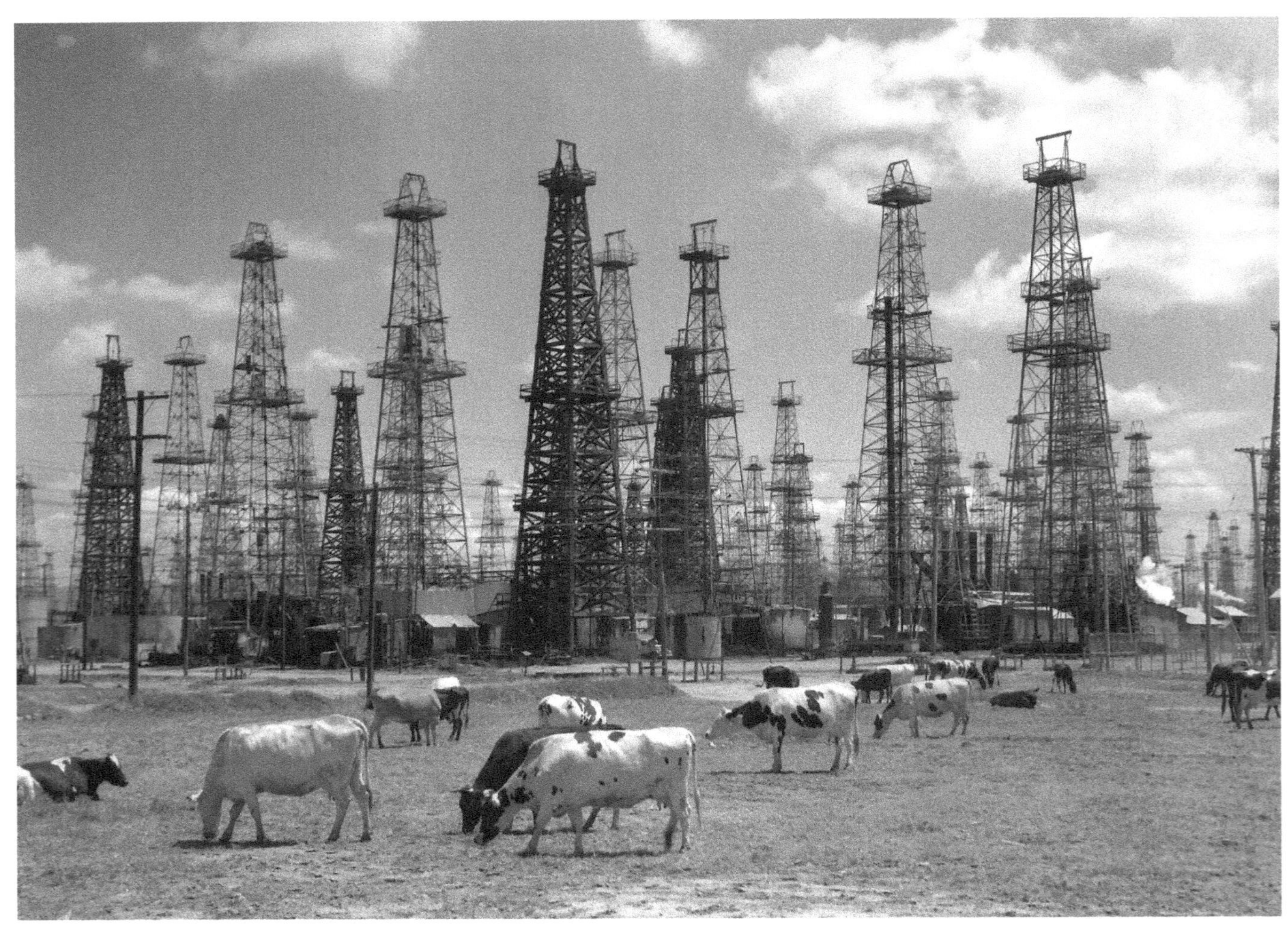

Only seventeen miles from downtown Los Angeles during World War II was the agricultural area of Norwalk and its oil-field backdrop. Like much of Southern California, Norwalk evolved from a rural area with dairy farms to a dense suburb of L.A.

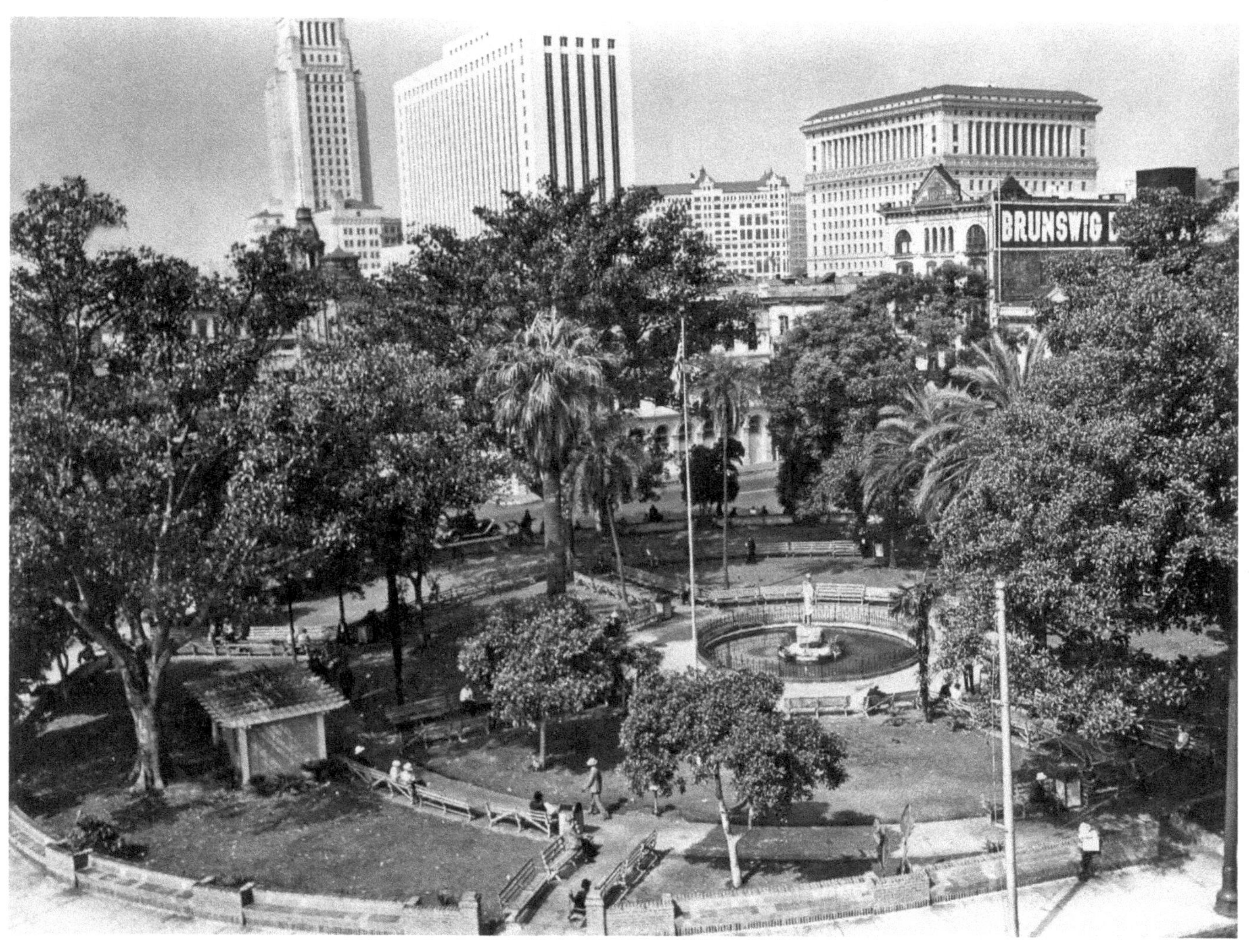

Plaza Park in the 1940s was bounded by Main, Los Angeles, and Marchessault streets, and Ferguson Alley. The fountain statue at center is of the city's founder, Governor Felipe de Neve, who laid out the first plaza in 1781 at a location to the northwest of this one.

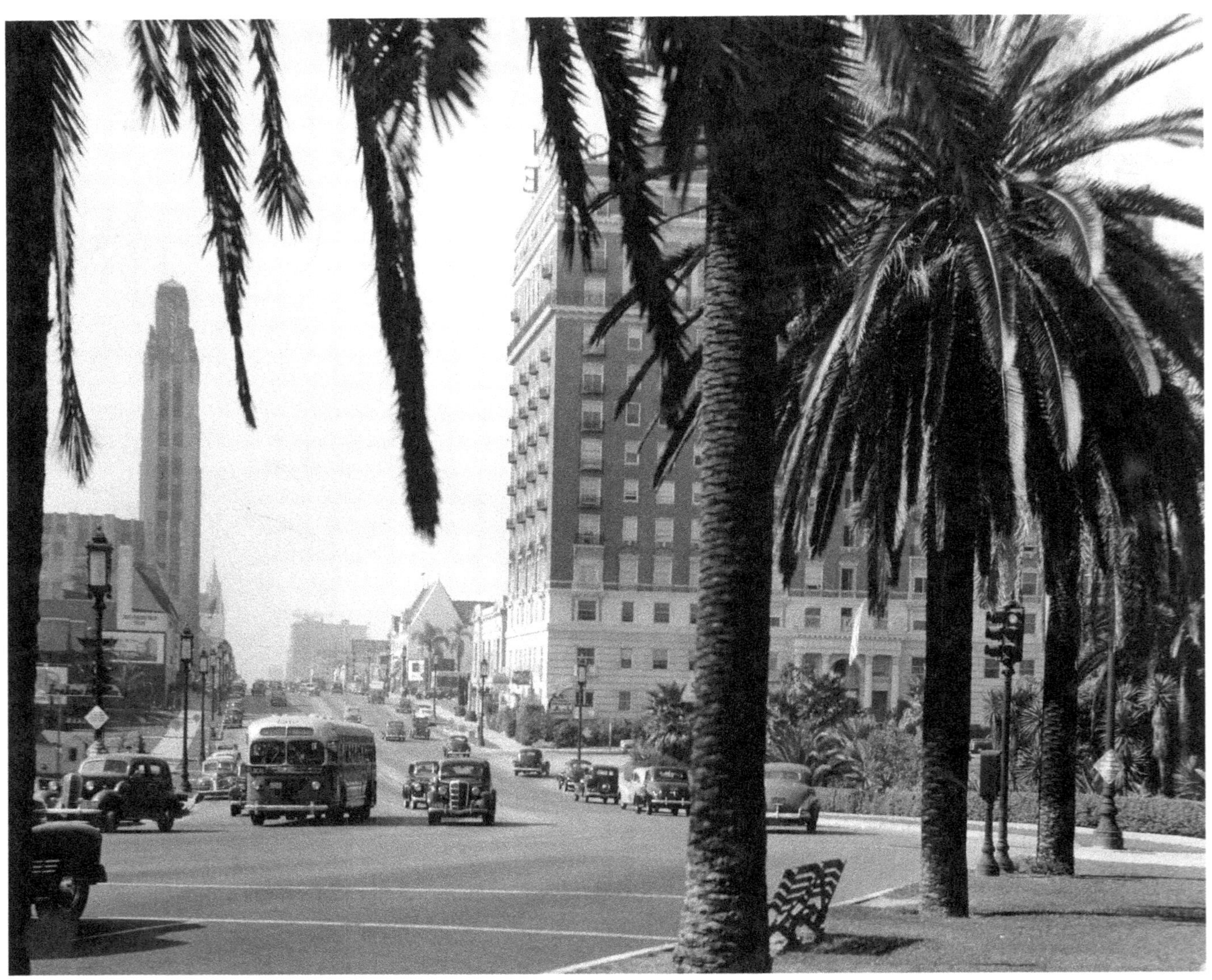

In 1940 L.A. was the fifth-largest city in the United States. By 1950, about the time of this photo, it passed Detroit in population. Writer Truman Capote (1924–1984) visited L.A. just after the war and found it "a dumping ground for all that is most exploitedly American: oil pumps pounding . . . avenues of used-car lots, supermarkets, motels, the . . . gee whiz wham of publicity, the biggest, broadest, best, sprawled and helplessly etherized by immaculate sunshine and sound of sea."

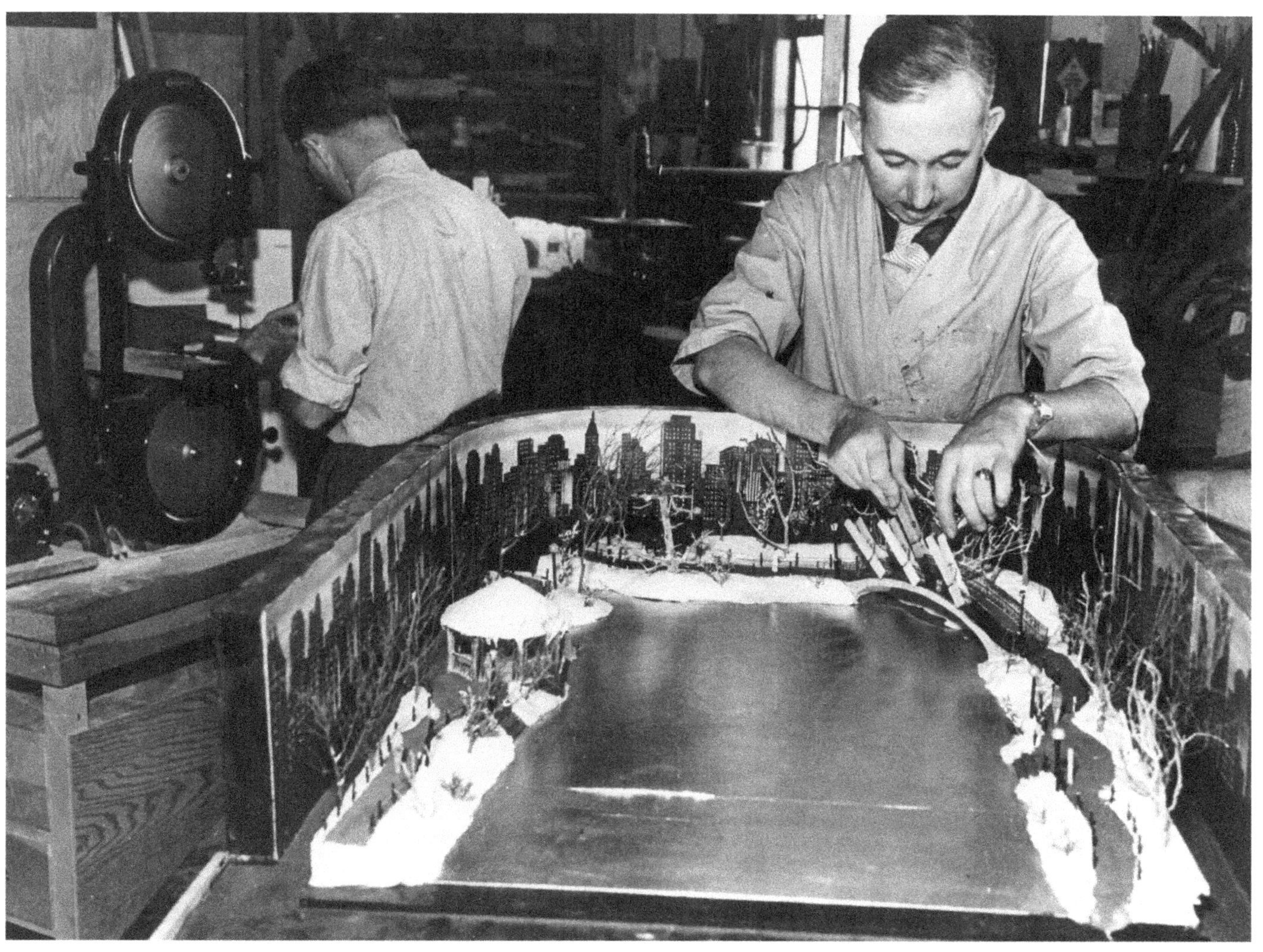

The movie stars, directors, producers, and writers were the most visible celebrities of Hollywood. However, they were outnumbered by an army of supporting workers whose efforts went unnoticed but were essential in the output of the nearly 500 major A- and B-level films each year. Here artists craft a scale replica of a winter scene in New York City's Central Park.

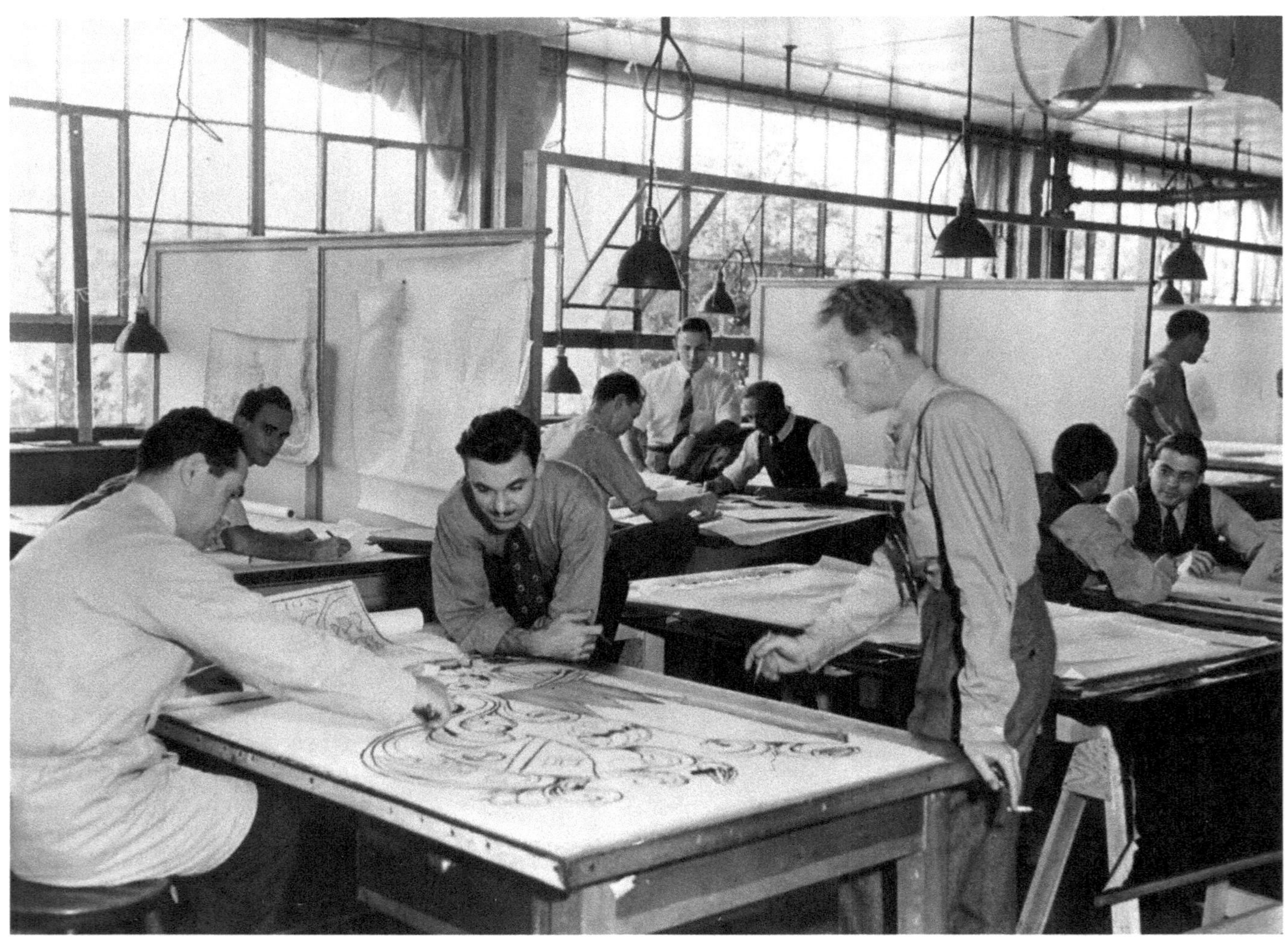

Despite the beautiful weather in Southern California, most films were shot on the studio lots on indoor stage sets. Intricate homes, official buildings, even caves and faux outdoor scenes were created on these sets, often from drawings created in the studio art departments by professionals such as these.

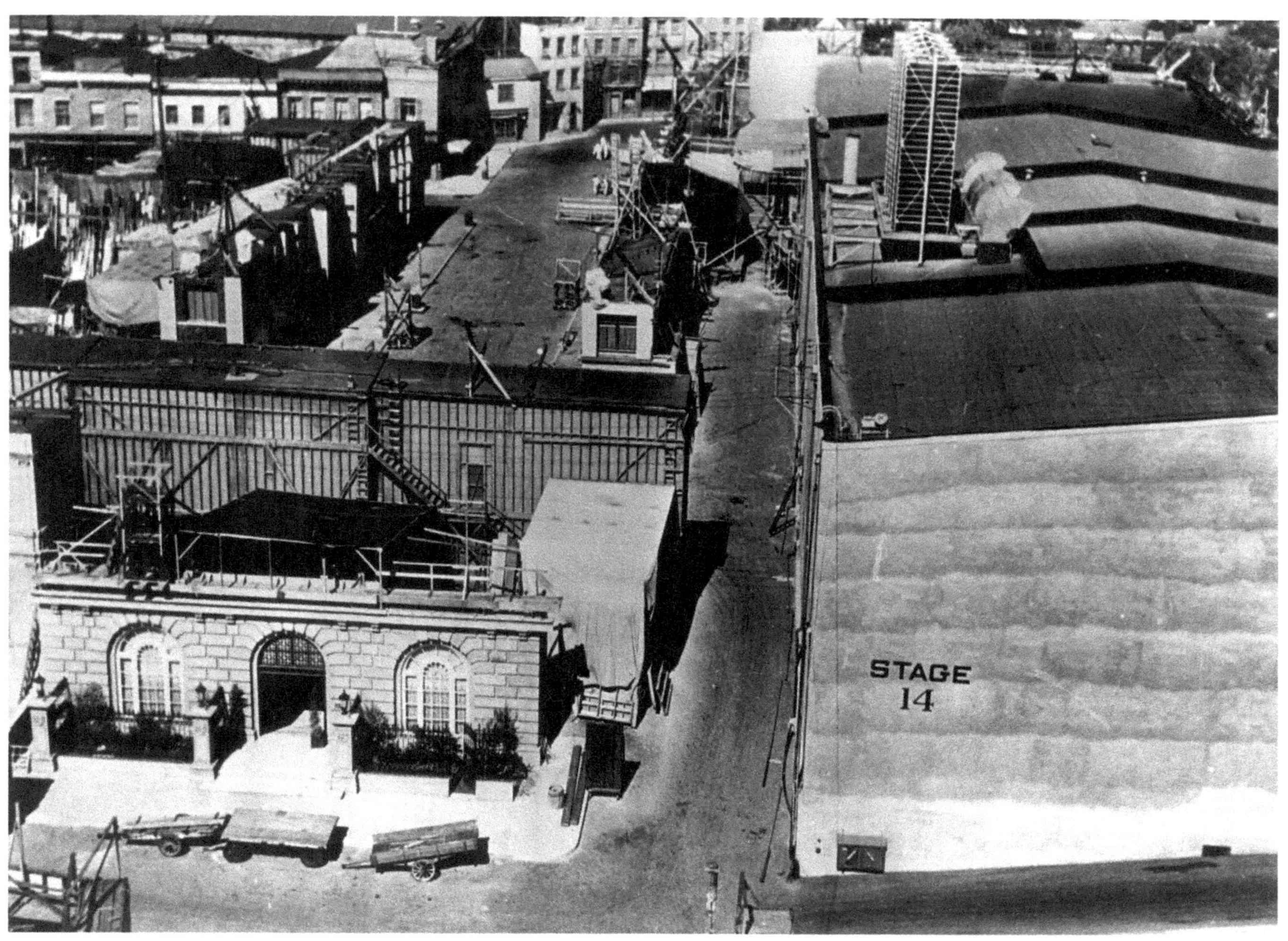

If a movie script required a city street scene, a simulated one was constructed outside on studio property. This overhead photo shows assorted false building fronts and replicated city streets where camera positions could be set up according to the backdrop or scenery required by the script. The "Stage 14" building served for shooting interior scenes.

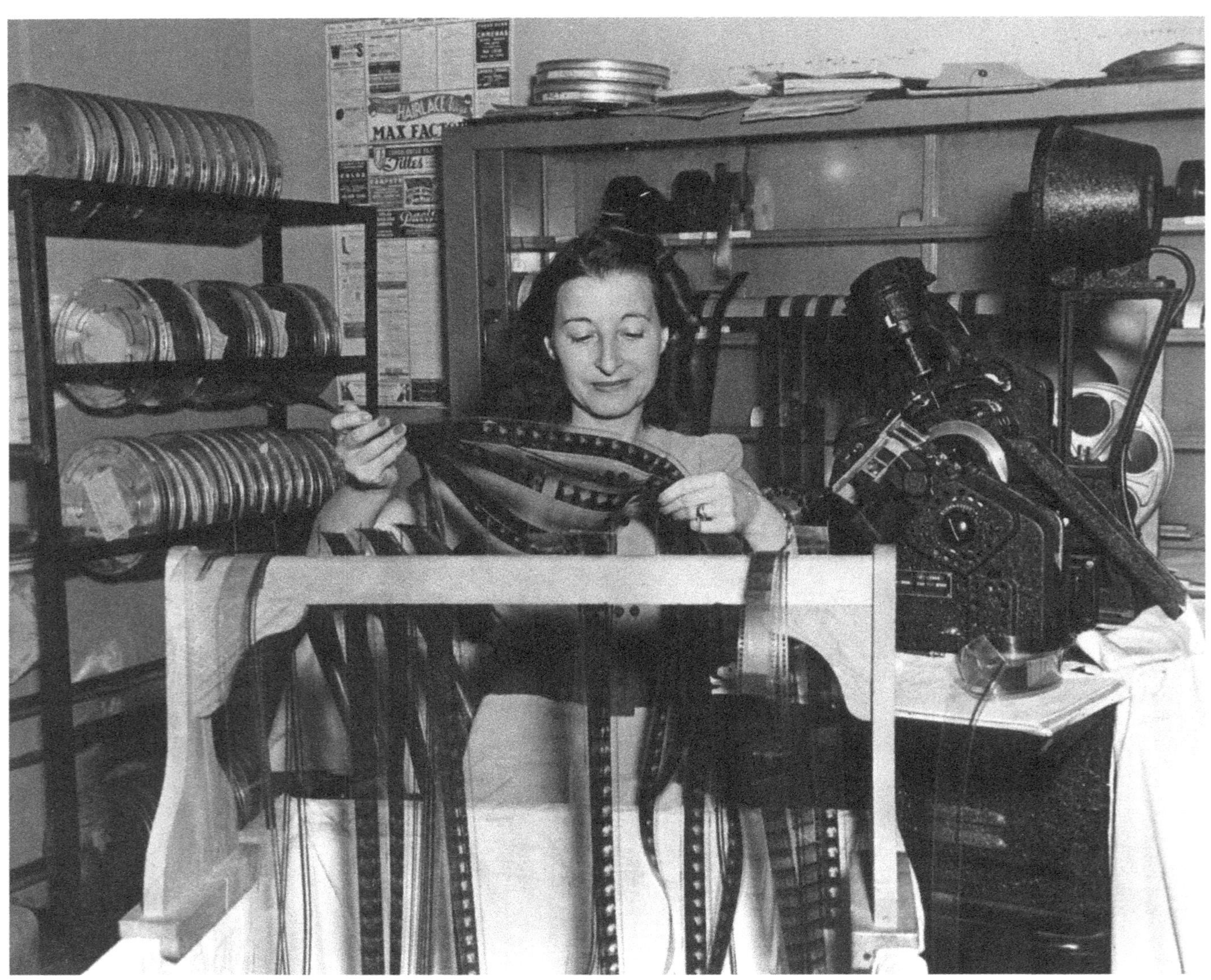

After filming but prior to release, a movie would be edited in a "cutting laboratory" and put into final sequence for projection. At first, moving picture film was shot and projected at various speeds using hand-cranked cameras and projectors. When sound film was introduced in the late 1920s, a constant speed was required, and 24 frames per second was chosen because it was the slowest and therefore cheapest speed that allowed for good sound quality.

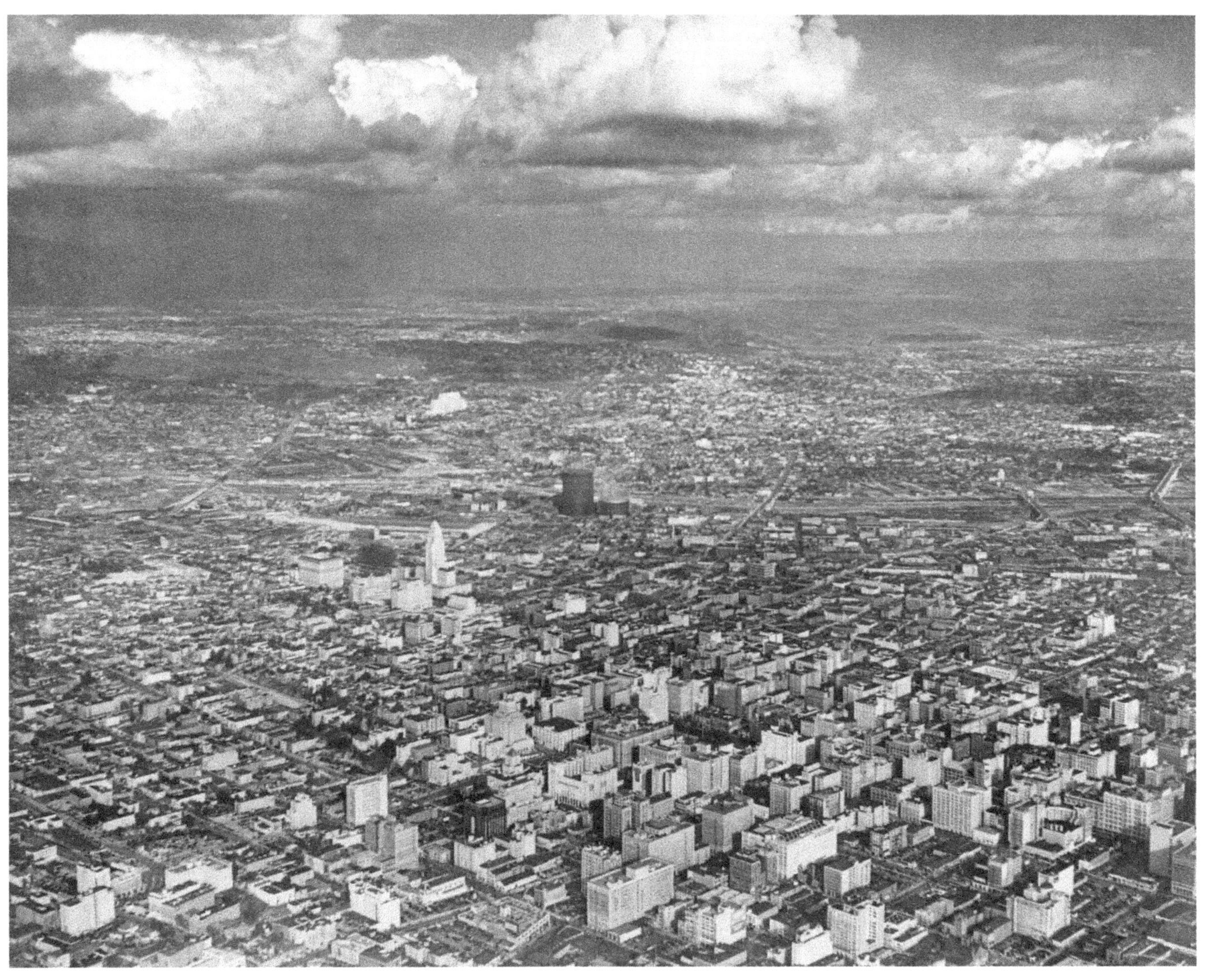

Between 1940 and 1950 the population density within the 400 square miles of Los Angeles was concentrated from downtown to Watts in the south, Inglewood in the west, Beverly Hills and Hollywood in the north, and East L.A. Except for Santa Monica, Long Beach, and Pasadena, the rest of Los Angeles County was sparsely populated. In 1940, nearly 70 percent of the 1.5 million residents lived in Central L.A.

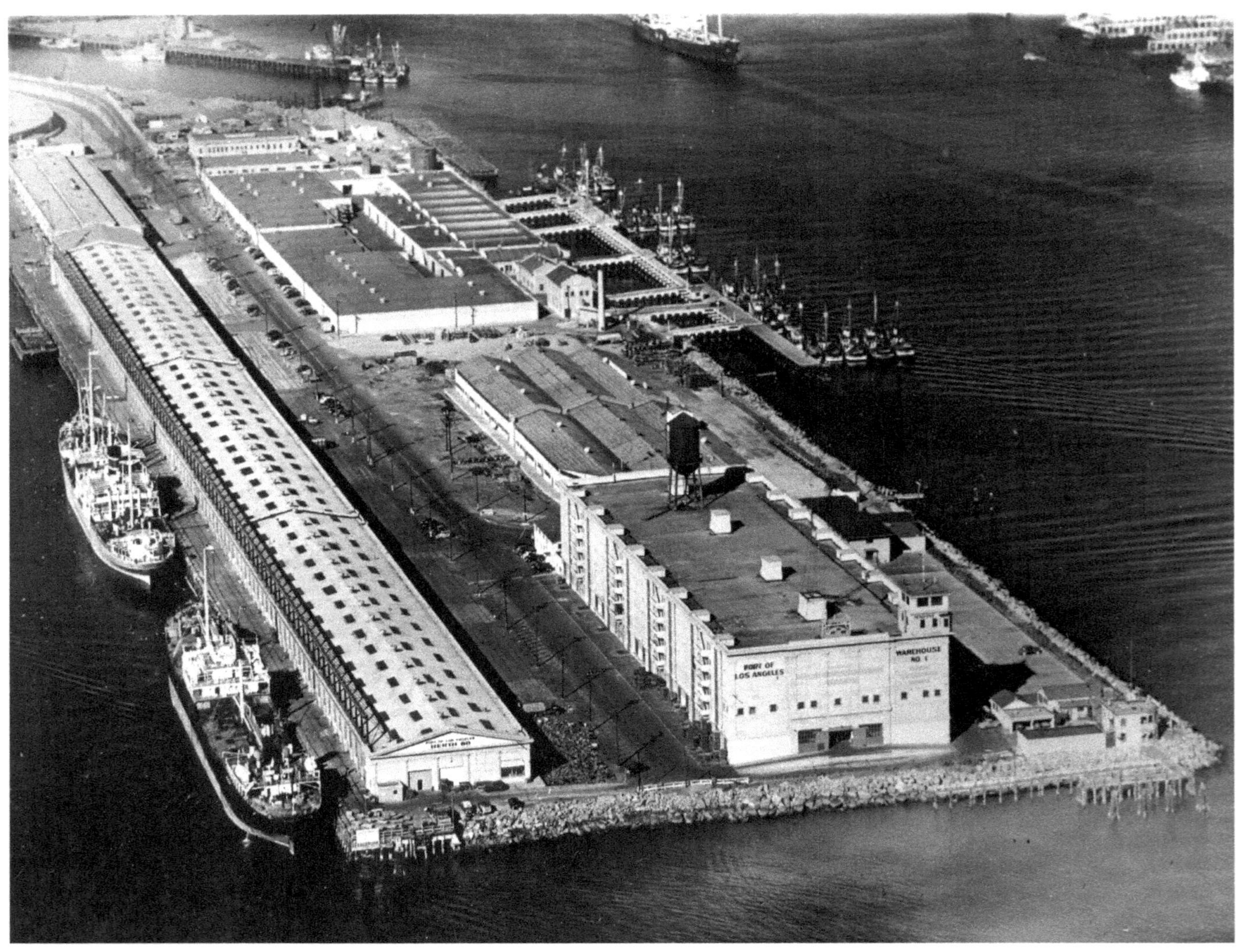

During World War II, San Pedro Bay shipyards employed more than 90,000 workers and produced hundreds of military and merchant vessels. Originally, Los Angeles' poor harbor at San Pedro Bay was a shallow mudflat, too soft to support a wharf. Visiting ships either had to stay far out at anchor and have their goods and passengers ferried to shore, or beach themselves. Dredging began in 1871, and the area was annexed to Los Angeles in 1909.

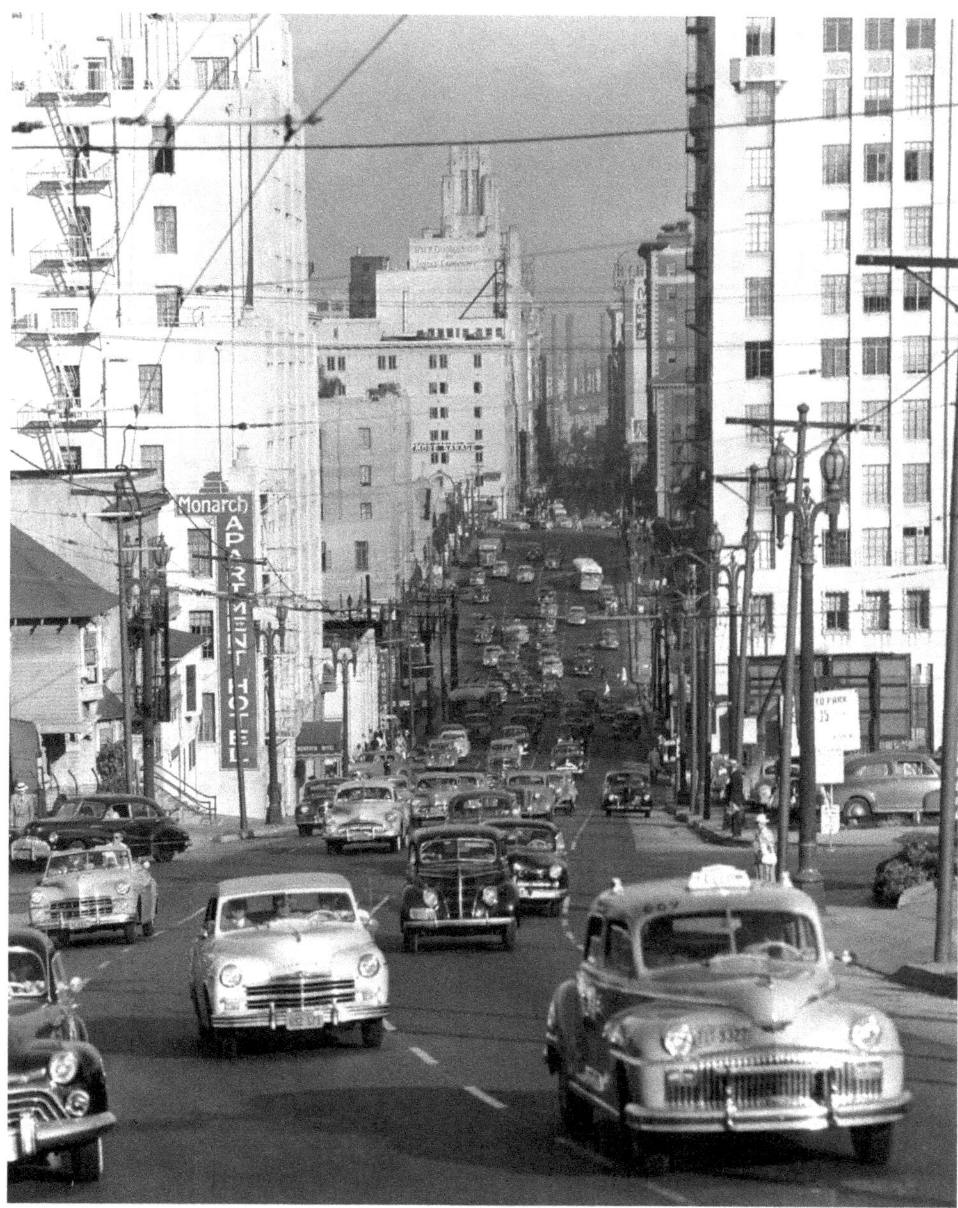

Like many multi-lane Los Angeles streets, this one, seen midtown at the end of the decade, was designated one-way to ease traffic movement. Urban planners also believed that the new freeway system could both engender suburban development and stop the decline of the inner city. In 1947, $300 million was legislated for the metropolitan freeway network, enough to build 105 miles of roadway.

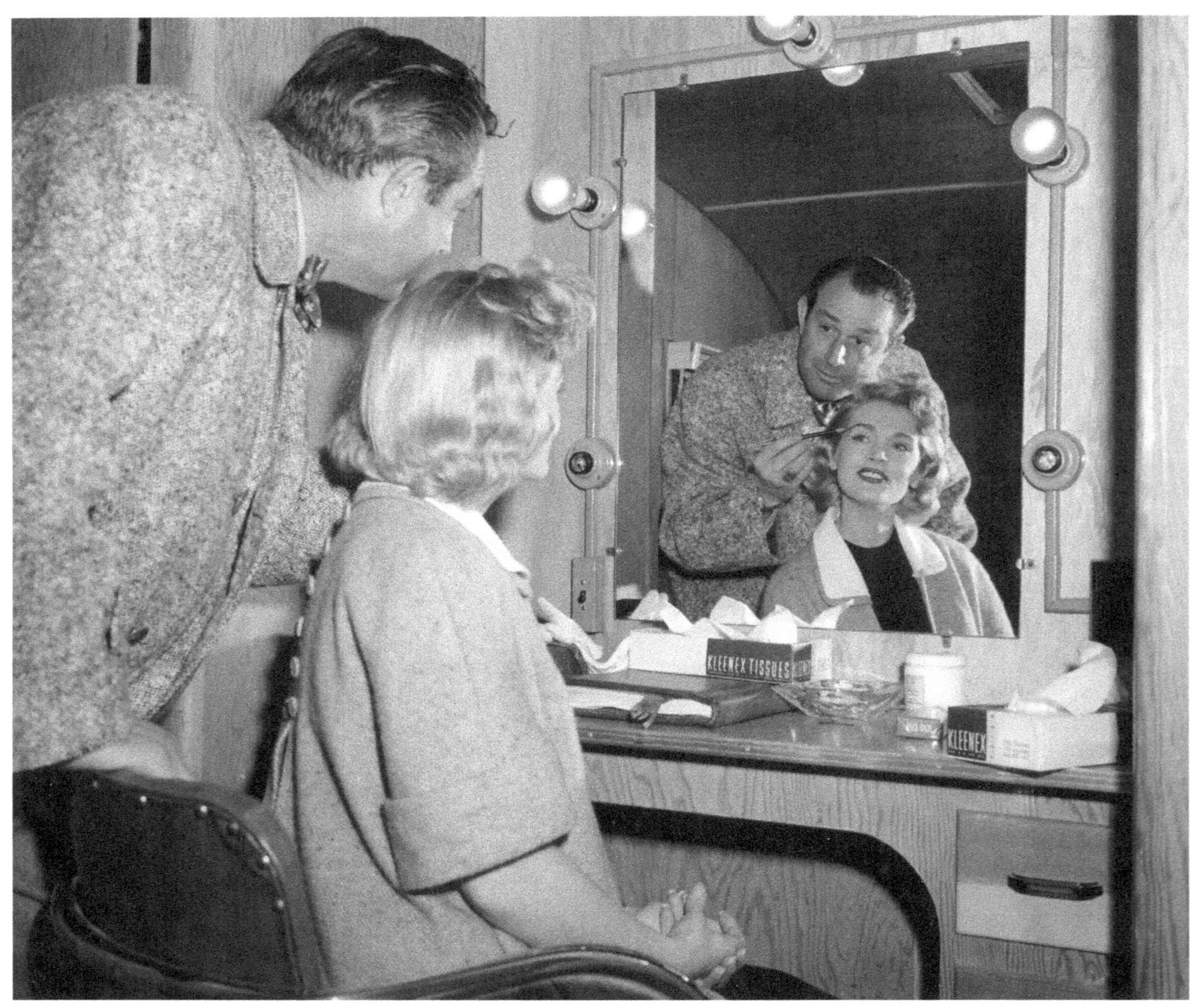

Layne “Shotgun” Britton, a makeup artist and actor in Hollywood from 1939 until 1989, works with Lizabeth Scott during the filming of *The Company She Keeps*, the story of Georgia Durante’s days with the Mafia. A willowy blonde with green eyes and a husky, smoky voice, Scott (1922–) excelled as a femme fatale in the genre known as film noir, the dark, angst-ridden films of the post–World War II era.

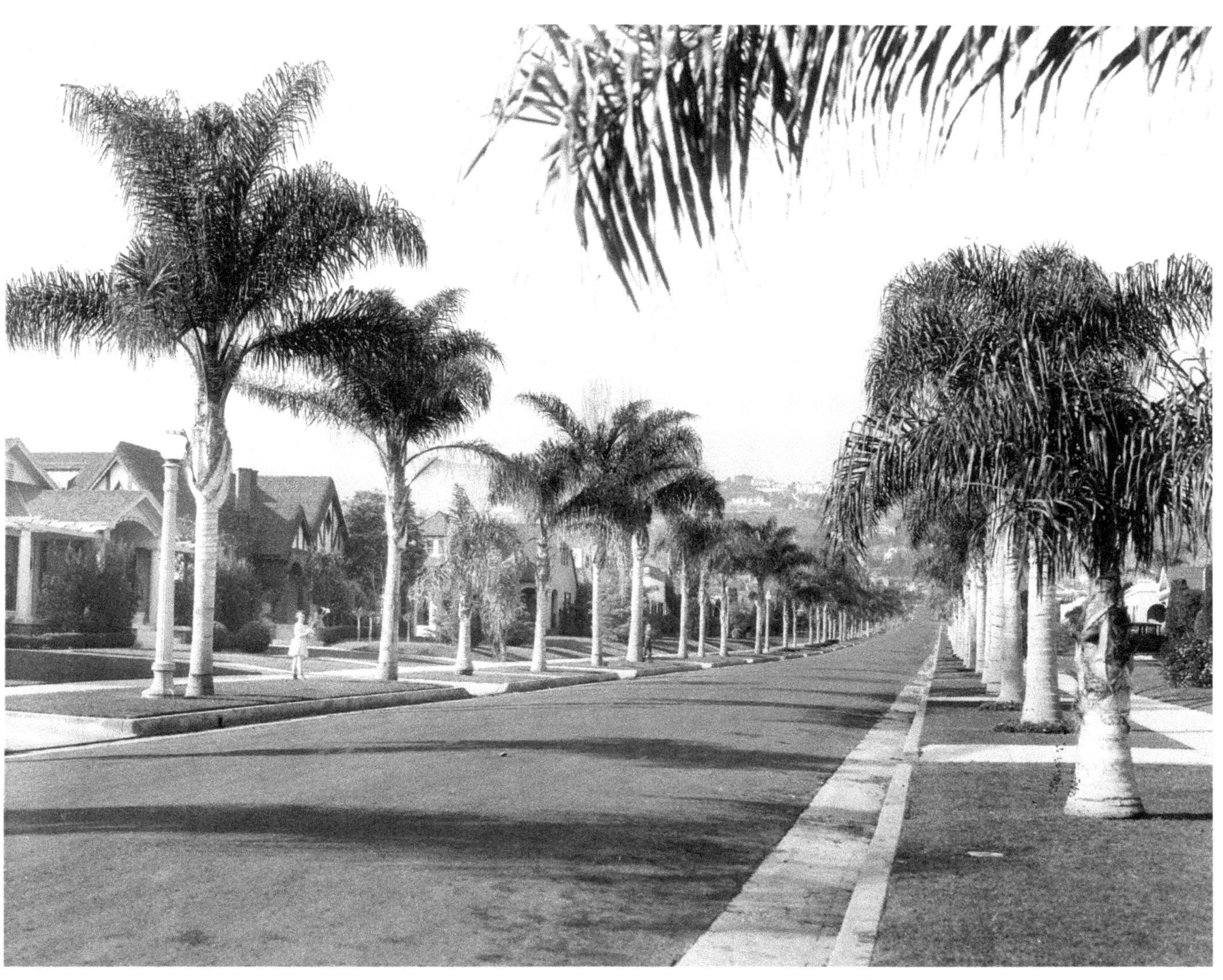

By the 1940s, most of Los Angeles consisted of suburbs such as this Hollywood neighborhood. Simone de Beauvoir (1908–1986) was a French author and philosopher whose 1949 treatise *The Second Sex*, a study of women's oppression, became a cornerstone of modern feminism. In 1947 she visited Los Angeles and wrote, "The city is unlike any other . . . nothing but suburbs. The city slips away like a phantom city . . . Los Angeles is far from possessing the beauty of New York or the depth of Chicago, and I understand why some French people spoke to me about it with such distaste."

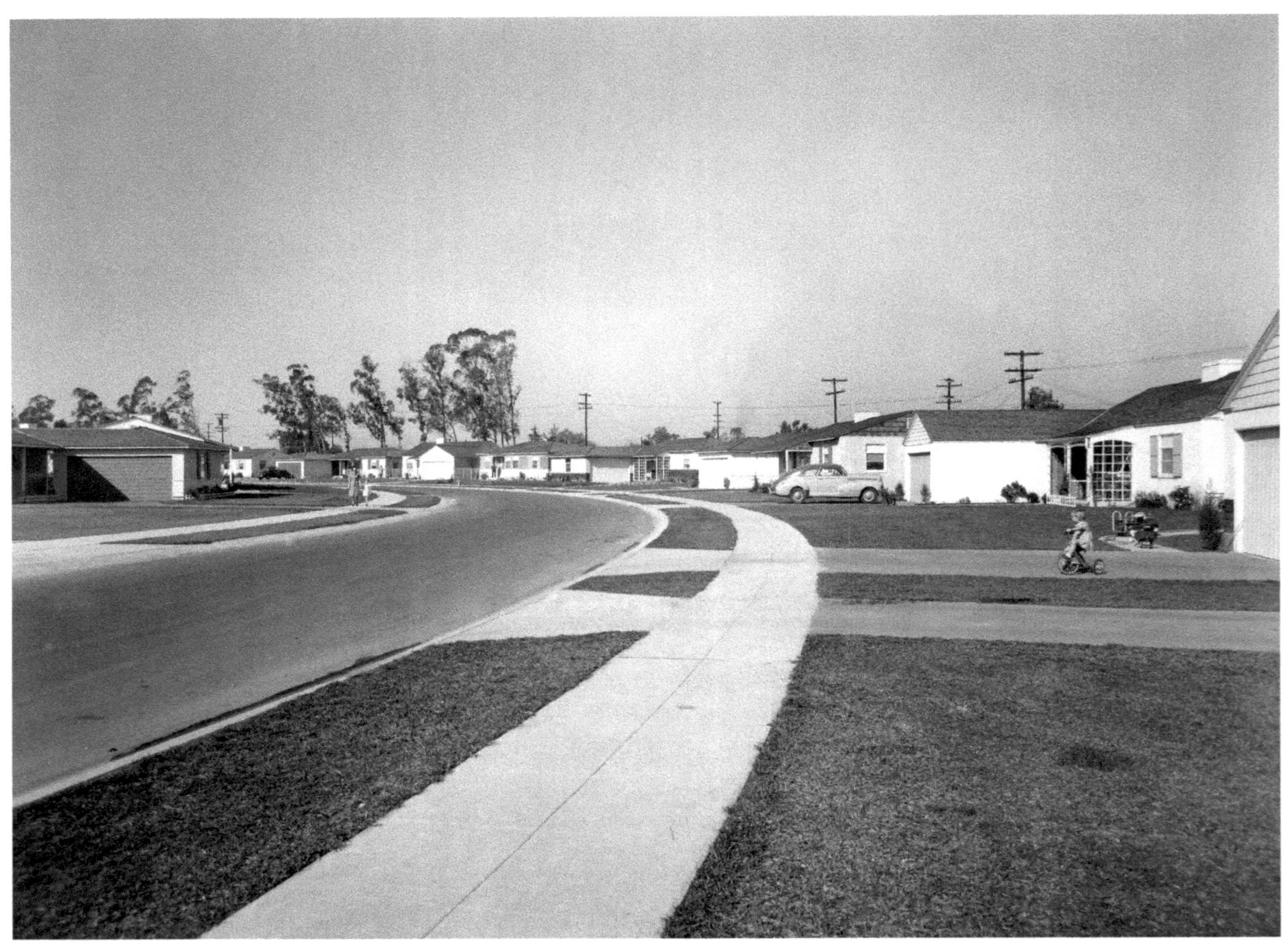

Because of the forty-five fault lines in California, the framed construction used in these "Kaiser Home" houses in the Westchester district provided "seismically sound structures," according to a scholarly study. Such metal-frame houses built in great numbers in Los Angeles in the 1940s and 1950s are considered part of the so-called modern movement in American architecture.

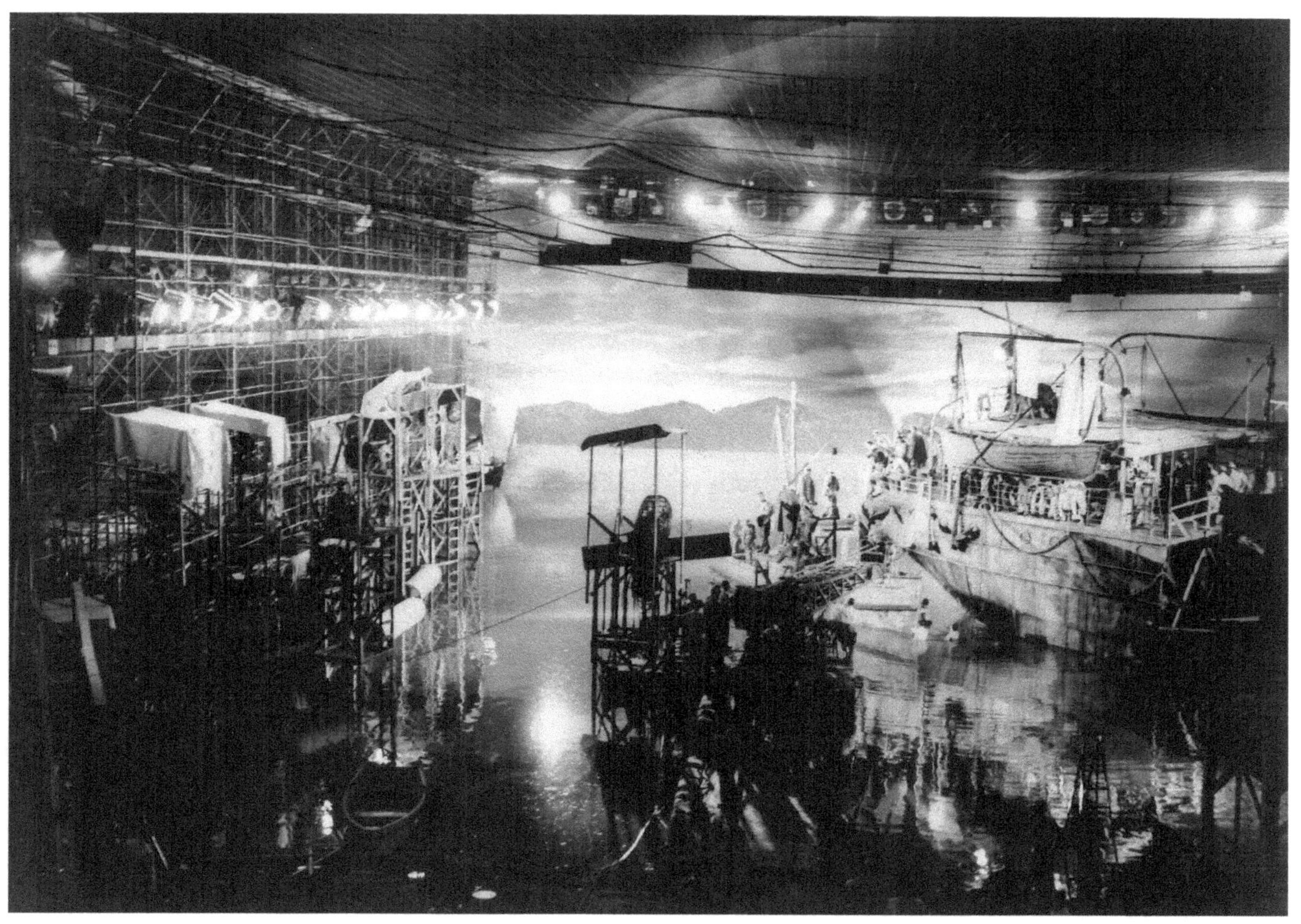

Though not evident from this scene on the Paramount Pictures lot, Hollywood's golden age began to decline in the late 1940s due to television, Hollywood blacklisting, and the newfound freedom of actors to sign with whatever studios they chose. A final blow to the industry's old ways occurred when antitrust suits were filed against the major studios in 1948.

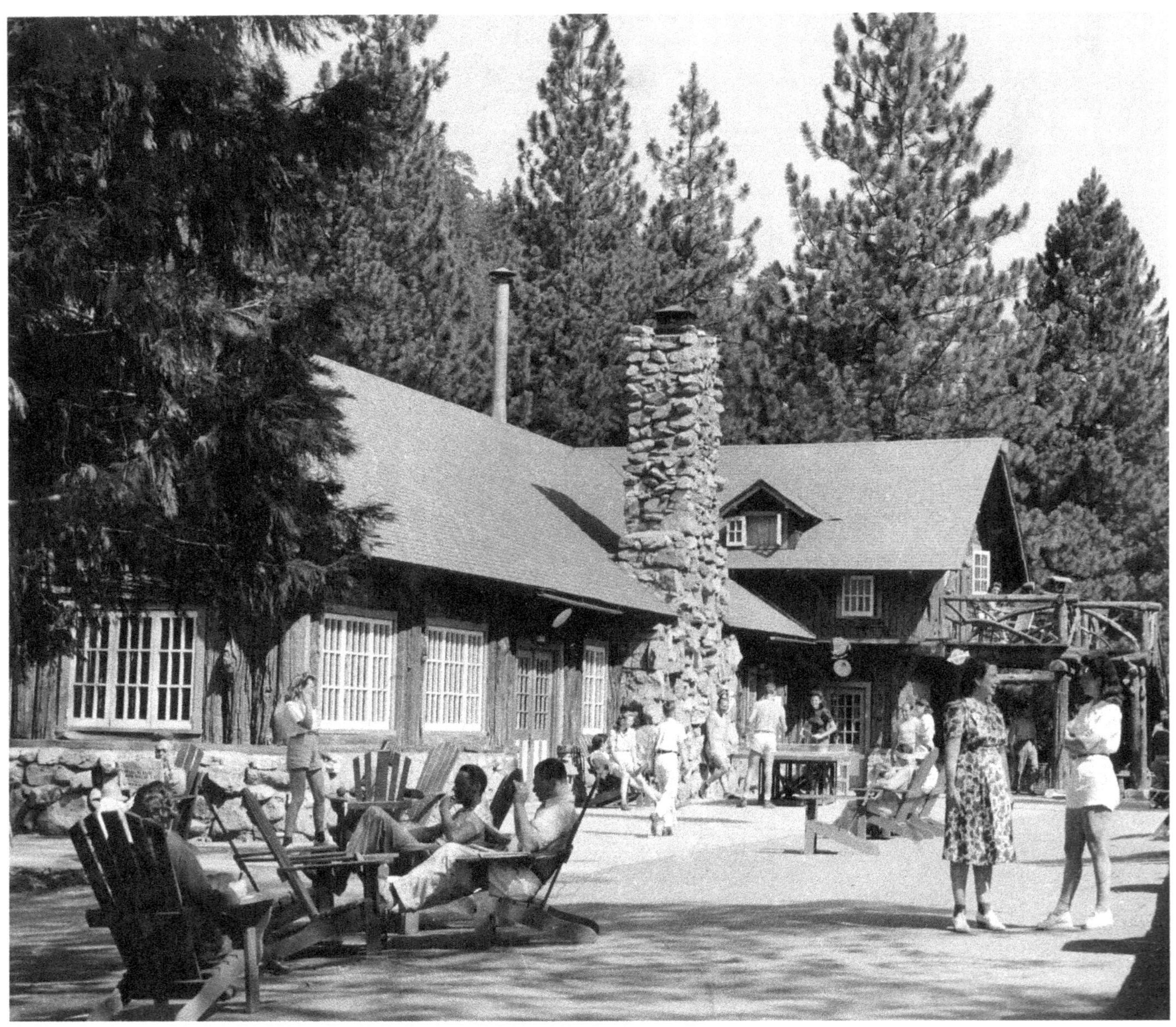

The end of World War II meant an end to rationing and a return to prewar leisure activities. In this case, vacationers relax in the sun and shade of Camp Beeley, one of more than a hundred resorts in the San Bernardino mountains.

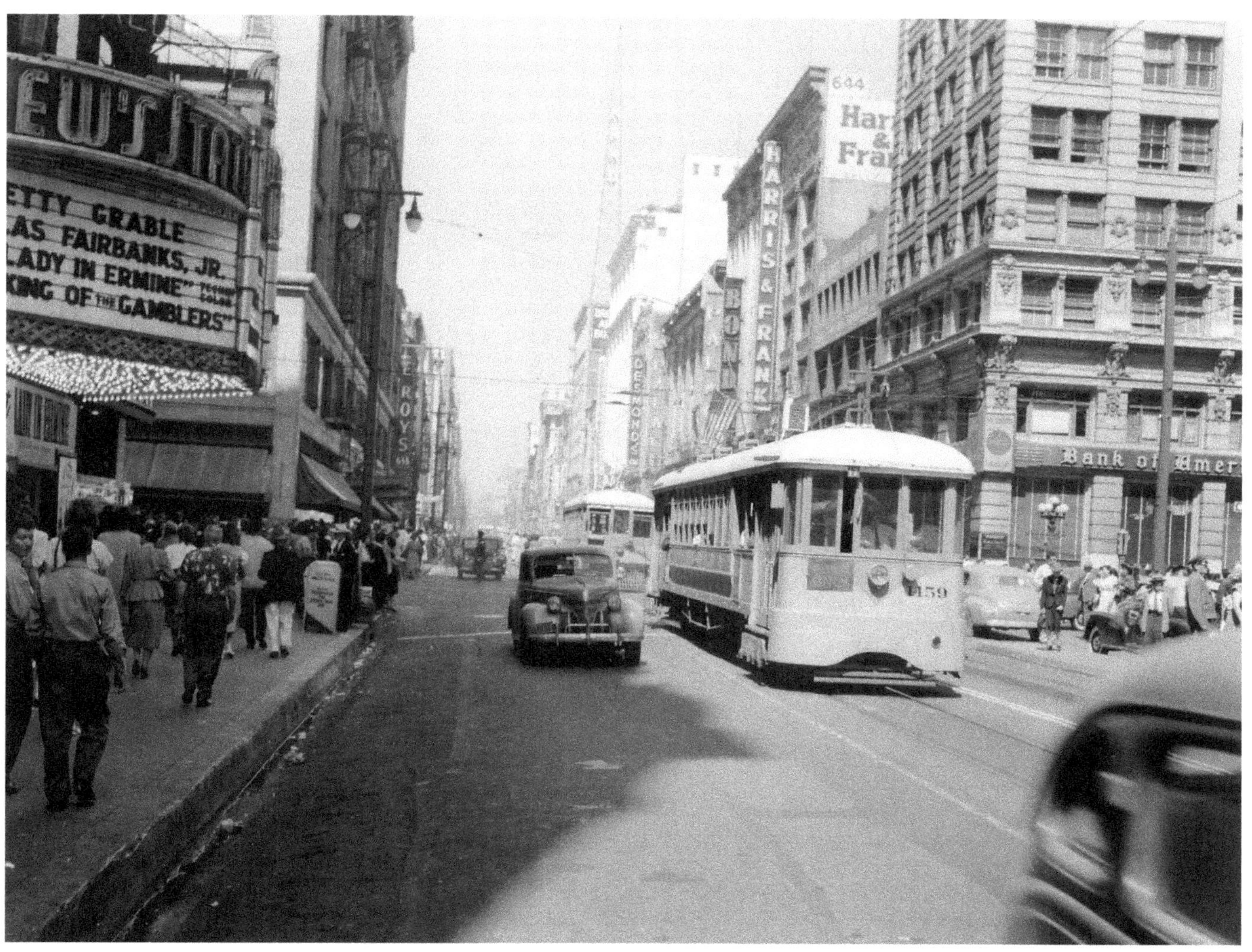

At the corner of 7th and Broadway in Los Angeles in 1948, no parking was permitted against the 10-inch curb. That year the Santa Ana–101 Freeway opened from Aliso Street to Soto Street. Aliso Village was one of the nation's first racially integrated public housing projects. The postwar housing crunch hit L.A. as U.S. servicemen, and Japanese Americans recently permitted to return to Little Tokyo, settled in the area.

Singer and actor Frank Sinatra (1915–1998) is shown getting his fingerprints taken in Hollywood in 1947 after he applied for permission to carry a gun. The popular vocalist became a solo artist with great success in the 1940s and is considered the first teen idol, but his career stalled in the 1950s until he won an Academy Award for Best Supporting Actor in 1954 for his role in the film *From Here to Eternity*.

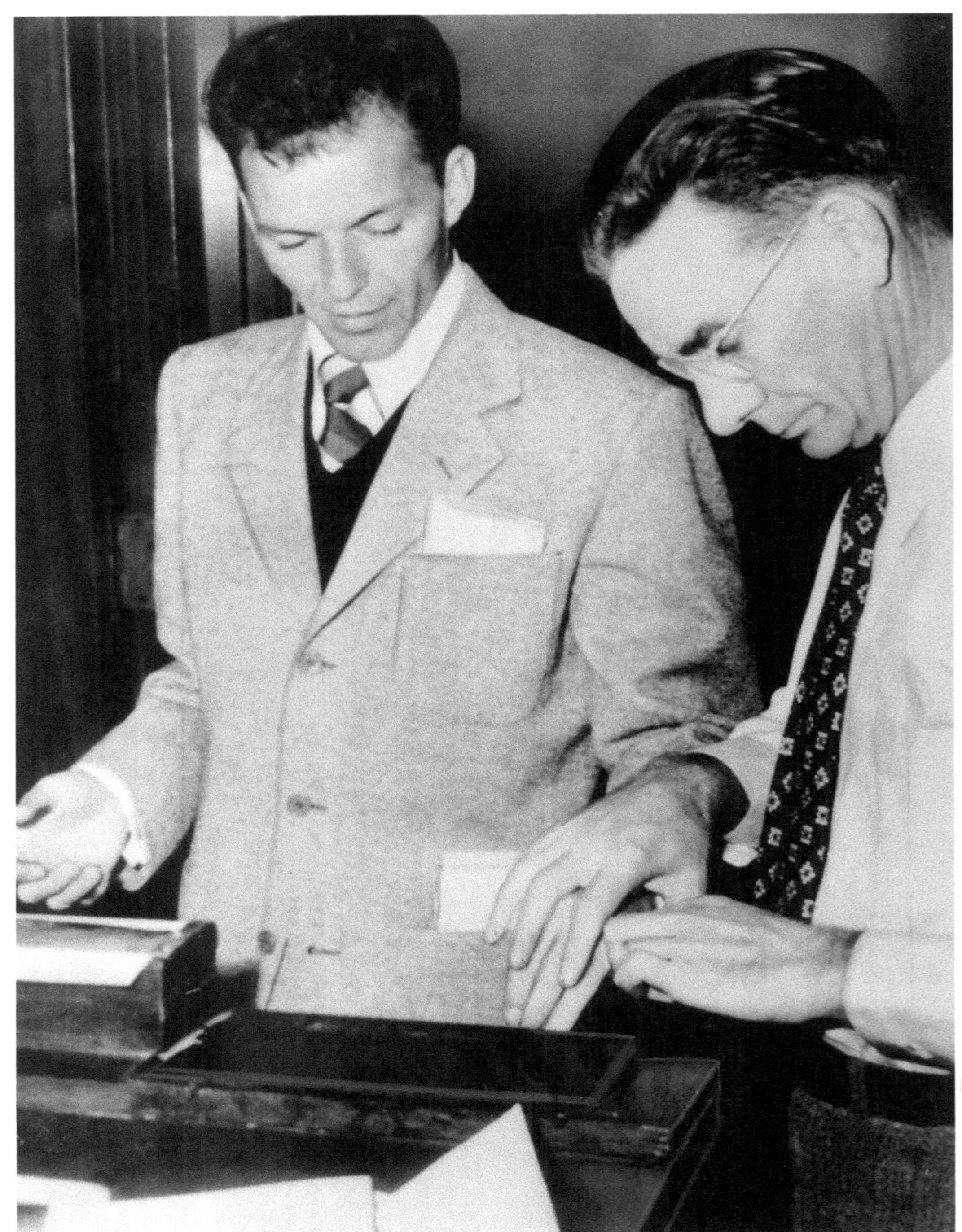

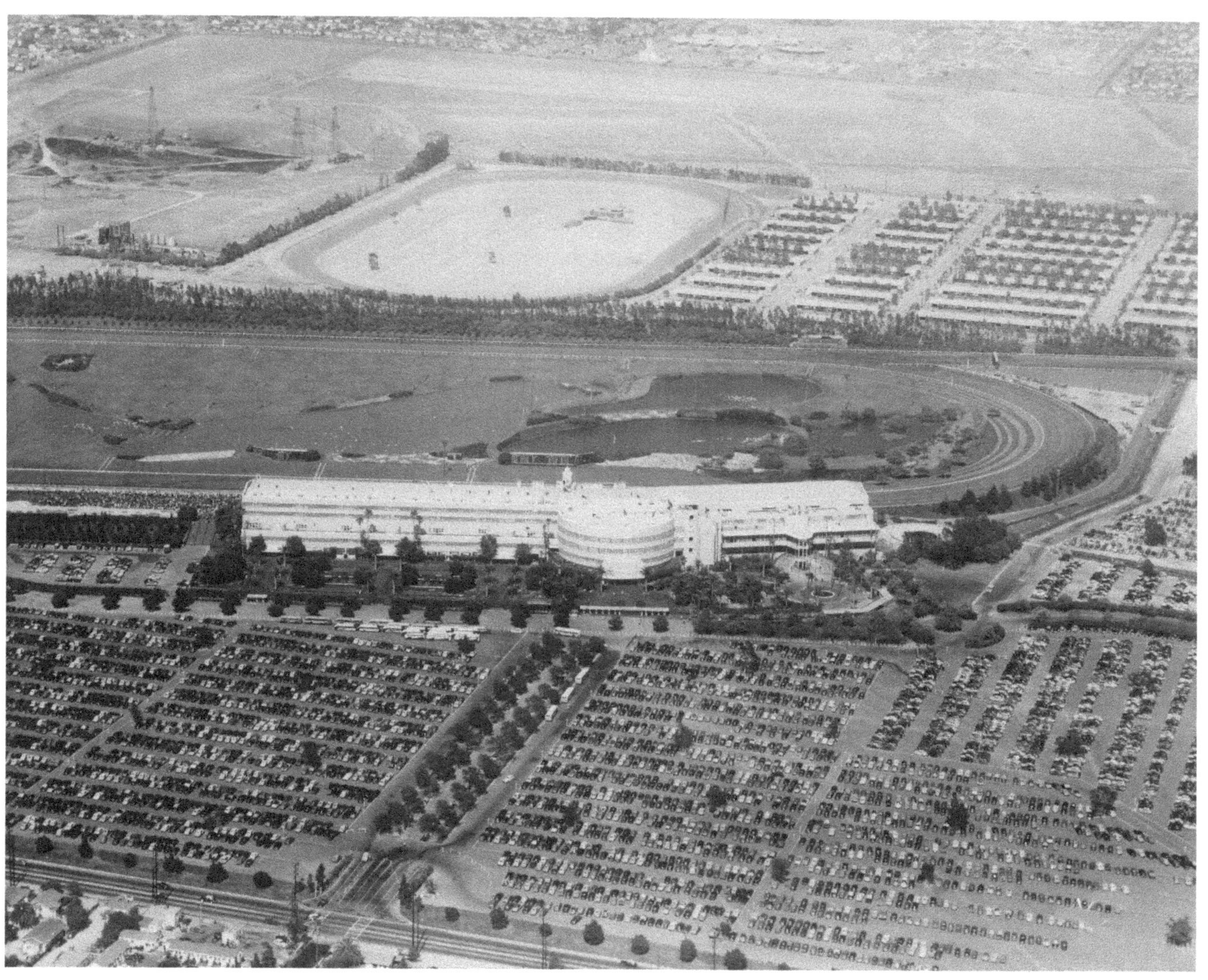

An aerial view of Hollywood Park Race Track. The track was opened in 1938 by the Hollywood Turf Club whose chairman was Jack Warner of Warner Brothers, and its 600 shareholders included many other Hollywood luminaries. It was closed from 1942 to 1944 due to the war, and in 1949 the grandstand and clubhouse were destroyed by a fire, but were rebuilt soon thereafter.

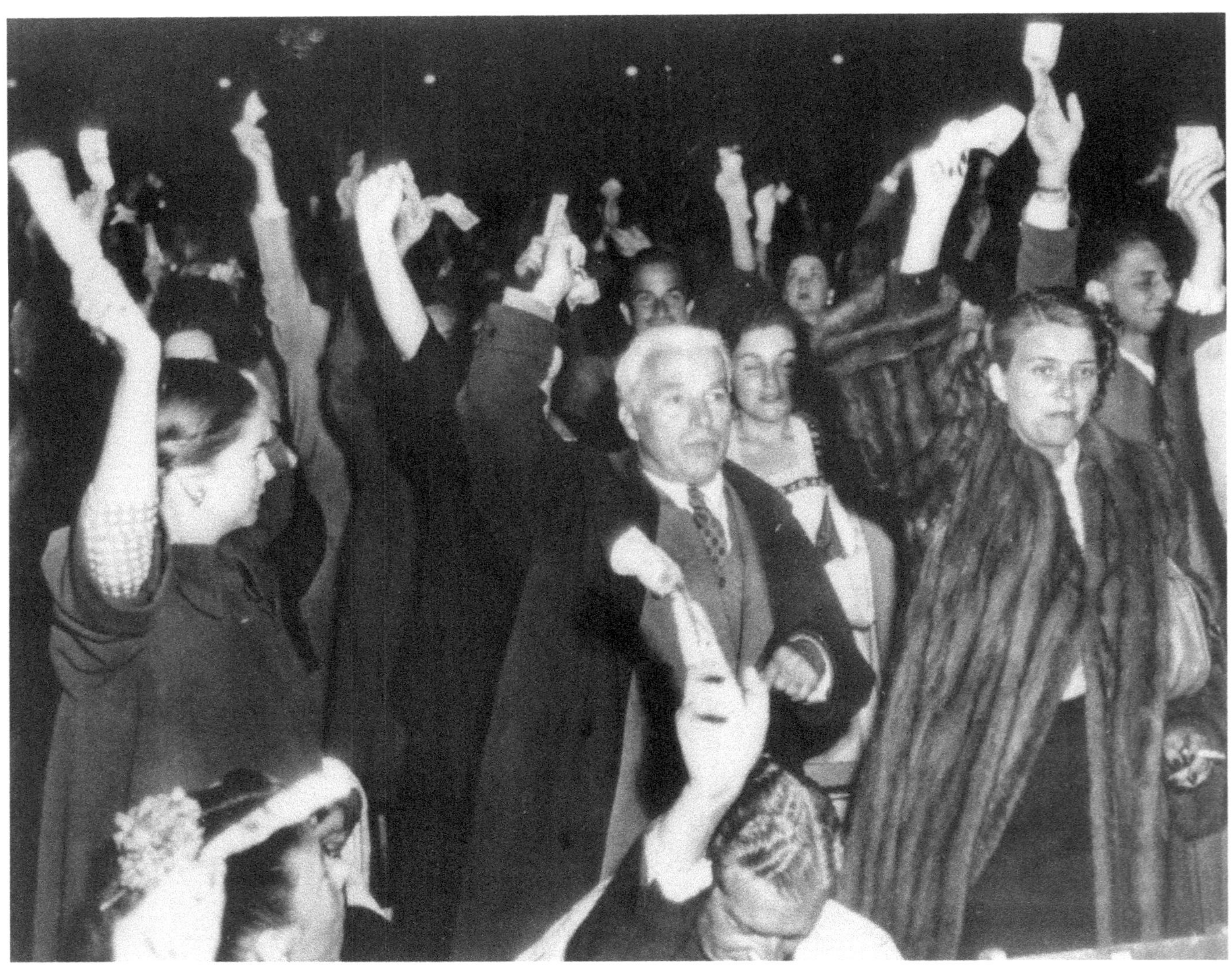

Actor, director, and composer Charlie Chaplin (1889–1977) with his wife Oona at a 1948 rally for the presidential campaign of Henry A. Wallace, the nominee of the Progressive Party. Wallace (1888–1965) was vice-president under Franklin D. Roosevelt from 1941, but Roosevelt replaced him as his running mate in 1944 with Harry S. Truman. Wallace then served as secretary of commerce until 1946 when he was fired by President Truman because of disagreements about U.S. policy towards the Soviet Union.

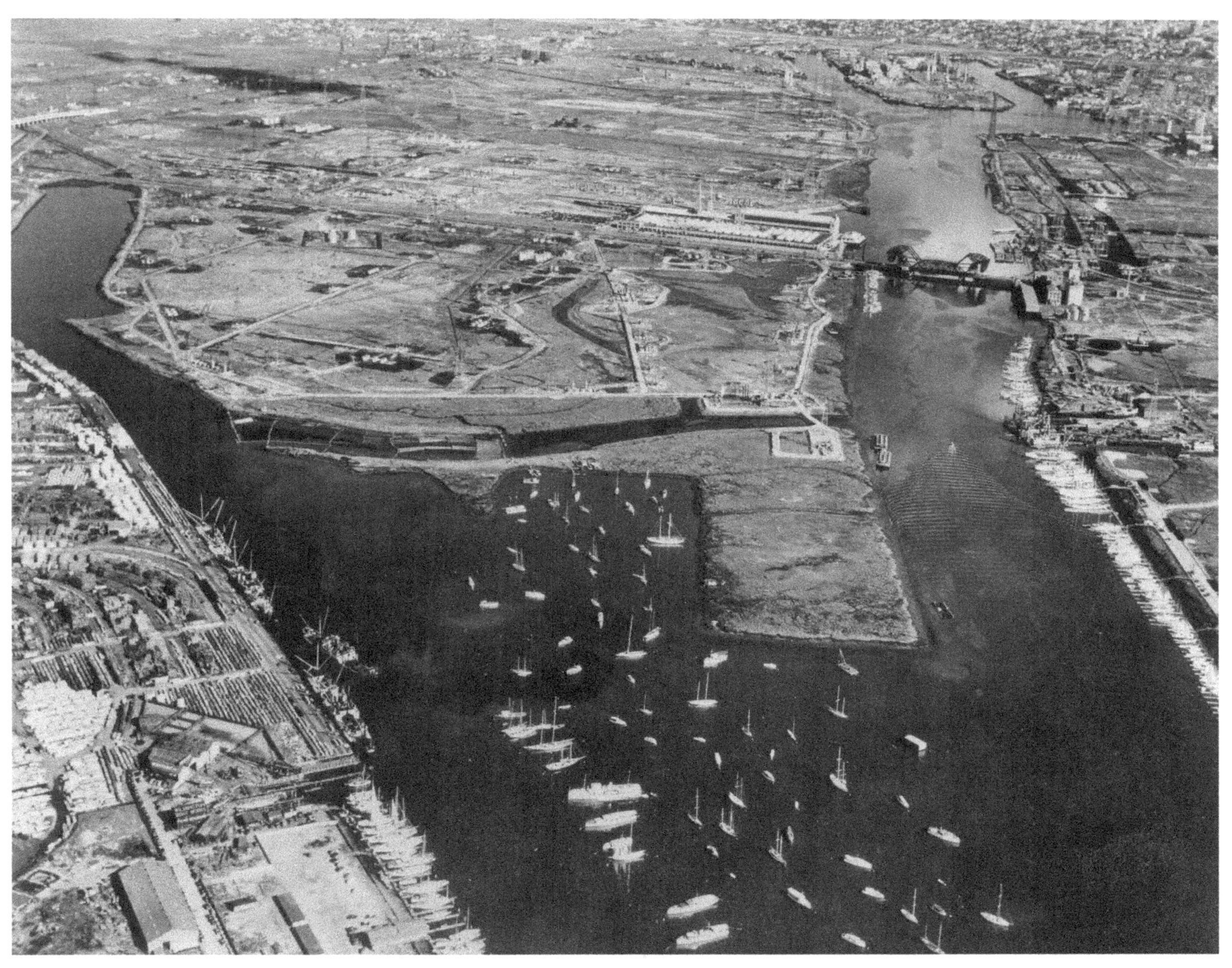

Los Angeles harbor viewed from above in 1949. That year saw the first Mexican American elected to the L.A. City Council in the twentieth century, Edward Roybal, who later represented his area in Congress until 1993.

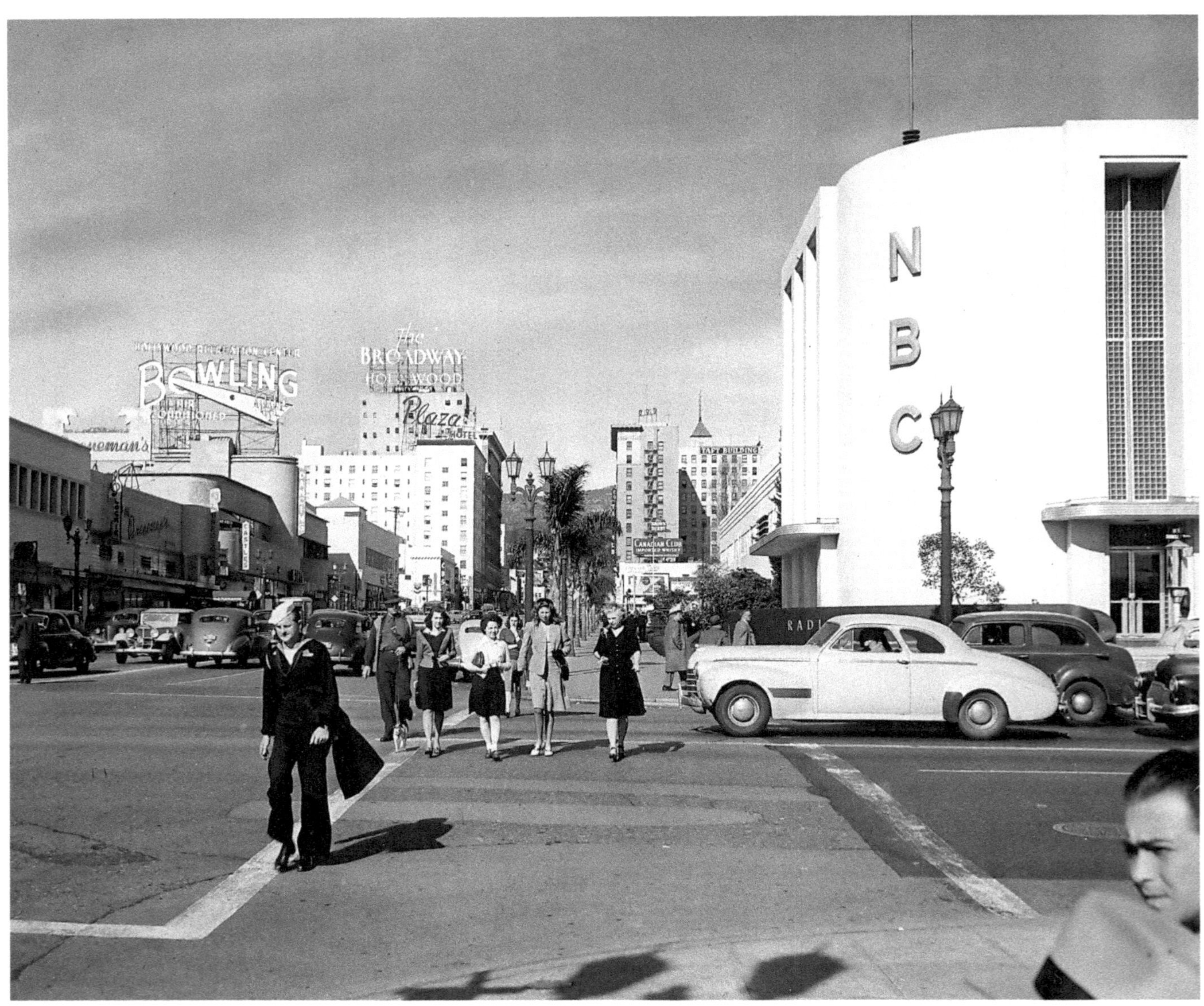

The National Broadcasting Company (NBC) building in Hollywood in 1951. In the 1950s, millions of Americans bought TVs, and NBC launched television's first superstar, Milton Berle (1908–2002), whose antics on the *Texaco Star Theater* drew massive audiences. During this decade television became the dominant mass media, and young people watched TV more hours than they went to school, a trend that is still the same in 2008.

Suburbs, Freeways, and a Cold War

(1950–1959)

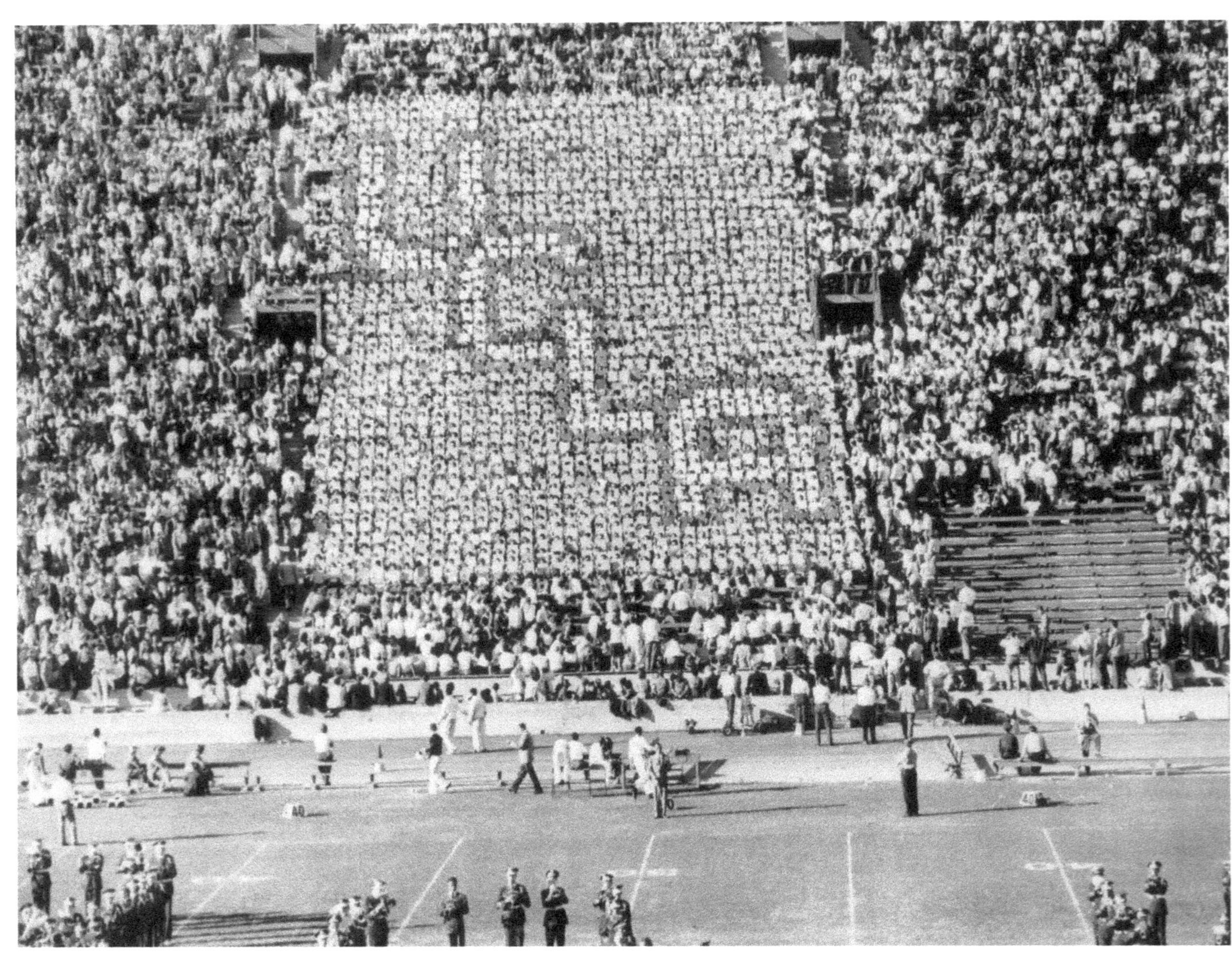

In what appears to be part of a football game halftime extravaganza, 15,000 students hold up cards spelling out "UCLA" in 1950. The University of California, Los Angeles, is a public research university established as a branch of the state university system in 1919. It is the second oldest campus in the UC system and has the largest enrollment of any university in California. In 2008 UCLA had more applicants than any other university in the United States.

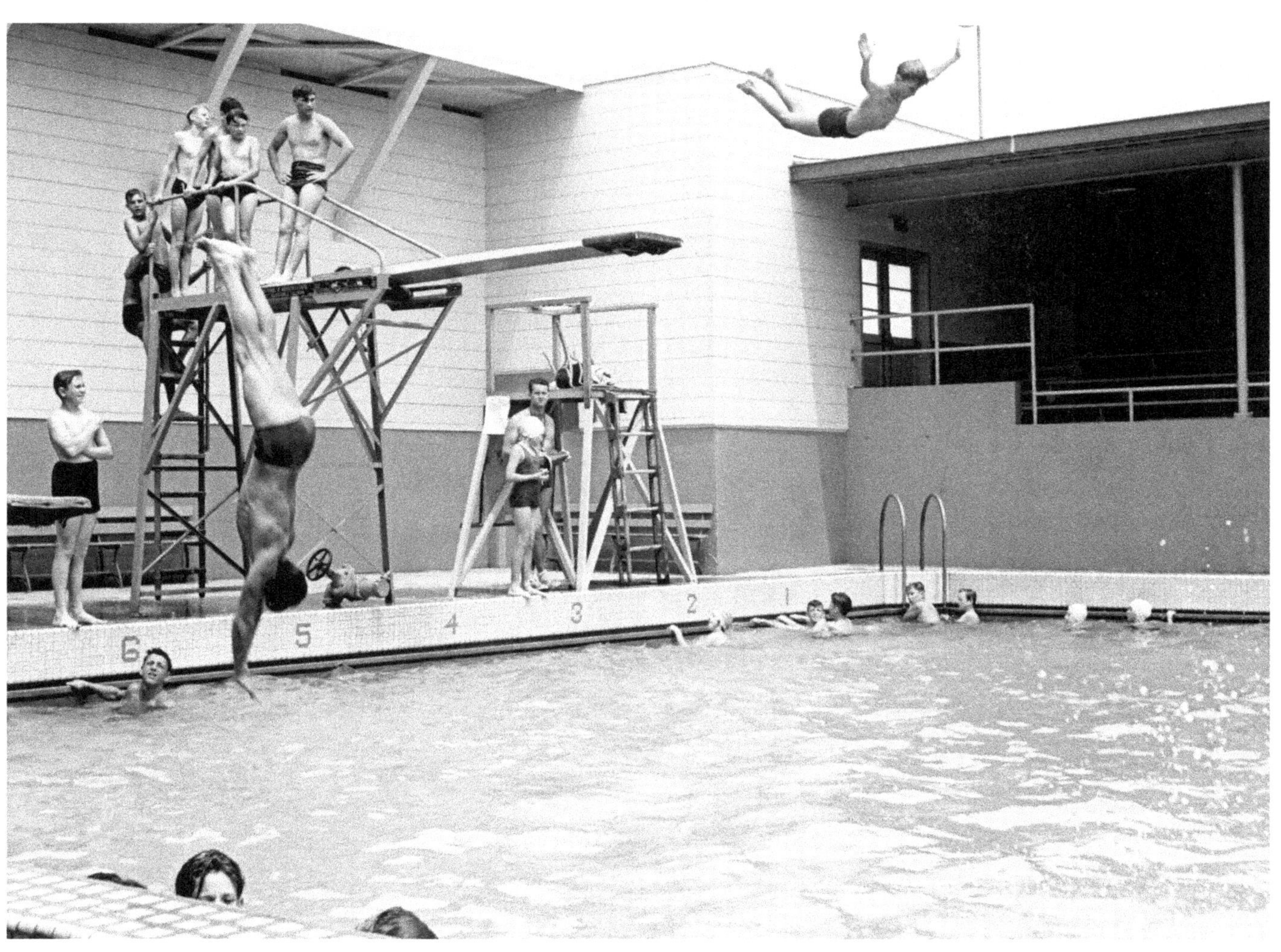

A public swimming pool of the Playground and Recreation Department in Compton. Los Angeles is not usually noted for such normal activities as diving at a public pool, but instead has been referred to as "La-La-Land," an expression that pokes fun at the supposed eccentricities of the city's residents.

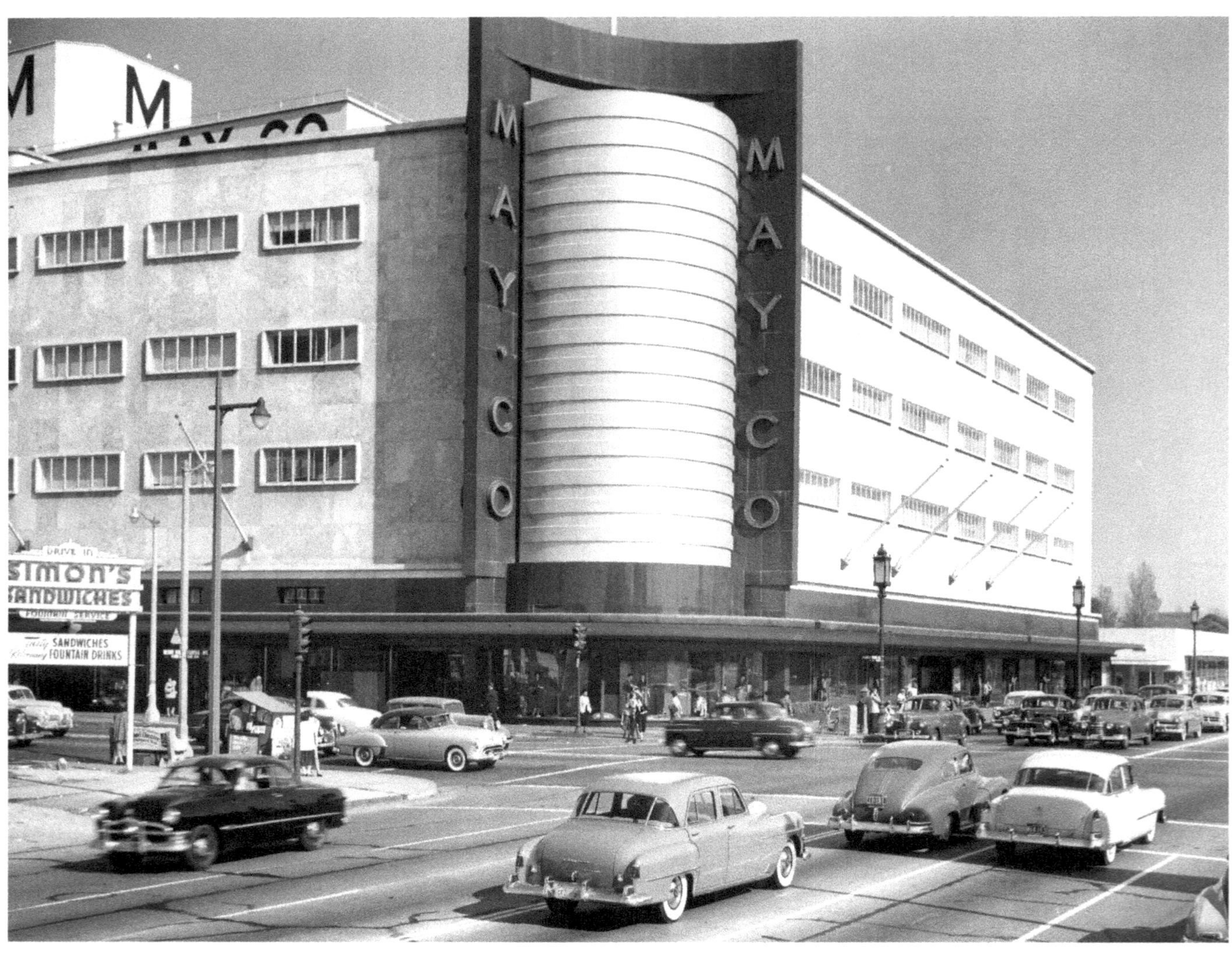

The May Company department store, seen here in 1956, was part of the Miracle Mile, the name given to the "super-modern" retail and service establishments along Wilshire Boulevard. In the early 1920s, Wilshire west of Western Avenue was an unpaved farm road. Developer A. W. Ross developed Wilshire as a car-oriented shopping district to compete with downtown Los Angeles. It was named Miracle Mile for its unprecedented and unlikely commercial success.

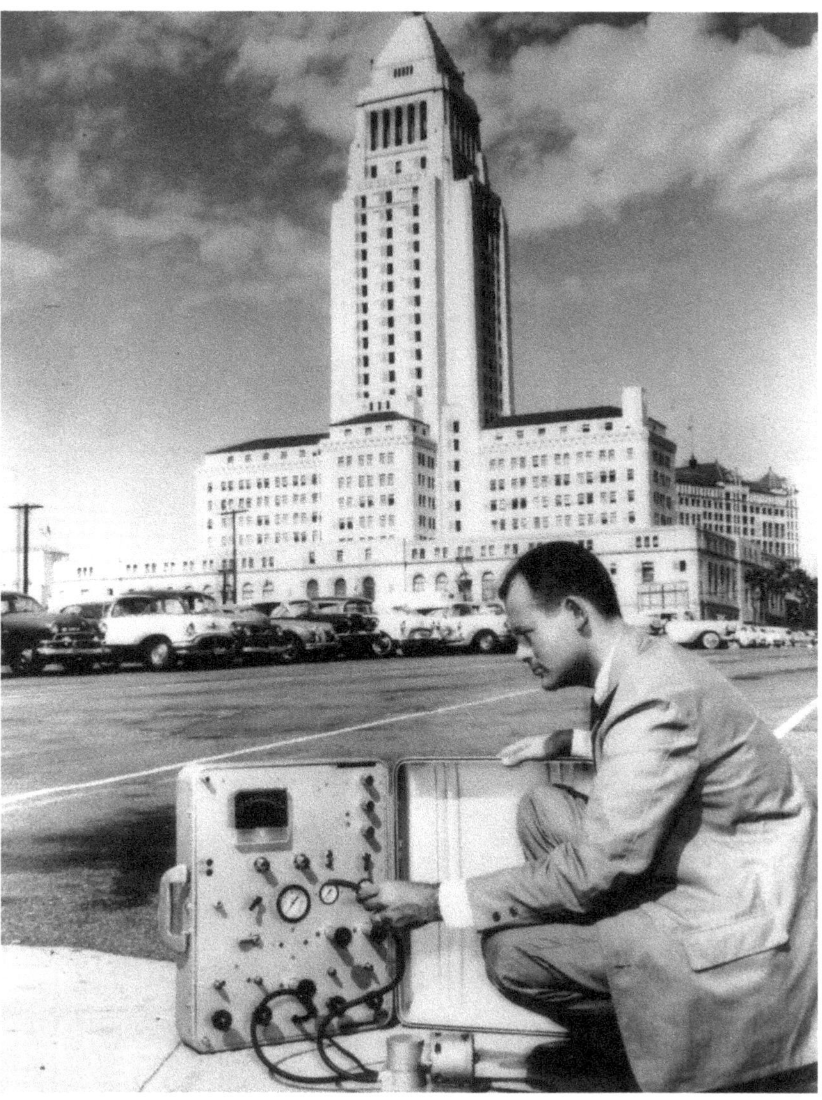

In October 1954, heavy smog shut down schools and industry in Los Angeles for most of the month. Historically, the word "smog" meant a blend of smoke and fog, but it became synonymous with automobile-exhaust air pollution in L.A. Here, engineer Newell Claudy measures carbon impurities in the L.A. atmosphere of 1959. Los Angeles City Hall is in the background.

Parked in the foreground outside the Van De Kamp Coffee Shop, down the block from the Prudential Insurance Building, on Wilshire Boulevard in Hollywood is a Chevrolet Corvette, the first all-American sports car, whose initial model ran from 1953 to 1962. The scene is 1956, but this is a pre-1956 Corvette with the early body design.

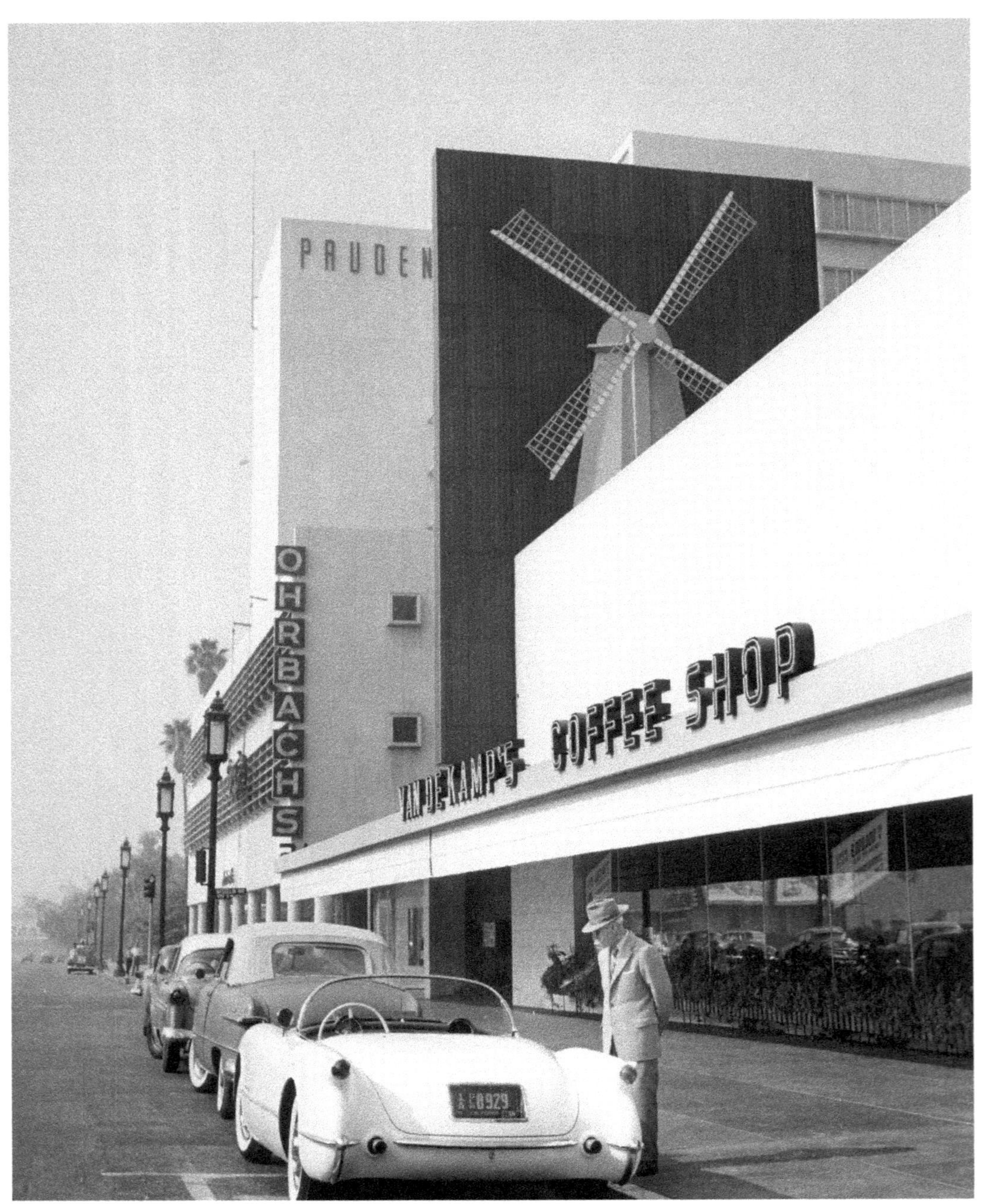

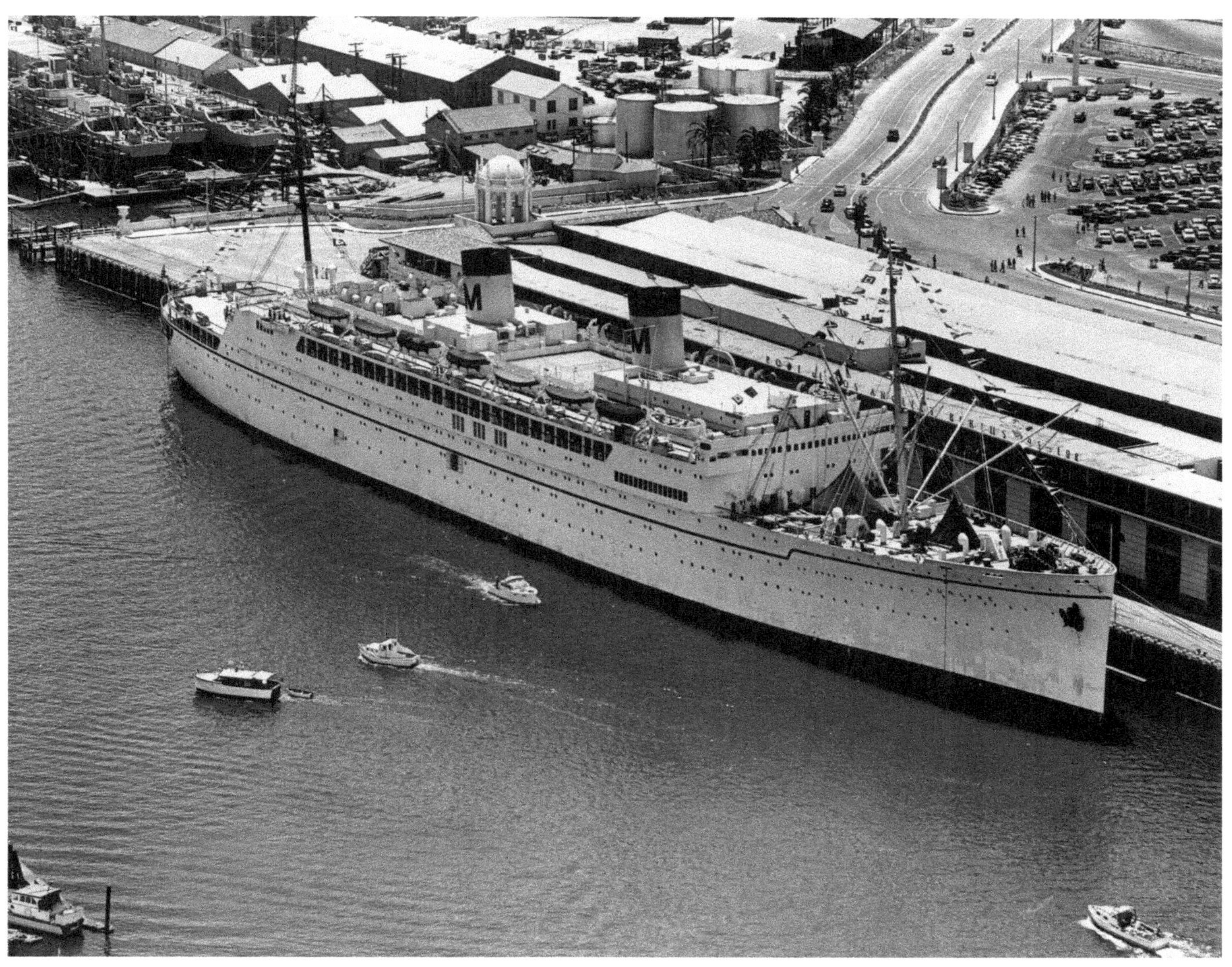

The passenger ship *Lurline* rests alongside the 70-foot wharf of the 48-acre terminal assigned to Matson Navigation Company during the 1950s. The *Lurline* was christened in 1931 and sailed the San Francisco, Honolulu, and Sydney, Australia, route. During World War II, the *Lurline* carried thousands of troops. After the war, and until 1970, the *Lurline* returned to passenger service as one of the four Matson luxury liners called "white ships" because of their color.

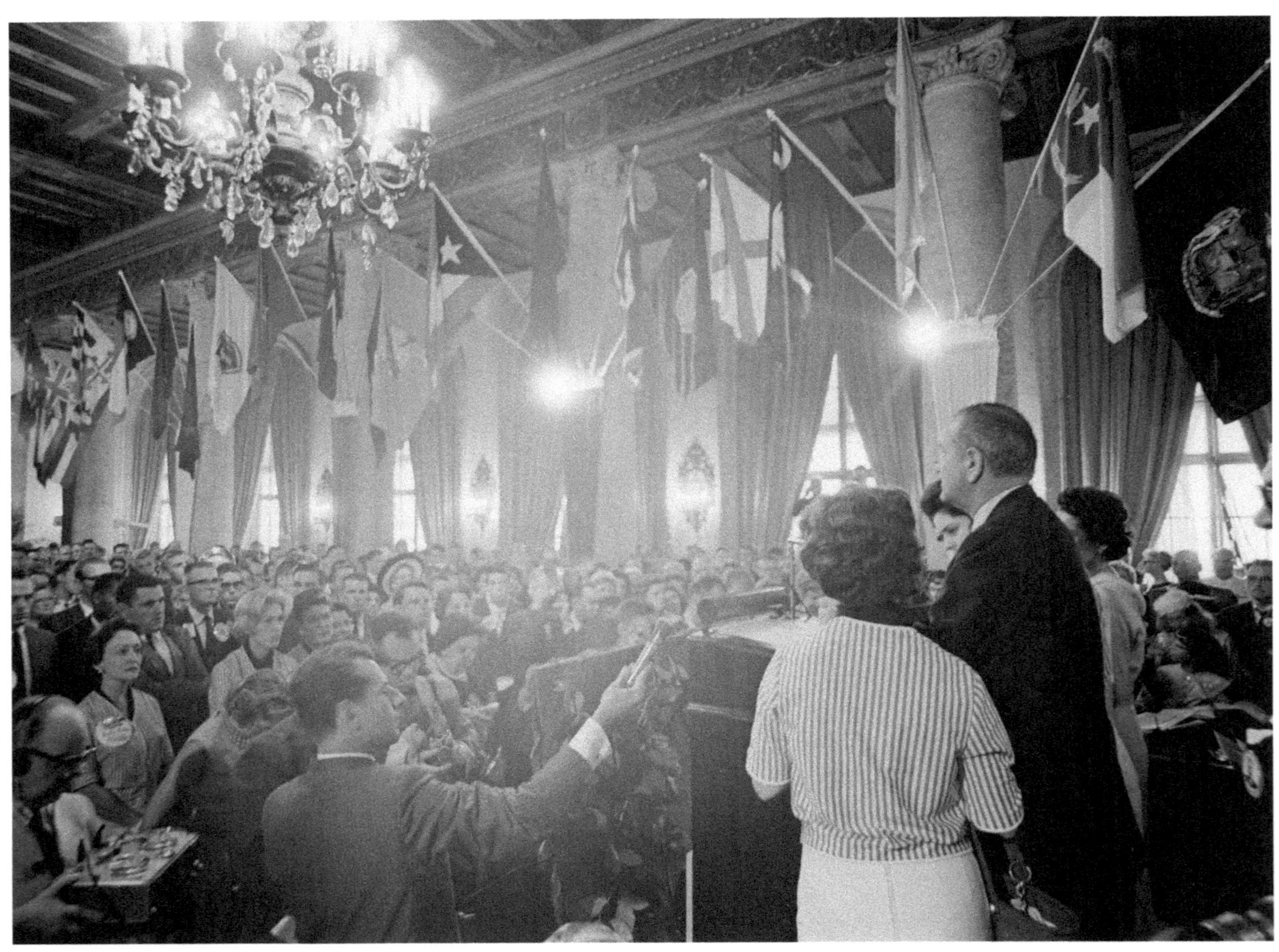

At a Biltmore Hotel reception on July 10, 1960, Senator Lyndon B. Johnson, with his wife beside him, campaigns for the Democratic nomination for president. The Democratic Convention was held in Los Angeles at the L.A. Memorial Sports Arena. Senator John F. Kennedy won the presidential nomination and asked Johnson to be his running mate, despite clashes between them during the primary elections. Kennedy needed Johnson's political strength in the South.

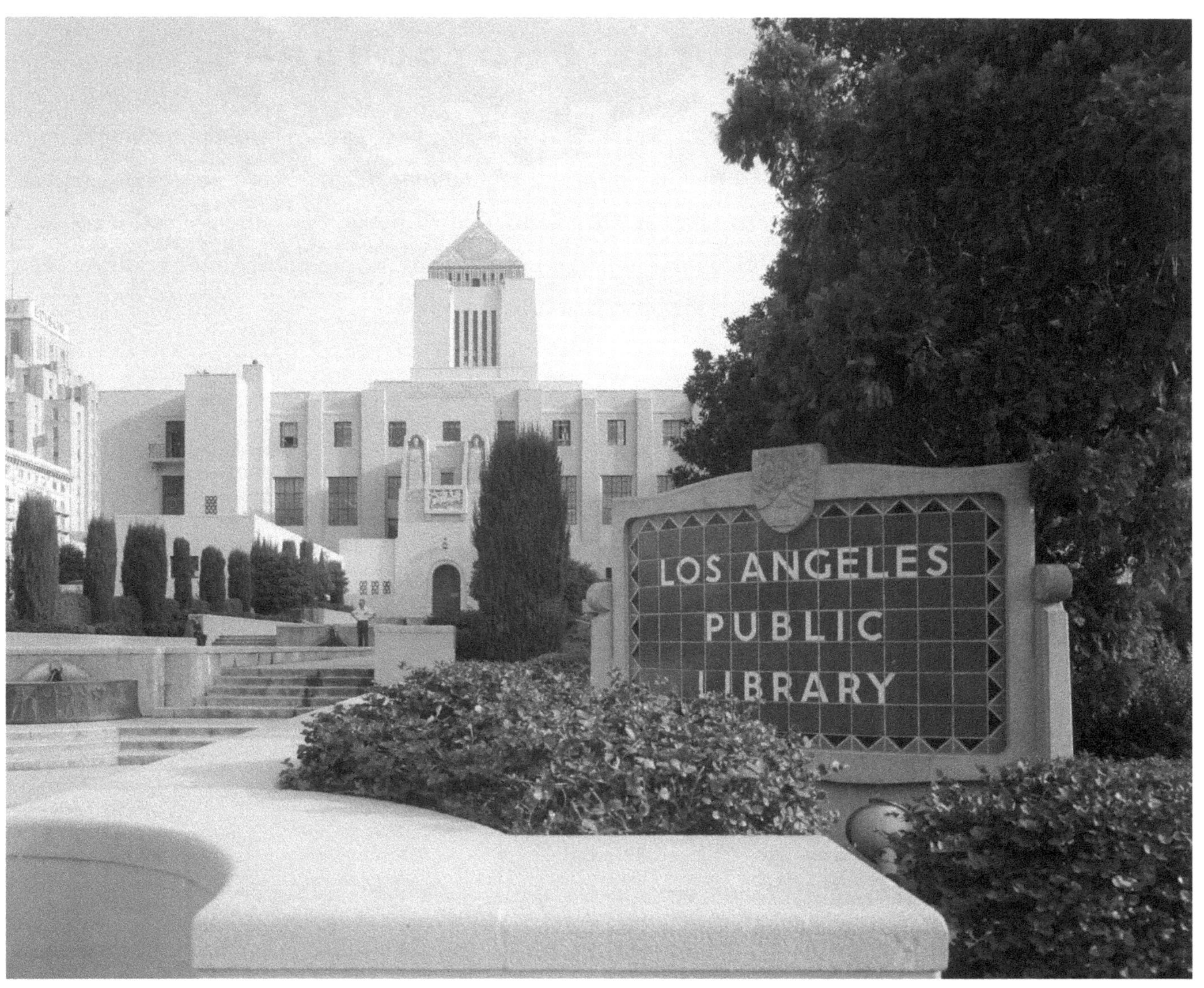

The Los Angeles Public Library, initially constructed in 1926, is a downtown landmark. In 2008 it is the third largest public library in the United States in terms of book and periodical holdings.

Notes on the Photographs

These notes, listed by page number, attempt to include all aspects known of the photographs. Each of the photographs is identified by the page number, photograph's title or description, photographer and collection, archive, and call or box number when applicable. Although every attempt was made to collect all available data, in some cases complete data was unavailable due to the age and condition of some of the photographs and records.

ii **North Carolina Countryside**
North Carolina State Archives
PhC68.1.538.1

vi **The Julia Bell**
North Carolina State Archives
PhC42.Bx6.Boats and Boating.F18

x **Two Men and Oystering Boat**
North Carolina State Archives
PhC42.Bx11.Fishes and Fishing.F39

2 **Battery Lamb, Fort Fisher**
Library of Congress
cwpb 04367u

3 **Purdie Battery, Fort Fisher**
Library of Congress
cwpb 01412u

4 **Fort Fisher Damaged Gun**
Library of Congress
cwpb 01411u

5 **Old Ferry over Yadkin River**
North Carolina State Archives
N.71.12.199

6 **Capitol and Oxcart**
North Carolina State Archives
N.53.15.353

7 **Elm Street in Greensboro**
North Carolina State Archives
PhC9_Bx10_F6_1

8 **Farmers Hauling Cotton to Charlotte**
North Carolina State Archives
PhC42.Bx21.Scenic CentralNC.F40

9 **The Ocracoke Lighthouse**
North Carolina State Archives
N_77_4_25

10 **Pea Island Life Station**
North Carolina State Archives
N_77_4_29

11 **Boykin's Bridge**
North Carolina State Archives
N_68_3_40

12 **Weather Bureau Station**
North Carolina State Archives
PhC42.Bx7.Cape Hatteras.F10

13 **Young Women in Sewing Class**
Library of Congress
cph 3c18917u

14 **Biltmore Estate**
Library of Congress
cph 3c05586u

16 **Cropping Tobacco in Nash County**
North Carolina State Archives
PhC42.Bx4. Agriculture. Tobacco.F2

17 **Columbus County Strawberries**
North Carolina State Archives
PhC42.Bx4. Agriculture. Strawberries.F15

18 **Family at Falls of Neuse River**
North Carolina State Archives
N_98_4_38

19 **Man on Beach Cart**
North Carolina State Archives
PhC42.Bx7.Cape Hatteras.F1

20 **Engine 535 and Crew**
North Carolina State Archives
N.89.4.28

21 **Mountain Scene Near Asheville**
Library of Congress
cph 3c17036u

22 **Sharecropping**
Library of Congress
cph 3c24329u

23 **Pee Dee Bank**
North Carolina State Archives
Postcard 181 Bank and Opera Hs Rockingham NC

24 **Big Kinnakeet**
North Carolina State Archives
PhC42.Bx10. Coastgaurd.F1-3

25 **Wright Brothers' First Flight**
North Carolina State Archives
N_63_9_27

26 **Family Farming Near Linville Falls**
North Carolina State Archives
N_83_2_83

27 **Cape Hatteras Lighthouse**
North Carolina State Archives
PhC42.Bx7.cape Hatteras.F6-3

28 **Cunningham Farm Tobacco**
North Carolina State Archives
Phc42.Bx4. Agriculture. Tobacco.F11

29 **Asheville in Buncombe County**
Library of Congress
cph 3c24130u

30 **Young Boy at Warping Machine**
Library of Congress
nclc 05391u

31 **Electric-powered Utility Truck**
North Carolina State Archives
PhC68.1.266.1

32 **Peuland Family of Scaly Gap**
Library of Congress
nclc 04572u

33 **Mountain Cabin**
North Carolina State Archives
N_98_3_409

34 **Prison Chain Gang**
Library of Congress
fsa 8e04044u

35 **Zebulon Street Scene**
North Carolina State Archives
N_76_4_38

36 **Engine 38 in Hamlet**
North Carolina State Archives
N.94.8.3

37 **Crowd on Steps of Lumina Pavilion**
North Carolina State Archives
PhC68.1.81.2

38 **Downtown Durham**
North Carolina State Archives
PhC68.1.25

39 **Fayetteville Street in Raleigh**
North Carolina State Archives
PhC68.1.89

40 **Asheville Street Scene**
North Carolina State Archives
PhC68.1.2.2

41 **Wilmington Street in Raleigh**
North Carolina State Archives
PhC68.1.126

42 **Replacing Wooden Poles**
North Carolina State Archives
PhC68.1.238

43 **Frederick Fritz Daeke**
North Carolina State Archives
PhC68.1.49

44 **Linemen and Crew with First Two-ton White Truck**
North Carolina State Archives
PhC68.1.239

46 **McCrary-Redding Hardware**
North Carolina State Archives
PhC68.1.1.2

47 **Women's Suffrage Headquarters**
North Carolina State Archives
N.53.16.6672

48 **Women's Suffrage Campaign**
North Carolina State Archives
N_60_4_38

49 **Farmyard in the Piedmont**
North Carolina State Archives
PhC_bBx4_F283

50 **Baled Cotton Crop Ready for Market**
North Carolina State Archives
PhC_121_50

51 **Cotton Starts Through the Mill**
North Carolina State Archives
N.85.10.119

52 **Flora McDonald Orchestra at Flora McDonald College**
North Carolina State Archives
N.53.16.3782

53 **Fayetteville Street Looking North**
North Carolina State Archives
PhC68.1.105

54 **Meredith Students on Old Campus**
North Carolina State Archives
N.53.17.270

55 **Wadesboro Business District**
North Carolina State Archives
PhC68.1.75

56 **Greensboro Sinclair Service Station**
North Carolina State Archives
PhC9_Bx4_F240

57 **Wrightsville Beach Float in Wilmington Parade**
North Carolina State Archives
PhC68.1.505

58 **Automobiles Waiting at Railroad Crossing**
North Carolina State Archives
PhC68.1.520

59 **Carolina Coach Company**
North Carolina State Archives
ConDevOSPrintsBx127 Buses 1

60 **Downtown Greensboro**
North Carolina State Archives
PhC9_Bx4_F267

61 **War Memorial Stadium Construction**
North Carolina State Archives
PhC9_Bx3_F197

62 **Hargett Street**
North Carolina State Archives
PhC68.1.112

63 **F. H. Krahnke, Jr., Clothing Store**
North Carolina State Archives
PhC9_Bx3_F200

64 **Kids Enjoying Ice Cream and Sodas**
North Carolina State Archives
PhC_121-54

65 **Goldsboro in Wayne County**
North Carolina State Archives
PhC68.1.37

66 **Jefferson Standard Building**
North Carolina State Archives
N_89_7_65

67 **Beached Whale on Wrightsville Beach**
North Carolina State Archives
N.75.7.229

68 **Yates Pond near Raleigh**
North Carolina State Archives
N.53.15.132

69 **Asheboro in Randolph County**
North Carolina State Archives
PhC68.1.1.5

70 **Armistice Day Parade in Greensboro**
North Carolina State Archives
PhC9_Bx10_F2

71 **Thanksgiving Parade**
North Carolina State Archives
PhC9_Bx10_F7-03

72 **Meyers Float in Thanksgiving Parade**
North Carolina State Archives
PhC9_Bx10_F7-01

73 **Santa Claus Float in Thanksgiving Parade**
North Carolina State Archives
PhC9_Bx10_F7-06

74 **Stein's Clothing Store**
North Carolina State Archives
PhC9_Bx3_F202

75 **Crowd at Night Baseball Game**
North Carolina State Archives
PhC9_Bx2_F98

76 **St. Patrick's Brawl Parade**
North Carolina State Archives
N.53.16.3691

77 **Armistice Day Parade**
North Carolina State Archives
PhC9_Bx10-03

78 **Band in Armistice Day Parade**
North Carolina State Archives
PhC9_Bx10-04

79 **Garnett Street at Night**
North Carolina State Archives
PhC68.1.48

80 **Amoco and Esso Service Stations**
North Carolina State Archives
N.53.15.5323

81 **R. J. Reynolds Tobacco Facility**
North Carolina State Archives
ConDevOSPrintsBx121

82 **North Person Street Service Station**
North Carolina State Archives
N.53.15.5321

83 **Wright Brothers Memorial at Kill Devil Hills**
North Carolina State Archives
PhC68.1.52.1

84 **Silver Moon Barbecue Restaurant**
North Carolina State Archives
N.86.9.52

85 **Pastoral Scene in Jackson County**
Library of Congress
fsa 8e03372u

86 **Cole Pottery**
North Carolina State Archives
N_73_2_106

87 **Two Children of Sharecroppers**
Library of Congress
fsa 8c30011u

88 **Women Tying Tobacco**
North Carolina State Archives
ConDev1244D

89 **Tobacco Auction**
North Carolina State Archives
ConDev1429A

90 **Tobacco Warehouse**
North Carolina State Archives
ConDev863A

91 **Blue Ridge Parkway**
North Carolina State Archives
ConDev2296C

92 **Gillikin Island**
North Carolina State Archives
PhC9_Bx7_F3.9

93 **Fishermen at Gillikin Island**
North Carolina State Archives
PhC9_Bx7_F2.1

94 **Menhaden Fishermen Aboard the Mace**
North Carolina State Archives
PhC9_Bx7_F16_20_18

95 **Fishermen from Onslow County**
North Carolina State Archives
PhC9_Bx7_F13_16_1

96 **Main Street in Jacksonville**
North Carolina State Archives
PhC9_Bx9_F77_87_9

97 **Family of Tobacco Sharecroppers**
Library of Congress
fsa 8b33728u

98 **MAIN STREET IN PITTSBORO**
Library of Congress
fsa 8b33858u

99 **BASEBALL PLAYERS AT FILLING STATION**
Library of Congress
fsa 8b34021u

100 **COTTON GIN**
North Carolina State Archives
PhC9_Bx7_F14_17_10

101 **DUCK HUNTING**
North Carolina State Archives
PhC9_Bx9_F62_75_26

102 **COASTLINE AT DUCK**
North Carolina State Archives
PhC9_Bx9_F72_85_45

104 **OBELISK MEMORIAL IN ASHEVILLE**
North Carolina State Archives
PhC68.1.9.2

105 **MAKING ICE CREAM**
Library of Congress
fsa 8a43752u

106 **TRAFFIC ON MAIN STREET IN FAYETTEVILLE**
Library of Congress
fsa 8c04721u

107 **NORTH CAROLINA STATE CAPITOL**
North Carolina State Archives
N.53.15.558

108 **SALVAGING TROLLEY TRACKS**
Library of Congress
fsa 8e11036u

109 **PRACTICING GAS MASK DRILL**
Library of Congress
fsa 8e04908u

110 **41ST ENGINEERS MARCHING AT FORT BRAGG**
Library of Congress
fsa 8e04920u

111 **FINAL PARADE AT FORT BRAGG**
Library of Congress
fsa 8e04904u

112 **PINEHURST GOLF CLUB**
North Carolina State Archives
PhC68.1.526.5

113 **WAR BOND SALES AND DISPLAY**
North Carolina State Archives
N.53.15.5988

114 **EAST HARGETT STREET**
North Carolina State Archives
PhC68.1.115

115 **CAMP LEJEUNE BASEBALL TEAM**
Library of Congress
fsa 8d16372u

116 **TOWN OF CHEROKEE**
North Carolina State Archives
ConDev4408B

117 **ALBEMARLE BEACH**
North Carolina State Archives
ConDev5191B

118 **WORLD WAR II TROOP RETURN**
North Carolina State Archives
N_2004_4_1

119 **PICKING BERRIES**
North Carolina State Archives
ConDev6287-B

120 **HOMING PIGEONS**
North Carolina State Archives
ConDevOSPrintsBx127

121 **FAYETTEVILLE STREET, 1948**
North Carolina State Archives
ConDev7063C

122 **BEAUFORT COUNTY TOBACCO WAREHOUSE**
North Carolina State Archives
ConDev7215A

123 **DOWNTOWN ASHEVILLE, 1949**
North Carolina State Archives
ConDev8157A

124 **MOUNTAIN DANCE AND FOLK FESTIVAL**
Library of Congress
ppmsc 00424u

125 **FORSYTH COUNTY CENTENNIAL**
North Carolina State Archives
ConDev7666D

126 **FAYETTEVILLE STREET AT NIGHT**
North Carolina State Archives
PhC68.1.137

127 **BRIGHT LEAF MOVIE OPENING**
North Carolina State Archives
ConDevOSPrintsBx127

128 **WRIGHT BROTHERS CELEBRATION, 1950**
North Carolina State Archives
ConDev8386A

129 **SEABOARD LOCOMOTIVE**
North Carolina State Archives
N.53.15.9616

130 **ROBESON COUNTY COURTHOUSE**
North Carolina State Archives
ConDevOSPrintsBx123

131 **DUKE VS. UNIVERSITY OF NORTH CAROLINA**
North Carolina State Archives
ConDev53-1194

www.ingramcontent.com/pod-product-compliance
Lightning Source LLC
LaVergne TN
LVHW060640110826
845147LV00018B/1012

* 9 7 8 1 6 8 3 3 6 8 5 1 9 *